Vayaged Yehonatan

THE EYBESHITZ HAGGADAH

Experiencing Redemption

by

Rabbi Shalom Hammer

Vayaged Yehonatan — The Eybeshitz Haggadah: Experiencing Redemption
Published by Devora Publishing Company

COVER DESIGN: Benjie Herskowitz
TYPESETTING AND BOOK DESIGN: Don Finkel, Leshon Limudim Ltd.
EDITORIAL AND PRODUCTION MANAGER: Daniella Barak
EDITOR: Rabbi Meshulam Gotlieb

Hard Cover ISBN: 978-1-934440-24-7
E-mail: publisher@devorapublishing.com
Web Site: devorapublishing.com

Printed in the United States of America

DEDICATED TO OUR CHILDREN

Bracha • Adena • Yaakov • Hamshush • Gila • Srulie

"What does Hashem your God ask of you? Only to fear Hashem, your God, to go in all His ways and to love Him, and to serve Hashem your God with all your heart and all your soul." *Devarim 10:12*

May the merit of the learning done with this sefer
and the merit of Rav Yehonatan Eybeshitz
lead you in this direction.

הרב דוב בערל ויין
שדרות בן מימון 15, ירושלים 92262

ל"ט ג'

October 25 2007
13 MarCheshvan 5768

Rabbi Shalom Hammer has collected, translated and explained many of Rabbi Yehonotan's works on Jewish thought and provided the English-speaking community with the opportunity to benefit from Rabbi Yehonatan's unique brilliance in an English format. This is especially true regarding Rabbi Yehonatan's Pesach Hagada.

Rabbi Hammer is a brilliant young Torah scholar, lecturer and teacher of Torah. His skills and knowledge have already gained for him an international reputation. Rabbi Yehonatan's Hagada is a combination of the great knowledge and talents of its author. It is a unique blend of agada, kabala, halacha, philosophy and keen insight into the Jewish past and the conditions of his own time and locale. It is not a simple book to deal with and understand and appreciate. Rabbi Hammer is to be complimented for his unusual ability to capture the flavor and nuances of the original work in his translation and commentary to the work. This is a book not only for the Seder table, for it certainly is that, but for study and perusal all the days of the year. The difficult is made understandable and the obtuse is clarified in this work. I highly recommend it.

Rabbi Berel Wein

דוד קאהן

ביהמ"ד גבול יעבץ
ברוקלין, נוא יארק

בס"ד

כבוד ידידי בן ידידי
הרב שלום אברהם המר שליט"א

מאד התענגתי לשמוע שהנך תי"ש עסק בידך ועוסק בכתיבת ספרים. ראיתי קטעים מעבודתך בקובץ-ליקוטי דיבורים ממרן הגאון רב יהונתן אייבשיץ זצ"ל על ההגדה של פסח, והנני רואה שתרגמת דבריו בטוב טעם ודעת. אין ספק אצלי שעולם התורה ישבעו ויתענגו מספרך זה שהנך מתכונן להוציא לאור.

והנני חותם בברכת שבכל אשר תפנה תשכיל

באהבה ויקר
דוד קאהן
יב' כסלו תשס"ח

דוד קאהן

ביהמ"ד גבול יעבץ
ברוקלין, נוא יארק

בס"ד

To my esteemed friend Rav Shalom Hammer שליט"א,

I was pleased to hear that you are planning to publish a compilation of the writings of Rav Yehonasan Eybeshitz זצ"ל on the Hagada. It goes without saying that this Titan's novelae need no approbation. Your translation and presentation is a marked contribution to Agadic-Hagadic literature. More Power to you!

I close with my profound wishes that you succeed in all your endeavors.

Dovid Cohen
Rav of Congregation
GVUL YAABETZ

SPONSORSHIPS

In loving memory

יצחק בן משה הלוי ז״ל — תמר בת צבי הירש ז״ל

MR. AND MRS. FRANK NUTIS, COLUMBUS, OHIO

In memory of our father and grandfather Robert Leitson

ראובן מנדל בן שמואל הכהן ז״ל

LAURA, IRA, SAM, JOE AND SARAH NUTIS, COLUMBUS, OHIO

לזכר נשמות הורינו היקרים

אברהם משה בן הרב שלמה זאלי ז״ל וגוטקה טובה בת רב אברהם דוד ע״ה

למשפחת בيננפלד

יהודה לייב בן אהרון זאב ז״ל וחוה מינה בת יצחק אייזיק ע״ה

למשפחת יוסדן

מוקדש ע״י ר׳ מנחם שמואל והדסה בيננפלד

In loving memory of our grandfather Jack Strulowitz ז״ל

In loving memory of our father and grandfather

Irving Zweier ישראל בן משה ז״ל

who loved to read the Haggadah

and tell the story of Pesach

to the family

FROM THE ZWEIER FAMILY

In loving memory of Solly Tager שאול בן אליהו זעליג הלוי ז״ל
a true physical and spiritual giant,
whose love and kindness
touched the lives of many

In memory of our brothers
Alvin Ruben ז״ל and Bernard Ruben ז״ל

SYLVIA AND MURRAY EBNER, COLUMBUS, OHIO

In memory of our parents
יעקב יחיאל בן אליעזר הלוי ז״ל — רשא בת אברהם פסח ז״ל
נפתלי בן משה ז״ל — צירל בת הרב שלמה זאלי ז״ל

In honor of our son Rabbi Shalom Hammer and his family

DAVID AND FLORENCE HAMMER, JERUSALEM, ISRAEL

In memory of our parents
מרים בת חיים זאב ז״ל   שלמה בן חיים צבי ז״ל
חפציבה בת רפאל ז״ל   פנחס בן אברהם ז״ל

In honor of our grandson Yaakov Hammer's bar mitzva
Gabi, Shalom and kids: We are so proud of your accomplishments.

MOM AND DAD, LONDON, ENGLAND

In honor of my grandchildren
Yechezkel Akivah, Gila Eden, Arielle Mia and Zecharia Shlomo

DR. SILVIO SPERBER, HOLLYWOOD, FLORIDA

In memory of David and Miriam Kramer
צבי דוד בן זאב דב ז"ל — מרים בת אברהם יעקב ז"ל

THE GROSS FAMILY

CONTENTS

ACKNOWLEDGMENTS

There are many people whose support and encouragement helped me complete this *sefer*. Simcha Publishing recognized the importance of this project, and they did such an excellent job on my first book, *The Family Parsha Book*, that I welcomed the opportunity to work with them again. I thank both Yaakov Peterseil, the publisher, and Daniella Barak, the general manager, for their patience and support. It has been a pleasure and a valuable learning experience working with you, and I look forward to working together on future projects.

This project required a special editor who was knowledgeable and well-versed in both Torah and English composition in order to make Rav Yehonatan's profound words and deep thoughts comprehensible and interesting. Rabbi Meshulam Gotlieb, a neighbor and a friend, is a talented editor as well as a wise and patient man. Working with him was both a pleasure and a unique learning experience for me.

I would also like to thank Rabbi Ari Zivotovsky, who took the time and effort to carefully read through the entire text, for his input and advice.

Baruch Hashem, I have been blessed with many friends and acquaintances throughout the world who are genuinely interested in and extremely supportive of my endeavors. Two outstanding families who I have been privileged to develop a special relationship with are Mr. and Mrs. Frank Nutis and Mr. and Mrs. Ira Nutis. The Nutis families are pillars of the Columbus Jewish community and they are extremely supportive of Jewish education and *Eretz Yisrael*.

The time I spent serving as a rabbi in Columbus, Ohio was challenging and the friendship that my family and I enjoyed with the Nutis families made it worthwhile. I was privileged to witness personally more than once the outstanding *chesed* and sincere kindness that the Nutis's have shown towards people in dire straits. They are always prepared to give and to help and they do so in an unassuming, unpretentious fashion. Without their efforts and support, not only this sefer but also many of my projects and aspirations could not be achieved.

Marvin and Dasi Beinenfeld are well-known supporters and contributors to many Jewish organizations and outstanding supporters of *Eretz Yisrael*. Most importantly, they are my dear cousins, who are very close to my parents, and with whom I to share a friendship.

David Harris and I went to school together for many years (people doubted whether either of us would make it). We were good friends then, and we continue to be good friends now. David is a kind, sensitive person and most importantly he is a *mentsh* par excellence. Mazal Tov to David and his wife "Chani" (I got it right!) on their recent marriage. Thanks for your generous support.

Other supporters who contributed to this sefer include Dr. and Mrs. Jay Zweier from Columbus, Ohio who not only befriended me, but whose children I had the pleasure of establishing a relationship with. I hope they will all visit us in Israel in the near future. Mr. and Mrs. Murray Ebner, my dear friends from Columbus, also deserve my thanks. Well-known contributors to many Jewish causes, Murray and Silvia never seek personal recognition, and as survivors of the Holocaust their sole interest is in perpetuating the Jewish future.

It was only recently that I had the privilege of spending time with and developing a special friendship with Doc Rob, Jon and the entire Tager family. Thank you for your encouragement and appreciation. "Howzit" to all of you!

Old friendships, regardless of whether or not you are regularly in touch, never sour or change; they simply continue to grow with time. Some of those friends who I cherish and thank for always being supportive include Dr. Silvio Sperber and, of course, my old, childhood friend and companion David Gross. Thank you Rita and David for your contribution. Nothing can compare with old friends.

The Pesach Seder is a family experience that both helps forge and makes one appreciate the ties that bind. My memories of the Seder at my Bubie and Zadie's house, may they rest in peace, in Harrisburg, Pennsylvania, are still fresh in my mind. My parents and in-laws continue to ensure that our children will have similar ones. They have always been so supportive, interested, and close to Gabi, our children, and myself.

A special thank you to my Rebbe, Rabbi Berel Wein, *shlita,* not only for the historical introduction to the sefer, but more importantly for agreeing to serve as my mentor, guide and confidant. I am truly blessed to benefit from working with and learning from a Rav of such caliber, and I sincerely cherish the closeness that we share.

My first sefer, *The Family Parsha Book,* was dedicated to my wife, Gabi, and at the time I wrote that she never ceases to amaze me. She holds it all together while juggling two jobs, raising six children and believing wholeheartedly in a husband who travels regularly, dreams endlessly, and is often just "not home." Thank you dear.

When I lecture, I often tell the story of someone I once sat next to on an airplane who asked me what I wanted out of life. Many people have made a living trying to answer this complex question: writing books, hosting shows, engaging in discourse and offering complex formulae to successfully handle what seems to be a complicated and challenging question. I answered this question with ease. I responded that I want my children to appreciate and understand the importance of being religious Jews, of living in Eretz Yisrael, and of the role they play in the future of the Jewish nation. This has always been the response of the Jewish people, and I know that Gabi and I pray that our children will always be able to answer this question with the same response, regardless of the challenges and hardships that they undoubtedly will face and the price they will pay for calling themselves religious Jews.

Thank you Hashem for providing me with this opportunity to reincarnate Rav Yehonatan. I pray that the merit of Rav Yehonatan's Torah will protect *Am Yisrael* and Eretz Yisrael and will help facilitate the deliverance of the Jewish people, as we proclaim at the conclusion of the Seder:

לשנה הבאה בירושלים הבנויה

FOREWORD

One of the great geniuses of rabbinic writing in the eighteenth century was Rabbi Yehonatan Eybeshitz. Rabbi Yehonatan was a prolific author and an acknowledged Talmudic scholar and halachic decisor in an age when such great scholars were abundant. His fabulous breadth of Jewish Torah knowledge combined with his gift of creativity and deep insight into the texts guaranteed him immortality among the students of Torah in all later times. In 1711, while still a very young man, he already headed the famed school of Talmud in Prague. He later served as a rabbi in Prague and was known throughout the Jewish world as Rabbi Yehonatan Prager. In 1740 he moved to Metz in the province of Alsace and then ten years later accepted the position of rabbi in the famed tri-community of AHU – Altona, Hamburg and Wandsbek – then part of the Danish kingdom. Living there at that time was Rabbi Yaakov Emden, an eminent scholar and a fierce polemicist against the remnants of the Shabtai Zevi sect of false messianists. Suspicious and contentious by nature, Rabbi Yaakov Emden was engaged in a zealous campaign against anyone he suspected of Shabbatean tendencies. It would not take long before he and Rabbi Yehonatan would clash.

Rabbi Yehonatan was known not only for his great intellectual accomplishments, but as an active kabbalist as well. He was especially famous for his kabbalistic amulets, which were in great demand. This practice of his raised the suspicion of Rabbi Yaakov Emden who upon studying the kabbalistic nature of one of the amulets proclaimed it to be of

Shabbatean origin and belief. Rabbi Yaakov Emden immediately called for a ban against such amulets and that Rabbi Yehonatan be enjoined from issuing any further amulets. Rabbi Yehonatan stoutly defended himself, denying all of the accusations made against him and continued with his kabbalistic practices. The dispute between the two great rabbis split the community of Altona, Hamburg and Wandsbek and eventually much of the European rabbinic world as well. The leaders of the community sided with their rabbi and forced Rabbi Yaakov Emden to leave the community. The dispute was so public and bitter that it came to the attention of the Danish king who sided with Rabbi Yaakov Emden and forced Rabbi Yehonatan to resign his position and leave his community. However, in 1756, the king reconsidered the matter and restored Rabbi Yehonatan to his post and the dispute finally simmered down.

Traditional Jewry has always sided with Rabbi Yehonatan and accepted his denials of all the charges made against him. Only in the rarified atmosphere of Judaic academia does the dispute still rage in our time. In the study halls of the yeshivot and the synagogues the issue was long ago settled, if not even forgotten. Rabbi Yehonatan's great halachic works are part of every rabbinic curriculum and his tumultuous life of controversy is completely subsumed and unrecognizable in his great works of Torah. He was not only a master of Halacha and Kabbala, but of Homiletics, Aggada, and Drush as well.

None of Rav Yehonatan's works have ever been translated into English. Rabbi Shalom Hammer collected, translated and explained many of Rav Yehonatan's works on Jewish thought and provides the English-speaking community with the opportunity to benefit from Rav Yehonatan's unique brilliance in the format of the Pesach Haggadah. Rabbi Hammer is a brilliant young Torah scholar, lecturer and teacher of Torah. His skills and knowledge have already gained him an international reputation. Rabbi Yehonatan's Torah on the Haggadah is a combination of the great knowledge and talents of its author. It is a unique blend of Aggada, Kabbala, Halacha, and Philosophy and presents keen insights into the Jewish past and the conditions of the author's own times and locale. It is not a simple book to deal with, to understand, and to appreciate. Rabbi Hammer is to be complimented for his unusual ability to catch the flavor and nuances of the original work in his translation and commentary to the work. This is a book not only for the Seder table, for it certainly is that, but for study and perusal all the days of the year. The difficult is made understandable and the obtuse is clarified in this work. I highly recommend it.

Rabbi Berel Wein

EDITOR'S NOTE

Rav Yehonatan's Torah functions on the levels of the forest and of the trees. His writings possess both an immense *hashkafic-halachic* breadth and a tremendous attention to the details of each and every halacha or biblical verse he chances to interpret. Demonstrating this breadth, Rav Yehonatan weaves together ideas and concepts from the Halacha and Aggada. Using the power of his imagination and his depth of knowledge, he seamlessly links sources from the Talmud and *Rishonim* with ones from the *Midrash* and the *Zohar*. Sources that, oftentimes, seem dissimilar or unrelated are woven together to generate one unified concept. Sometimes he uses the Halacha to bolster an *aggadic* insight and sometimes he uses an aggadic insight to explain the Halacha.

However, Rav Yehonatan's true brilliance is revealed in his ability to find a basis for these hashkafic-halachic insights in the *pesukim* themselves. His close reading of every word in these verses – either to substantiate or to create his hashkafic-halachic insights – leads to homiletical interpretations which at times strain the bounds of *peshat* and, indeed, often the boundaries of anything close to a literal reading of the verse. However, what these readings lack in peshat, they gain from the clever, oftentimes, brilliantly associative way, they manage to read these verses. Personally, I will never be able to recite "the cornerstone which the builders despised" quite the same way after being exposed to Rav Yehonatan's brilliant interpretations. First, based on a *Gemara* and a Tosafot, he explains how it refers to Chava and then he explains how Rabbi Abbahu uses it to refer to the *ba'al teshuva* and the *tzaddik*. In the end, Rav Yehonatan always manages to create a solid homiletical foundation for his *hashkafa* in the Written Torah, itself.

So as you begin delving into Rav Yehonatan's Torah, pay careful attention both to the themes he develops, and to the method he uses to read these messages out of, or into, the biblical and haggadic texts at his disposal, for the beauty and complexity of his Torah is to be found not only in his messages but also in how he derives them.

Rabbi Meshulam Gotlieb

INTRODUCTION

Rabbi Yehonatan Eybeshitz, was an outstanding eighteenth century Talmudist, Halachist and Kabbalist. He served as *Dayan* of Prague, and later as Rabbi of the "Three Communities," Altona, Hamburg and Wandsbek. Famed not only for his Torah wisdom and greatness but also for his worldly knowledge, Rav Yehonatan, as he was affectionately known, was in contact with the Christian leaders of his day, debating religious and philosophical issues with them.

Notwithstanding his Torah greatness, Rav Yehonatan's fame also stems from his notoriety, as his pulpit was put in jeopardy, after he was accused of being a secret adherent of Shabbateanism, a movement revolving around the false messiah, Shabtai Zevi. Rav Yaakov Emden, himself, an influential figure and scholar in the Jewish community of Hamburg was one of Rav Yehonatan's principal accusers. Despite Rav Yehonatan's support for the excommunication of all Shabbateans, and his publication of a sefer entitled, *Luchot Ha'edut*, which contained letters from many of the most distinguished Rabbis of his time defending and praising him, he was twice removed from his pulpit by these unsubstantiated accusations. While he was finally reinstated as Rav of Altona, Hamburg and Wandsbek – a position he retained for the rest of his life – over time the controversy spread to all major Jewish communities and attacks by Rav Yehonatan's opponents continued unabated until his death in 1764.

I mention this heated debate not only because I owe it to my readers to place all the facts on the table but also because

I want my readers to appreciate the inner strength and resilience of this Torah giant. As Rabbi Berel Wein writes:

> Rabbi Yehonatan rallied his disciples and colleagues to his defense. Such great personages as Rabbi Yechezkel Landau (known as the Noda B'Yehuda) of Prague and Rabbi Elijah, the Gaon of Vilna, defended him ... The innocence of Rabbi Yehonatan Eybeshitz has been established and his great works on the Talmud and Jewish law are still studied and admired. (*Triumph of Survival*, 34)

Whatever the reason for the attacks upon him, the immense amount of Torah Rav Yehonatan taught and the level of learning he attained vitiate any accusations against him. Rav Yehonatan's breadth of knowledge and the ease with which he handled the many diverse disciplines of Torah study are virtually unparalleled. Many of his sefarim remain basic staples in the library of the Torah scholar to this very day. He wrote the *Kreiti Upleiti* on *Yore Dea, Tiferet Yisrael* on the laws of *nidda, Urim Vetumim* on *Choshen Mishpat, Ya'arot Devash* – a compilation of sermons, *Bina Le'itim* on the Rambam's *Hilchot Yom Tov, Tiferet Yehonatan* on the *Chumash, Ahavat Yehonatan* on the weekly *Haftorah* portions, *Alon Bachut* on *Megillat Eicha, Midrash Yehonatan* on *midrash aggada* and *midrash halacha, Shem Olam* on Kabbala, and a commentary on "*Chad Gadya.*" All but one of Rav Yehonatan's works were published posthumously. The posthumous printing of so many of his works is testimony to the profound influence his oral teachings and character had on his contemporaries.

I only discovered Rav Yehonatan's sefarim a few years after I began my professional career as a teacher and a rebbe. Teaching a weekly *shiur* on Haftorah, I was always on the lookout for commentaries dedicated to studying the Haftorah itself, as opposed to that particular section of the *Navi*. I came across the *Ahavat Yehonatan*, and I was mesmerized. While parts of the commentary were difficult for me to understand because of their kabbalistic nature (typical of many of Rav Yehonatan's sefarim), I was enthralled by its richness as it synthesized many diverse Torah disciplines, creating an organic web linking all areas of Torah. Rav Yehonatan's brilliance and expertise in so many diverse areas of Torah grabbed my interest and fuelled my fascination with his commentaries.

I began to read the *Ahavat Yehonatan*, the *Tiferet Yehonatan* on the weekly *parsha* and the *Ye'arot Devash*. The latter contains thematically based discourses, fourteen or fifteen pages long. Their contents is complex and diverse, containing an analysis of many areas of Torah and science. Most works commenting upon Torah focus upon a specific area of Torah, such as Halacha or Aggada, *Tanach* or Talmud, *Parshanut* or *Midrash*. Rarely does a commentator integrate and weave all of these seemingly diverse fields into one discourse. Witnessing Rav Yehonatan's mastery in addressing a midrash, linking it to a portion of the Talmud, following the Talmud's lead to a *Zohar*, and then connecting this to the codified laws in the *Shulchan Aruch* was an awe inspiring experience. Rav Yehonatan connected ideas that would otherwise have seemed dissimilar.

As I continued studying Rav Yehonatan's Torah, I realized that his creative genius was truly extraordinary. His urge to know all of Torah and innovatively weave it together seemed almost uncontrollable. I tried to envision this great, Torah giant addressing his *kehilla* in Prague or Hamburg, speaking for hours on end, weaving together the complexities of Jewish philosophy and of Jewish law in front of a mesmerized crowd (many of whom presumably had very little or no understanding of what he was truly saying). When I realized that the yeshiva world was not as familiar with the teachings of Rav Yehonatan as it should have been, I began teaching classes on the *Ye'arot Devash*.

While over the last few years the situation has improved drastically with a new printing of *Ye'arot Devash*, the printing of Rav Yehonatan's novellae on the Talmud and the new version of the *Tiferet Yehonatan*, the lack is still felt. Particularly within the English-speaking world, both those with a strong background in learning and those with a weaker one lack sufficient familiarity with Rav Yehonatan and his commentaries, and I felt that this situation had to be rectified. To deprive the world of Rav Yehonatan's breadth and unique style is to deprive the world of a unique way of appreciating the scope and depth of Torah.

I came to believe that the best way to introduce the Torah of Rav Yehonatan to the Jewish world (particularly the English-speaking one) was by compiling a Haggadah. This format would provide me with the opportunity to draw upon many of Rav Yehonatan's unique works and would provide me with a framework in which to arrange his complex *Divrei Torah* in an organized fashion, so that they would be easier to access and understand. Since every Pesach, people look for new insights to share around the Seder table, by formulating Rav Yehonatan's thoughts as a commentary upon the Haggadah, I also hoped to ensure that many people would be exposed to them.

Rav Yehonatan did not write an official commentary on the Haggadah (although he did write a lengthy and extremely complex commentary on "*Chad Gadya*"), but using the Haggadah's text as a guide, I planned to choose and organize a multitude of different sources and ideas from his sefarim in the format of a commentary upon the Haggadah. As I was mulling this plan over, I met a friend from the United States who was visiting Israel for Pesach. I discussed my plans with him and he told me that at the Pesach Seder his uncle, Rabbi Moshe Meiselman, Rosh Yeshiva of *Torat Moshe* in Jerusalem, used the *Rav Yehonatan Eybeshitz Haggadah*. Sure enough, someone had already gathered, compiled and, to some extent, paraphrased

Divrei Torah from Rav Yehonatan's books into a Hebrew commentary upon the Haggadah. This edition of the Haggadah was printed in 1985, but the print run must have been very limited because the booksellers I approached had never heard of it, let alone stocked it. Therefore, I decided to translate this commentary. Rabbi Meiselman was kind enough to lend me his edition, so I could work on the translation. Without his cooperation this project would not have begun.

Excitedly I approached a number of peers and colleagues about the Haggadah only to be greeted with the same reaction. They explained to me that the reason Rav Yehonatan's sefarim were never translated into English was because they were too difficult to understand even in Hebrew, translating them into English was futile. I remained determined but as I continued my work, I quickly realized that not all of the material collected by the Haggadah's author was suitable or necessary for attaining my goal of providing an introduction to Rav Yehonatan's thought. In addition, other material related to the Haggadah and Pesach, essential for presenting Rav Yehonatan's thought, was missing. So I decided that rather than translating the Hebrew original, I would base myself loosely upon it: embellishing and elaborating upon some of Rav Yehonatan's original commentary omitting some material cited therein, but unnecessary to fulfilling my goals, adding a series of discourses printed in the *Ye'arot Devash*, and contributing my own brief essays concerning issues raised by Rav Yehonatan.

As my peers and colleagues noted, translating or even paraphrasing Rav Yehonatan's writings is extremely difficult both for substantive and stylistic reasons. When I began reviewing the material with my editor, the reasons for their hesitation became even more apparent. Unraveling Rav Yehonatan's complex and intertwined ideas, so that they not only make sense but are also readable is a tremendous challenge. The act of translating a commentary of this complex nature, itself necessitates departing from the structure of the original sentences for Rav Yehonatan's style, particularly when translated fairly literally, is oftentimes incomprehensible.

When working on the discourses, I began by reading each discourse a number of times. Then I would begin restructuring the relationship between the questions and answers in order to increase the overall clarity. There are a number of concepts which Rav Yehonatan refers to whose sources I did not manage to discover and, in order to create a logical, flowing text, we (the editor and myself) had to either omit some of Rav Yehonatan's ideas or explain them by turning to other places in his writings, always taking care not to distort Rav Yehonatan's original intent. If I omitted parts that should have remained, or if I left in parts that could have been omitted, I apologize both to Rav Yehonatan and to the reader. However, I sincerely believe that the gains accrued from exposing the public to Rav Yehonatan's brilliance far outweigh the losses incurred by editing and adapting his works into this Haggadah commentary format.

As mentioned above, following Rav Yehonatan's commentary on particular sections of the Haggadah, I sometimes incorporated my own brief essays, based upon other commentaries and personal insights that I felt related to Rav Yehonatan's ideas. They will be typographically differentiated from Rav Yehonatan's original commentary. My objective for doing this was twofold. First and foremost I wanted to demonstrate how many of Rav Yehonatan's ideas can relate to other commentaries, as well as to concepts and challenges within contemporary society. Secondly, these are Divrei Torah that can be shared around the Seder table and will hopefully encourage more discussion and discourse.

Most of my expressions of gratitude are included in the acknowledgment section of this book; however, I felt I would be remiss to not include one special acknowledgment in the Haggadah's "Introduction." I once learned that having read a particular Rabbi's sefarim and learned from them, one is entitled to call this author his Rebbe, even if he is deceased. That being the case, I must acknowledge and express my sincerest gratitude to my Rebbe, Rav Yehonatan Eybeshitz. I hope I did justice to his works, and I pray that my readers will benefit and appreciate his Torah knowledge and genius as much as I have.

Bevracha
Shalom Hammer

THE HAGGADAH WITH COMMENTARY

סדר ביעור חמץ

Before the search the following blessing is recited:

בָּרוּךְ אַתָּה יְיָ אֱלֹהֵינוּ מֶלֶךְ הָעוֹלָם אֲשֶׁר קִדְּשָׁנוּ בְּמִצְוֹתָיו וְצִוָּנוּ עַל בִּעוּר חָמֵץ:

Immediately after the search the following declaration is made:

כָּל חֲמִירָא דְּאִיתֵיהּ בִּרְשׁוּתִי דְּלָא חֲזִיתֵיהּ וּדְלָא בִיעַרְתֵּיהּ לִבָּטֵיל וְלֶיהֱוֵי הֶפְקֵר כְּעַפְרָא דְאַרְעָא:

After burning the chametz on the morning before Pesach, the following declaration is made:

כָּל חֲמִירָא דְאִיתֵיהּ בִּרְשׁוּתִי דַּחֲזִיתֵיהּ וּדְלָא חֲזִיתֵיהּ, דְּבִיעַרְתֵּיהּ וּדְלָא בִיעַרְתֵּיהּ. לִבָּטֵיל וְלֶיהֱוֵי הֶפְקֵר כְּעַפְרָא דְאַרְעָא:

סדר עירוב תבשילין

When a holiday falls out on a Friday (or Thursday and Friday) an Eruv Tavshilin must be performed in order to permit preparations for the Shabbat to be done on the holiday. A cooked food and a piece of matza are set aside (if one does not intend to bake, then a cooked food without a piece of matza is sufficient), and the following blessing is recited:

בָּרוּךְ אַתָּה יְיָ אֱלֹהֵינוּ מֶלֶךְ הָעוֹלָם אֲשֶׁר קִדְּשָׁנוּ בְּמִצְוֹתָיו וְצִוָּנוּ עַל מִצְוַת עֵירוּב:

Then the following declaration of intent is recited:

בְּדֵין עֵרוּבָא יְהֵא שָׁרָא לָן לְאֲפוּיֵי וּלְבִישּׁוּלֵי וּלְאַטְמוּנֵי וּלְאַדְלוּקֵי שְׁרָגָא וּלְתַקָּנָא וּלְמֶעְבַּד כָּל צָרְכָּנָא מִיּוֹם טוֹב לְשַׁבָּת לָנָא וּלְכָל בְּנֵי הָעִיר הַזֹּאת:

The Search for Chametz

Blessed are You, Lord, our God, King of the universe, who has sanctified us with His commandments, and commanded us concerning the removal of *chametz*.

All sourdough and *chametz* that is in my possession, which I have not seen nor disposed of, and about which I am unaware, is hereby nullified, and shall be ownerless as the dust of the earth.

All sourdough or *chametz* that is in my possession, whether I have seen it or not, whether I have disposed of it or not, is hereby nullified, and shall be ownerless as the dust of the earth.

Eruv Tavshilin

Blessed are You, Lord, our God, King of the universe, Who has sanctified us through His commandments, and commanded us concerning the precept of the *eruv*.

Then the following declaration of intent is recited:

By this *eruv* it shall be permitted for us to bake, to cook, to insulate pots of hot food, to light candles, to make preparations, and to do all that is necessary on the festival in preparation for the Sabbath – for us and for all the Jews who live in this city.

קַדֵּשׁ

Before reciting kiddush, bear in mind that you are about to fulfill the mitzva of kiddush and the mitzva of the first of the four cups of wine. Lift the cup of wine, and say the following: (On Shabbat the words in parentheses are added.)

(וַיְהִי עֶרֶב וַיְהִי בֹקֶר

יוֹם הַשִּׁשִּׁי. וַיְכֻלּוּ הַשָּׁמַיִם וְהָאָרֶץ וְכָל צְבָאָם. וַיְכַל אֱלֹהִים בַּיּוֹם הַשְּׁבִיעִי מְלַאכְתּוֹ אֲשֶׁר עָשָׂה, וַיִּשְׁבֹּת בַּיּוֹם הַשְּׁבִיעִי מִכָּל מְלַאכְתּוֹ אֲשֶׁר עָשָׂה. וַיְבָרֶךְ אֱלֹהִים אֶת יוֹם הַשְּׁבִיעִי וַיְקַדֵּשׁ אֹתוֹ, כִּי בוֹ שָׁבַת מִכָּל מְלַאכְתּוֹ אֲשֶׁר בָּרָא אֱלֹהִים לַעֲשׂוֹת:)

The Purpose of Creation

ויכולו השמים והארץ Why does the Torah describe Hashem's completion of Creation using two different words: *vayechulu*[1] and *vayechal*[2]? While both words can be translated as "completed," Targum Onkelos points out a more subtle nuance: *vayechulu* means finished, while *vayechal* means perfected. By using both terms, the Torah teaches us that Hashem not only finished but also perfected Creation by the end of the sixth day. Indeed, Rav Yehonatan explains that at the end of the previous verse, the sixth day of Creation is referred to as *yom hashishi* – the sixth day – to emphasize that on the sixth day Hashem perfected the world. According to Rav Yehonatan, the Torah uses the definite article "the" to remind us that on another sixth day – far in the future – the sixth day of Sivan, Hashem would raise the world to an even higher level of perfection by giving

Kaddesh

(And it was evening and it was morning, the sixth day.
The heavens and the earth and all their hosts were completed. God completed on the seventh day His work which He had done, and He rested on the seventh day from all His work which He had done. God blessed the seventh day and sanctified it, for on it He rested from all His work which God had created to make. *[Bereishit 1:31-2:3]*)

the Torah to the Jewish people, for by studying the Torah, the Jews would further perfect the world and give it meaning.[3]

The *Midrash* teaches that when Hashem gave the Torah to the Jewish people, the Torah protested that the Jews would always be busy working and would never have time to study. Hashem replied that there would be a day reserved for Torah study, the Shabbat.[4] For this reason the Torah declares, "On the seventh day Hashem perfected His work." Hashem finished perfecting Creation on the sixth day, but on the seventh day – dedicated to Torah study – declared that an even higher level of perfection could be reached. As Hashem says in *Yirmiyahu*, "My covenant with the night and with the day would not be, had I not set up the laws of heaven and earth."[5] Meaning, were it not for My covenant with the Jewish people who study Torah day and night, I would not have created the world. Hashem created the world and man perfects it together with Him by learning Torah.

סַבְרִי מָרָנָן וְרַבָּנָן וְרַבּוֹתַי

בָּרוּךְ אַתָּה יְיָ, אֱלֹהֵינוּ מֶלֶךְ הָעוֹלָם, בּוֹרֵא פְּרִי הַגָּפֶן:

בָּרוּךְ אַתָּה יְיָ, אֱלֹהֵינוּ מֶלֶךְ הָעוֹלָם, אֲשֶׁר בָּחַר בָּנוּ מִכָּל עָם, וְרוֹמְמָנוּ מִכָּל לָשׁוֹן, וְקִדְּשָׁנוּ בְּמִצְוֹתָיו. וַתִּתֶּן לָנוּ יְיָ אֱלֹהֵינוּ, בְּאַהֲבָה (שַׁבָּתוֹת לִמְנוּחָה וּ)מוֹעֲדִים לְשִׂמְחָה, חַגִּים וּזְמַנִּים לְשָׂשׂוֹן, אֶת יוֹם (הַשַּׁבָּת הַזֶּה וְאֶת יוֹם) חַג הַמַּצּוֹת הַזֶּה, זְמַן חֵרוּתֵנוּ (בְּאַהֲבָה), מִקְרָא קֹדֶשׁ זֵכֶר לִיצִיאַת מִצְרָיִם, כִּי בָנוּ בָחַרְתָּ וְאוֹתָנוּ קִדַּשְׁתָּ מִכָּל הָעַמִּים (וְשַׁבָּת) וּמוֹעֲדֵי קָדְשֶׁךָ (בְּאַהֲבָה וּבְרָצוֹן) בְּשִׂמְחָה וּבְשָׂשׂוֹן הִנְחַלְתָּנוּ. בָּרוּךְ אַתָּה יְיָ, מְקַדֵּשׁ (הַשַּׁבָּת וְ)יִשְׂרָאֵל וְהַזְּמַנִּים:

AUTHOR'S COMMENTS Seder night begins with the kiddush, a rite that both describes Hashem's creation of the world and shows how the Jewish people testify to it by studying Torah. On Seder night we fulfill the commandment of learning Torah and, in so doing, tell the story of our Exodus from Egypt.

The Origins of the Sanctity of Shabbat

ויקדש אותו Was the Shabbat an intrinsically holy day, or did Hashem sanctify it by abstaining from work? Our

With your permission, Gentlemen.

Blessed are You, Lord, our God, King of the universe, Who creates the fruit of the vine.

Blessed are You, Lord, our God, King of the universe, who has chosen us from all the nations, and raised us above all nationalities, and made us holy through His commandments. You, Lord, our God, gave us in love (*Shabbat for rest and*) holidays for rejoicing, festivals and festive seasons for gladness – (*this Shabbat day and*) this day of the Festival of Matzot, the season of our freedom (*with love*), a holy convocation, in commemoration of the Exodus from Egypt. For You have chosen us and sanctified us from all the nations, and You have bestowed upon us Your holy (*Shabbat and*) festivals, (*with love and favor*), with happiness and joy. Blessed are You, Lord, who sanctifies (*the Shabbat and*) Israel and the festive seasons.

verse answers this question by concluding, "He abstained from all His work which He had created to make."[6] By ending this verse with the infinitive "to make," the Torah implies that there was more work to be done. Hashem stopped working only because of the Shabbat's intrinsic sanctity. Emulating Hashem, *Bnei Yisrael* also testify to the sanctity of Shabbat by refraining from work.[7]

On Saturday night, add the following section before reciting Shehecheyanu.

בָּרוּךְ אַתָּה יְיָ, אֱלֹהֵינוּ מֶלֶךְ הָעוֹלָם, בּוֹרֵא מְאוֹרֵי הָאֵשׁ:

בָּרוּךְ אַתָּה יְיָ, אֱלֹהֵינוּ מֶלֶךְ הָעוֹלָם, הַמַּבְדִּיל בֵּין קֹדֶשׁ לְחֹל, בֵּין אוֹר לְחֹשֶׁךְ, בֵּין יִשְׂרָאֵל לָעַמִּים, בֵּין יוֹם הַשְּׁבִיעִי לְשֵׁשֶׁת יְמֵי הַמַּעֲשֶׂה. בֵּין קְדֻשַּׁת שַׁבָּת לִקְדֻשַּׁת יוֹם טוֹב הִבְדַּלְתָּ, וְאֶת יוֹם הַשְּׁבִיעִי מִשֵּׁשֶׁת יְמֵי הַמַּעֲשֶׂה קִדַּשְׁתָּ, הִבְדַּלְתָּ וְקִדַּשְׁתָּ אֶת עַמְּךָ יִשְׂרָאֵל בִּקְדֻשָּׁתֶךָ. בָּרוּךְ אַתָּה יְיָ, הַמַּבְדִּיל בֵּין קֹדֶשׁ לְקֹדֶשׁ:

בָּרוּךְ אַתָּה יְיָ, אֱלֹהֵינוּ מֶלֶךְ הָעוֹלָם, שֶׁהֶחֱיָנוּ וְקִיְּמָנוּ וְהִגִּיעָנוּ לַזְּמַן הַזֶּה:

Now drink the wine, while reclining on your left side.

Blessed are You, Lord, our God, King of the universe, Who creates the radiances of fire.

Blessed are You, Lord, our God, King of the universe, who distinguishes between the sacred and the profane, between light and darkness, between Israel and the nations, and between the seventh day and the six workdays. You distinguished between the holiness of the Sabbath and the holiness of the festivals, and You have sanctified the seventh day above the six workdays. You have distinguished and sanctified Your people Israel through Your holiness. Blessed are You, Lord, who distinguishes between [one level of] holiness and [another level of] holiness.)

Blessed are You, Lord, our God, King of the universe, who has granted us life, sustained us, and allowed us to reach this occasion.

וּרְחַץ

Wash your hands with a cup of water, but do not recite the blessing.

כַּרְפַּס

Dip a vegetable smaller than a kezayit in salt water and recite the following blessing.
Bear in mind that this blessing is also for the maror that will be eaten later:

בָּרוּךְ אַתָּה יְיָ, אֱלֹהֵינוּ מֶלֶךְ הָעוֹלָם, בּוֹרֵא פְּרִי הָאֲדָמָה:

Eat the vegetable.

יַחַץ

The Seder leader breaks the middle matza in two. The smaller piece is returned to its place in the Seder plate, and the larger piece is set aside for use as the afikoman.

מַגִּיד

The Haggadah must be recited in a language that is understood by the participants at the Seder. Before reciting the Haggadah, bear in mind that this recital fulfills the mitzva of recounting the Exodus from Egypt. The Haggadah is recited with reverence, and not while reclining.

Urechatz

Wash your hands with a cup of water, but do not recite the blessing.

Karpas

Dip a vegetable smaller than a kezayit in salt water and recite the following blessing.
Bear in mind that this blessing is also for the maror that will be eaten later:

Blessed are You, Lord, our God, King of the universe, who creates the produce of the ground.

Eat the vegetable.

Yachatz

The Seder leader breaks the middle matza in two. The smaller piece is returned to its place in the Seder plate, and the larger piece is set aside for use as the afikoman.

Maggid

The Haggadah must be recited in a language that is understood by the participants at the Seder. Before reciting the Haggadah, bear in mind that this recital fulfills the mitzva of recounting the Exodus from Egypt. The Haggadah is recited with reverence, and not while reclining.

The plate with the matza is raised, and the following paragraph is said:

הָא לַחְמָא עַנְיָא דִּי אֲכָלוּ אַבְהָתָנָא בְּאַרְעָא דְמִצְרָיִם. כָּל דִּכְפִין יֵיתֵי וְיֵיכוֹל, כָּל דִּצְרִיךְ יֵיתֵי וְיִפְסַח. הָשַׁתָּא הָכָא, לְשָׁנָה הַבָּאָה בְּאַרְעָא דְיִשְׂרָאֵל. הָשַׁתָּא עַבְדֵי, לְשָׁנָה הַבָּאָה בְּנֵי חוֹרִין:

In Anticipation of Celebrating Pesach Next Year in Jerusalem

הא לחמא עניא The Haggadah instructs us to invite both the hungry and the needy to our Pesach Seder. Is there a difference between these two types of individuals? To provide the theoretical basis for his answer, Rav Yehonatan directs our attention to a Talmudic ruling regarding Pesach eve: "On Pesach eve close to *mincha* [the afternoon prayer] one should not eat until it is dark."[8]

In discussing this ruling, the Talmud investigates why the Rabbis forbade eating and whether the prohibition extends from the time of *mincha gedola* – when mincha is recited earlier in the day – or from the time of *mincha ketana,* when mincha is recited later in the day. The Talmud concludes that if the Sages forbade eating from mincha gedola, they did so to free up *Am Yisrael*'s time to offer the Pesach sacrifice. If they forbade eating from mincha ketana, they did so to ensure that Am Yisrael would be hungry and eager to eat matza on Seder night.

Notwithstanding these two logical possibilities, by not specifying which mincha it refers to, the mishna also seems to imply that on all Pesach eves, including those after the Destruction of the Temple, Am Yisrael must observe this prohibition. Since after the Destruction, no sacrifices would be offered, this should mean that the prohibition has nothing to do with offering

This is the bread of affliction that our fathers ate in the land of Egypt. Whoever is hungry, let him come and eat; whoever is needy, let him come and partake from the Pesach sacrifice. Now we are here, but next year may we be in the Land of Israel. Now [we are] slaves, but next year may we be freed men.

the sacrifice. If so, why does the Talmud debate the two options?

Rav Yehonatan explains that the Talmudic dispute teaches us that even after the Destruction both reasons for the prohibition remain, for even after the Destruction the Rabbis commanded Am Yisrael to follow as many of the Temple laws as possible; the Jews' observance illustrating how eagerly they await the Temple's rebuilding, as they proclaim throughout the year, "May the Temple be rebuilt speedily in our days."[9]

Applying the Talmudic distinction between not eating in order to promote hunger and not eating in order to remember the Temple sacrifice, Rav Yehonatan explains why we symbolically invite the hungry and the needy. The hungry man symbolizes the requirement that we be hungry in order to fulfill the commandment of eating the matza properly. The needy man, invited, as the Haggadah puts it, to "come and partake from the Pesach sacrifice," symbolizes our eternal hope that the Temple will soon be rebuilt. We even proclaim at the end of this section of the Haggadah, "Now we are here, but next year may we be in the Land of Israel."

In Anticipation of the Third Temple

כָּל דִּכְפִין יֵיתֵי וְיֵיכוֹל Rav Yehonatan comments upon the seemingly repetitive command to invite the

Remove the plate with the matza temporarily from the table, or set it down on the far end of the table, and pour the second cup of wine, then have a child ask the following four questions. (If no child is present, another participant should ask the questions.)

מַה נִּשְׁתַּנָּה הַלַּיְלָה הַזֶּה מִכָּל הַלֵּילוֹת?

שֶׁבְּכָל הַלֵּילוֹת אָנוּ אוֹכְלִין חָמֵץ וּמַצָּה, הַלַּיְלָה הַזֶּה כֻּלּוֹ מַצָּה:

שֶׁבְּכָל הַלֵּילוֹת אָנוּ אוֹכְלִין שְׁאָר יְרָקוֹת, הַלַּיְלָה הַזֶּה מָרוֹר:

שֶׁבְּכָל הַלֵּילוֹת אֵין אָנוּ מַטְבִּילִין אֲפִלּוּ פַּעַם אֶחָת, הַלַּיְלָה הַזֶּה שְׁתֵּי פְעָמִים:

שֶׁבְּכָל הַלֵּילוֹת אָנוּ אוֹכְלִין בֵּין יוֹשְׁבִין וּבֵין מְסֻבִּין, הַלַּיְלָה הַזֶּה כֻּלָּנוּ מְסֻבִּין:

hungry to "come and eat" and the needy to "come and partake from the Pesach sacrifice." He explains how these two commands remind us of the Sages' advice regarding how to comply with the Torah's command, "and you shall not break a bone in it [i.e., the Pesach sacrifice]"[10]: first the Jew must eat so that he is not hungry and then he may partake of the sacrifice. Thus, for instance, the Jerusalem Talmud advises the Jew to eat before partaking of the Pesach sacrifice, so that in his haste to satiate himself, he does not accidentally break a bone.

Even though this law only applies to Temple times when the sacrifice was offered, our Sages have applied it to the afikoman as well, for the afikoman represents the Pesach sacrifice at the Seder. The Sages are concerned that if we do not maintain this practice when eating the

Why is this night different from all other nights?

For on all nights we eat either *chametz* or matza,
but on this night only matza!

For on all nights we eat other vegetables,
and on this night bitter herbs!

For on all nights we do not dip our food even once,
on this night we do it twice!

For on all nights we eat either sitting upright or reclining, and on this night we all recline!

afikoman, than next year, in Jerusalem – when we partake of the sacrifice – we might err.

On Seder night we not only commemorate the historical event of the Exodus but also envision our future when we will offer the Pesach sacrifice once again in the Temple. We adhere to the proper halachic requirements as if the Temple was still standing,[11] so we begin by proclaiming, "whoever is hungry let him come and eat," because we are required to eat before partaking from the Pesach sacrifice. Once our stomachs are full and we are confident that no one will eat in a rush and break a bone we say "whoever is needy, let him come and partake from the Pesach sacrifice." Eagerly awaiting the rebuilding of the Temple, we conclude this passage of the Haggadah with, "Now we are here, but next year [when the Temple is rebuilt] may we be in the Land of Israel."

Return the plate with the matzot to the table and uncover the matzot. The recitation of the Haggadah continues:

עֲבָדִים הָיִינוּ לְפַרְעֹה בְּמִצְרָיִם, וַיּוֹצִיאֵנוּ יְיָ אֱלֹהֵינוּ מִשָּׁם בְּיָד חֲזָקָה וּבִזְרוֹעַ נְטוּיָה. וְאִלּוּ לֹא הוֹצִיא הַקָּדוֹשׁ בָּרוּךְ הוּא אֶת אֲבוֹתֵינוּ מִמִּצְרַיִם, הֲרֵי אָנוּ וּבָנֵינוּ וּבְנֵי בָנֵינוּ מְשֻׁעְבָּדִים הָיִינוּ לְפַרְעֹה בְּמִצְרָיִם. וַאֲפִלּוּ כֻּלָּנוּ חֲכָמִים, כֻּלָּנוּ נְבוֹנִים, כֻּלָּנוּ זְקֵנִים, כֻּלָּנוּ יוֹדְעִים אֶת הַתּוֹרָה מִצְוָה עָלֵינוּ לְסַפֵּר בִּיצִיאַת מִצְרָיִם. וְכָל הַמַּרְבֶּה לְסַפֵּר בִּיצִיאַת מִצְרַיִם, הֲרֵי זֶה מְשֻׁבָּח:

From Redemption to Revelation

עבדים היינו לפרעה במצרים With the words "we were slaves to Pharaoh in Egypt," we begin our response to the four questions. Yet several questions remain unaddressed. For instance, the Jewish people observed Pesach in Egypt for one day and left Egypt during the daytime. In commemorating this event, why do we commemorate the Exodus at nighttime with the Seder and celebrate Pesach for seven days?

While it is true that the Exodus from Egypt commenced at night with the slaying of the firstborn, it concluded seven days later, on the twenty-first of Nissan, with the parting of the Red Sea. In Egypt, Hashem revealed His *etzba Elohim* by slaying the firstborn, but at the Red Sea He revealed His *yad hagedola*, as it is written, "*Bnei Yisrael* saw the great hand that Hashem inflicted upon Egypt."[12] Thus, in performing the Seder at night and observing Pesach for seven days, we mark both the beginning and the completion of the Exodus from Egypt.

We were slaves to Pharaoh in Egypt, and the Lord, our God, took us out from there with a strong hand and with an outstretched arm. And if God had not taken our ancestors out of Egypt, then we, our children and our children's children would still be subservient to Pharaoh in Egypt. Even if we were all wise, or we were all full of understanding, or we were all elders, or we were all knowledgeable in the Torah, it would still be incumbent upon us to recount the story of the Exodus from Egypt – and whoever expands upon the recounting of the story of the Exodus from Egypt is praiseworthy.

The Purpose of Redemption

ויוציאנו ה' אלוהינו משם The Torah teaches, "And he took us out of there in order to bring us, to give us the land that He swore to our forefathers."[13] This verse teaches us that Hashem took the Jews out of Egypt so that He could bring them to *Eretz Yisrael*. The Rabbis explain that just as the redemption from Egypt commenced on Seder night, so too the future redemption of the Jewish people will transpire on Seder night when He will transport Bnei Yisrael to Eretz Yisrael on the wings of eagles and bring about the ultimate purpose of redemption.

Prioritizing Life

ואילו לא הוציא The obligation to transgress in order to save a life is fundamental to Judaism, as demonstrated by the story about Elisha, the prophet, who miraculously brought a deceased child back to life. Tosafot relates that Elisha, even though he was a priest – forbidden from

מַעֲשֶׂה בְּרַבִּי אֱלִיעֶזֶר וְרַבִּי יְהוֹשֻׁעַ וְרַבִּי אֶלְעָזָר בֶּן עֲזַרְיָה וְרַבִּי עֲקִיבָא וְרַבִּי טַרְפוֹן, שֶׁהָיוּ מְסֻבִּין בִּבְנֵי בְרַק, וְהָיוּ מְסַפְּרִים בִּיצִיאַת מִצְרַיִם כָּל אוֹתוֹ הַלַּיְלָה, עַד שֶׁבָּאוּ תַלְמִידֵיהֶם וְאָמְרוּ לָהֶם: רַבּוֹתֵינוּ, הִגִּיעַ זְמַן קְרִיאַת שְׁמַע שֶׁל שַׁחֲרִית:

אָמַר רַבִּי אֶלְעָזָר בֶּן עֲזַרְיָה: הֲרֵי אֲנִי כְּבֶן שִׁבְעִים שָׁנָה, וְלֹא זָכִיתִי שֶׁתֵּאָמֵר יְצִיאַת מִצְרַיִם בַּלֵּילוֹת, עַד שֶׁדְּרָשָׁהּ בֶּן זוֹמָא, שֶׁנֶּאֱמַר: לְמַעַן תִּזְכֹּר אֶת יוֹם צֵאתְךָ מֵאֶרֶץ מִצְרַיִם

coming into contact with a corpse – exposed himself to this ritual impurity to save a life.[14] Elisha may have learned to apply this exemption by observing Hashem's actions in Egypt.

By the time the Jewish people left Egypt they had descended to the forty-ninth level of impurity. Had they descended to the fiftieth and lowest spiritual level, they would have been lost forever. Hashem descended into the cesspool of Egyptian impurity in order to save both the physical and spiritual lives of the Jewish nation.

As the Haggadah relates, "Hashem, our God, took us out from there." One might have asked: "Why did Hashem enter Egypt, exposing Himself to ritual impurity?" The Haggadah answers: "Had Hakadosh Baruch Hu not [immediately] taken our fathers out from Egypt," the Jewish people would have descended to the fiftieth level of impurity and they would have been wiped out.

Redemption and the Purpose of the Jew

אמר רבי אלעזר בן עזריה Bnei Yisrael did not leave Egypt in order to escape physical, or, even, spiritual servitude. Bnei

An incident happened with Rabbi Eliezer, Rabbi Yehoshua, Rabbi Elazar ben Azaryah, Rabbi Akiva and Rabbi Tarfon. They were reclining at the [Seder] table in B'nei Brak, and they were recounting the story of the Exodus from Egypt all that night, until their students came in and told them: "Our rabbis! The time for reciting the morning *Shema* has arrived!"

Rabbi Eleazar ben Azaryah said: I am like a seventy-year-old man, yet I did not merit [to understand why] the Exodus from Egypt should be mentioned every night, until Ben Zoma explained it: It says *(Devarim 16:3)*, "So that you remember the day you left Egypt all the days of your life." Just "the days

Yisrael left Egypt in order to receive the Torah, which would enable them to serve Hashem through Torah study and observance. The *Midrash* recounts that when Moshe ascended to the heavens to receive the Torah, the angels argued that man was unworthy. Moshe rebutted the angel's protests by reminding them that Hashem wrote in His Torah, "I am your God who has taken you out of Egypt."[15] Moshe reminded the angels that Bnei Yisrael could appreciate the Torah because they had experienced slavery and redemption. Immediately following Rabbi Elazar ben Azarya's teaching obligating us to remember the Exodus at night, we remind ourselves of why we were redeemed by reciting, "Blessed is the One who has given the Torah to His people Yisrael."

Remembering the Exodus From Egypt

עד שדרשה בן זומא Why does Ben Zoma interpret the phrase "all the days of your life" to obligate us to

כֹּל יְמֵי חַיֶּיךָ. יְמֵי חַיֶּיךָ הַיָּמִים. כֹּל יְמֵי חַיֶּיךָ הַלֵּילוֹת. וַחֲכָמִים אוֹמְרִים: יְמֵי חַיֶּיךָ הָעוֹלָם הַזֶּה. כֹּל יְמֵי חַיֶּיךָ לְהָבִיא לִימוֹת הַמָּשִׁיחַ:

בָּרוּךְ הַמָּקוֹם, בָּרוּךְ הוּא. בָּרוּךְ שֶׁנָּתַן תּוֹרָה לְעַמּוֹ יִשְׂרָאֵל, בָּרוּךְ הוּא:

כְּנֶגֶד אַרְבָּעָה בָנִים דִּבְּרָה תוֹרָה:

אֶחָד חָכָם, וְאֶחָד רָשָׁע, וְאֶחָד תָּם, וְאֶחָד שֶׁאֵינוֹ יוֹדֵעַ לִשְׁאוֹל:

remember the Exodus from Egypt both during the daytime and the nighttime, while the Rabbis declare that it obligates us to remember the Exodus both during the contemporary and the Messianic eras? The roots of this dispute may be found in Shmuel's declaration in the *Gemara*: "There is no difference between the contemporary era and the Messianic era other than the Jewish nation's servitude to foreign nations."[16] Rabbeinu Asher explains that Shmuel's contention is that even during the Messianic era, the Jews will be obligated to fulfill all of the Torah's commandments. Ben Zoma, like Shmuel, is of the opinion that all the mitzvot will continue to apply even after the Messiah's arrival, so there is no need for a special verse teaching that the Exodus must be remembered in the Messianic era. According to Ben Zoma, this verse teaches the obligation to also remember the Exodus at night.

of your life" would have referred to the days; "all the days of your life" therefore refers to the nights as well. But the other sages say that just "the days of your life" would have referred to the present world; the addition of the word "all" comes to include the Messianic era as well.

Blessed be God! Blessed be He! Blessed is the One Who gave the Torah to His people Israel! Blessed be He!

The Torah speaks of four different kinds of sons:

One who is wise, one who is wicked, one who is simple, and one who does not know enough to ask questions.

Calculating the Years of Servitude

יציאת מצרים בלילות During the *Berit ben Habetarim,* Hashem told Avraham that Bnei Yisrael would be enslaved for four hundred years.[17] Yet Bnei Yisrael were only enslaved for two hundred and ten years.[18] Some commentators explain that since the Egyptians forced Bnei Yisrael to work day and night, Hashem counted the two hundred and ten years as if they were four hundred. In commemorating this round-the-clock servitude, we must remember the Exodus from Egypt both during the day and during the night.

חָכָם מַה הוּא אוֹמֵר? מָה הָעֵדֹת וְהַחֻקִּים וְהַמִּשְׁפָּטִים, אֲשֶׁר צִוָּה יְיָ אֱלֹהֵינוּ אֶתְכֶם. וְאַף אַתָּה אֱמָר לוֹ כְּהִלְכוֹת הַפֶּסַח: אֵין מַפְטִירִין אַחַר הַפֶּסַח אֲפִיקוֹמָן:

The Wise Son and the Wicked Son – A Distinct Difference

חכם מה הוא אומר The author of the Haggadah criticizes the wicked son for excluding himself from the Jewish community by asking, "Of what purpose is this service to you?" The words "to you" imply that he has disenfranchised himself from the community of believers; however, the wise son uses a surprisingly similar phrase – "has commanded *you*" (italics added) – and escapes rebuke. Rav Yehonatan explains that the reason for the Haggadah's seemingly contradictory reactions to the wise son and the wicked son's questions lies in their biblical sources.

The Torah introduces the wise son's question with the crucial term "saying": "If your child asks you tomorrow *saying*, 'What are the testimonies, statutes, and laws...?' "(italics added)[19] Rav Yehonatan explains that the word "saying" encourages the parent to respond and implies further inquiry. The wise son asks with the intention of becoming better equipped to answer his own questions, of arriving at a deeper understanding of Torah and mitzvot. His question illustrates genuine interest, a yearning to strengthen his connection to the community. The wicked son does not incorporate any such expression of interest because he is not searching for a response. He asks in order to challenge the Torah and uproot it. He intentionally separates himself from the community.

AUTHOR'S COMMENTS The mitzva of redeeming one's firstborn, male child commemorates the slaying of the firstborn, which led to the deliverance of Bnei

What does the wise son say? "What are the testimonies and the statutes and the laws that Hashem, our God, has commanded you?" *(Devarim 6:20)*. You, in turn, should tell him all about the laws of the Pesach sacrifice, [for instance]: "One may not eat dessert, the afikoman, after the final taste of the offering."

Yisrael from Egypt. The Torah instructs parents to tell their children about this mitzva:

> 'And it shall be when your son asks you at some future time, 'What is this?' you shall say to him, 'With a strong hand Hashem removed us from Egypt from the house of bondage. And it happened when Pharaoh stubbornly refused to send us out, that Hashem killed all the firstborn in the land of Egypt, from the firstborn of man to the firstborn of beast. Therefore I offer to Hashem all male first issue of the womb, and I shall redeem all the firstborn of my sons.'[20]

Rashi comments that this response suits the child who does not know how to ask. Rav Shlomo Aviner observes that the Haggadah's author provides the wicked son with the same response. While the child who does not know how to ask is no scholar, is it fair to compare him with the wicked son? Why are these two sons assigned the same answer?

Rav Aviner explains that central to the concept of Jewish education is the tenet that nobody can remain in neutral, slowly stagnating. Judaism believes that an individual either progresses or regresses. Judaism does not define positive growth quantitatively, by the number of answers an individual possesses. Instead, Judaism defines positive growth qualitatively, by the increase of an individual's innate desire to ask questions and give free reign to his intellectual curiosity. Therefore, the child who does not know how to ask is not yet wicked, but his indifference towards questioning and his

רָשָׁע מַה הוּא אוֹמֵר? מָה הָעֲבֹדָה הַזֹּאת לָכֶם? לָכֶם וְלֹא לוֹ. וּלְפִי שֶׁהוֹצִיא אֶת עַצְמוֹ מִן הַכְּלָל, כָּפַר בְּעִקָּר:

lack of interest indicate that he may become so. This is why the Haggadah instructs the parent: "As for the son who is unable to ask, you must initiate the subject for him [literally, 'open his mouth'], as it is written: "You shall tell your son on that day: 'It is because of this that Hashem did so for me when I went out of Egypt.' "[21]

Many commentators interpret the Haggadah's advice to mean that the parent must "open the mouth of the child," providing him with answers, but this is not the case. The parent must cultivate the child's mind in order to promote inquiry. A responsible Jewish parent cannot allow a child steeped in apathy to drift towards wickedness. Parents must find ways to peak their children's curiosity and encourage inquisitiveness.

We must learn not to always expect answers either from ourselves or from our children because in order to espouse the profoundest of ideas, in order to transmit *devar Hashem* to the next generation, we must focus upon not losing the desire to question. This trait has been essential to our identity for so many generations. This is the trait being cultivated, honed, and honored throughout the many facets of the Seder ceremony.

Remembering the Past as the Key to Perpetuating the Future

רשע מה הוא אומר Yirmiyahu, the prophet, wrote in *Eicha*:

> Jerusalem remembered in the days of her affliction and of her anguish all her treasures that she had from the days of old; now that her people fall by the hand of the adversary and no one helps her, the adversaries have seen her, they have mocked at her desolations.[22]

What does the wicked son say? "Of what purpose is this service to you?" *(Shemot 12:26)* **– implying "to you," but not "to him"! Because he excludes himself from the rest of the community he has denied a fundamental principle.**

Yirmiyahu begged the Jews to keep Jerusalem alive in their memories, both her "days of affliction and anguish" and "her treasures from the days of old." One who does so is praiseworthy; one who does not do so joins the ranks of the wicked, who "mocked" Jerusalem in her desolation doing nothing to perpetuate her memory. Yirmiyahu reminded the Jewish people of the importance of remembering its history. The Jewish people's first taste of suffering took place in Egypt; therefore, every Shabbat and Jewish holiday is dedicated to commemorating the Exodus from Egypt. The Jews believe that remembering and recounting the past will facilitate their future redemption.

The wicked son sees no significance in remembering or learning from history. He rejects the entire notion of the Seder because he cannot understand why the Jewish people is commanded to remember the Exodus when still stuck in exile. Unfortunately, he fails to realize that by remembering their history, Jews strengthen their allegiance to their people and ensure a Jewish future.

AUTHOR'S COMMENTS When Balak, the king of Moav, wanted to dispose of Bnei Yisrael, he hired Bilaam, a wicked prophet, to curse them. Balak's messengers described Bnei Yisrael as "a people [that] has come out of Egypt."[23] Bilaam, in speaking with Hashem about his mission, described Bnei Yisrael as "the people coming out of Egypt."[24] Rav Moshe Feinstein, z"l, points out that Balak's messenger's described Bnei Yisrael using the grammatically correct past tense, as a people who had come out of Egypt. Bilaam surprisingly

וְאַף אַתָּה הַקְהֵה אֶת שִׁנָּיו וֶאֱמָר לוֹ: בַּעֲבוּר זֶה עָשָׂה יְיָ לִי בְּצֵאתִי מִמִּצְרָיִם. לִי וְלֹא לוֹ. אִלּוּ הָיָה שָׁם, לֹא הָיָה נִגְאָל:

used the present tense to describe Bnei Yisrael as a people coming out of Egypt. Why did he do so if Bnei Yisrael had left Egypt almost forty years ago?

Rav Moshe explains that Bnei Yisrael relives its history on a daily basis. History is not only the story of the past; it is the key to ensuring the future. Bilaam was aware of this exceptional Jewish ability. He understood that Bnei Yisrael would commemorate their Exodus from Egypt every day because celebrating their past is central to their greatness. When contemplating his mission to curse Bnei Yisrael, Bilaam described Bnei Yisrael as a people still coming out of Egypt because these words recall the unique force he would have to battle against.[25]

I once visited Auschwitz with a group of students. As we entered the ruins housing the gas chambers, I noticed a sign on the entrance that quoted twentieth-century philosopher, George Santayana: "If we do not learn from history, then history is doomed to repeat itself." The Jewish people has known this truth for over two millennia. No matter how unpleasant and disheartening its history has been, it has always been expected to remember its time in exile in order to facilitate its ultimate redemption.

The Difference Between Being Hashem's Servants and Being Pharaoh's Slaves

רשע מה הוא אומר What is the difference between a servant of Hashem and the average slave or servant forced to work for a human master? In defining Hashem's faithful servant, the *Midrash* relates: "One should not say, 'I cannot eat pig [because it is bad for my health or I dislike its taste],' ... but rather [one should say], 'I can eat [it], but what can I do, my Father, Who is in Heaven, decreed

You, in turn, should set his teeth on edge (i.e., cause him aggravation) and tell him: "Because of this Hashem did for me when I left Egypt" *(ibid. 13:8)* **– implying "for me," but not "for him"! If he had been there then, he would not have been redeemed.**

that I may not to do so.' "[26] The *Midrash* teaches that Hashem's servants should not perform the mitzvot to benefit themselves; rather, they should observe the mitzvot because Hashem commanded them to, even if they do not understand the reasons for performing them.

The wicked son views the world pragmatically and cannot comprehend purely ideological motivations. Thus, he asks: "Of what purpose is this service to you?" He sets himself apart from the Jewish nation, a people basing its life upon the ideology of serving Hashem.

The Haggadah's response to the wicked son delineates the difference between being enslaved to a human being and serving Hashem. Pharaoh enslaved us to aggrandize himself by creating monuments in stone for him. Hashem liberated us so that we would be free to serve Him by developing ourselves spiritually and by committing ourselves to a life based upon ideological fulfillment.

AUTHOR'S COMMENTS Even today, we continue to struggle with the notion of becoming Hashem's servants. The hedonistic society we live in is founded upon self-indulgence, not ideological commitment. Our lives revolve around modern conveniences, such as the internet, which enable instant gratification. Success is measured by how much money we earn, not by our lofty ideological ambitions. I recall asking a group of Jewish high schoolers what they wanted to do when they grew up. One of them sincerely responded that he wanted to become a corporate raider and make his first million in his first year on the job.

תָּם מַה הוּא אוֹמֵר. מַה זֹּאת? וְאָמַרְתָּ אֵלָיו: בְּחֹזֶק יָד הוֹצִיאָנוּ יְיָ מִמִּצְרַיִם מִבֵּית עֲבָדִים:

וְשֶׁאֵינוֹ יוֹדֵעַ לִשְׁאוֹל אַתְּ פְּתַח לוֹ שֶׁנֶּאֱמַר: וְהִגַּדְתָּ לְבִנְךָ בַּיּוֹם הַהוּא לֵאמֹר: בַּעֲבוּר זֶה עָשָׂה יְיָ לִי בְּצֵאתִי מִמִּצְרָיִם:

יָכוֹל מֵרֹאשׁ חֹדֶשׁ. תַּלְמוּד לוֹמַר בַּיּוֹם הַהוּא. אִי בַּיּוֹם הַהוּא, יָכוֹל מִבְּעוֹד יוֹם, תַּלְמוּד לוֹמַר בַּעֲבוּר זֶה. בַּעֲבוּר זֶה לֹא אָמַרְתִּי, אֶלָּא בְּשָׁעָה שֶׁיֵּשׁ מַצָּה וּמָרוֹר מֻנָּחִים לְפָנֶיךָ:

There was a time, not long ago, when such an answer was deemed unacceptable. Previous generations understood what it meant to work for a living. They appreciated an opportunity to dedicate themselves to a cause without demanding personal self-gratification. The State of Israel owes its existence to a generation of *halutzim* who were willing to risk and even sacrifice their lives in order to create a Jewish homeland. The halutzim drained the swamps and farmed the land. They toiled to actualize a vision they were unlikely to witness in their lifetimes, a beautiful, thriving homeland destined for the use of future generations.

Ideologically, Religious Zionism takes a similar path. All religious Jews believe that the Jewish state should be founded upon Torah principles and should base itself upon the Halacha. Religious Zionists understand that while this vision has not yet come to pass, we need to commit

What does the simple son say? "What is this?" *(ibid. 13:14)*. "And you shall say to him: With a strong hand Hashem the Lord took us out of Egypt, from the house of bondage" *(ibid.)*.

As for the one who does not know enough to ask questions – you must initiate the subject for him (lit., open 'his mouth'), as it says, "You shall tell your child on that day: Because of this Hashem did for me when I left Egypt" *(Shemot 13:8)*.

One might think that it (the recounting of the Exodus to one's children) should be done from the first of the month. Therefore the Torah says, "On that day" *(ibid.)*. But based on the words "On that *day*" one might think that it should be done while it is still daytime. Therefore the Torah says, "It is because of *this*" *(ibid.)*, implying that "I am speaking only of the time when matza and maror are spread out before you."

ourselves to building up Eretz Yisrael today, so that this dream can become a reality tomorrow. Taking this path means truly becoming Hashem's servant.

On Seder night we must remind ourselves of our true aspirations. We must internalize the experience of being Hashem's servants and teach ourselves to adhere to the Torah recipe for religious and spiritual growth.

מְתְּחִלָּה עוֹבְדֵי עֲבוֹדָה זָרָה הָיוּ אֲבוֹתֵינוּ, וְעַכְשָׁו קֵרְבָנוּ הַמָּקוֹם לַעֲבוֹדָתוֹ, שֶׁנֶּאֱמַר: וַיֹּאמֶר יְהוֹשֻׁעַ אֶל כָּל הָעָם: כֹּה אָמַר יְיָ אֱלֹהֵי יִשְׂרָאֵל: בְּעֵבֶר הַנָּהָר יָשְׁבוּ אֲבוֹתֵיכֶם מֵעוֹלָם, תֶּרַח אֲבִי אַבְרָהָם וַאֲבִי נָחוֹר, וַיַּעַבְדוּ אֱלֹהִים אֲחֵרִים. וָאֶקַּח אֶת אֲבִיכֶם אֶת אַבְרָהָם מֵעֵבֶר הַנָּהָר, וָאוֹלֵךְ אוֹתוֹ בְּכָל אֶרֶץ כְּנָעַן, וָאַרְבֶּה אֶת זַרְעוֹ, וָאֶתֶּן לוֹ אֶת יִצְחָק: וָאֶתֵּן לְיִצְחָק אֶת יַעֲקֹב וְאֶת עֵשָׂו, וָאֶתֵּן לְעֵשָׂו אֶת הַר שֵׂעִיר לָרֶשֶׁת אוֹתוֹ, וְיַעֲקֹב וּבָנָיו יָרְדוּ מִצְרָיִם:

The Significance of Yitzchak's Name

מתחילה עובדי עבודה זרה היו When Sarah overheard Hashem informing Avraham that he would have a son, she laughed. As a reminder of Sarah's lapse of faith and Hashem's displeasure, Hashem named this son Yitzchak, a name stemming from the verb *litzchok* – to laugh. In order to discourage us from further criticizing Sarah, Hashem incorporated in the name Yitzchak various positive connotations. For example, according to the *Midrash*, the letters comprising the name, Yitzchak, are intrinsically significant. The *yud* has the numeric value of ten, recalling the Ten Commandments. The *tzadi* has the numeric value of ninety, hinting at how old Sarah was when she gave birth to Yitzchak. The *chet* has the numeric value of eight, recalling the eight days leading up to circumcision, and the *kuf* has the numeric value of one hundred, hinting at how old Avraham was when Yitzchak was born.[27]

Another midrash teaches us how various Hebrew letters longed to appear in Sarah's name. The midrash

Originally our ancestors were idol-worshippers, but now God has drawn us near to His service. Thus it says, "Joshua said to all the people: Thus said Hashem, the God of Israel: Your ancestors had always dwelt on the other side of the river – Terah, the father of Avraham and the father of Nahor – and they worshipped other gods. Then I took your father Avraham from the other side of the [Euphrates] River, and I had him travel throughout all of the land of Canaan. I increased his offspring and gave him Yitzchak, and to Yitzchak I gave Jacob and Esau. To Esau I gave Mount Seir to take possession of, and Jacob and his sons went down to Egypt" *(Yehoshua 24:2-4)*.

teaches that the yud from Sarah's original name, Sarai, was upset that it had been replaced by the *heh*. To console the yud, Hashem placed it at the beginning of Yitzchak's name. As the Torah confirms: "Avraham called the name of his son, who was born to him whom Sarah had borne him – Yitzchak."[28] The Torah explicitly notes that Sarah, with a heh, bore Avraham a son named Yitzchak.[29]

Regardless of What the Nations of the World Believe, the Jewish People is the Chosen People

ואתן ליצחק את יעקב ואת עשו The Torah recounts: "Then [when they heard about the parting of the Red Sea] were the chiefs of Edom confounded; trembling gripped the powers of Moav, all the inhabitants of Canaan dissolved."[30] This verse mentions three nations that were enemies of the Jewish people: Edom, Moav and Canaan. After hearing about Hashem's parting of the Red Sea, they were frigh-

ברוך שומר הבטחתו לישראל, ברוך הוא. שהקדוש ברוך הוא חשב את הקץ לעשות כמה שאמר לאברהם אבינו בברית בין הבתרים, שנאמר: ויאמר לאברם: ידע תדע כי גר יהיה זרעך בארץ לא להם, ועבדום וענו אתם ארבע מאות שנה, וגם את הגוי אשר יעבדו דן אנכי, ואחרי כן יצאו ברכש גדול:

tened of Him. Rav Yehonatan explains why this specific miracle terrified them.

At first, the Edomites did not fear the Jewish people at all because they felt virtuous, wronged by Yaakov's theft of Esav's blessings. When Bnei Yisrael was enslaved in Egypt, the Edomites rejoiced. Apparently, the blessing that Hashem gave to Avraham, that his descendants would "spread towards the sea," constantly growing in number, was not coming true. When the Edomites heard that Hashem had parted the Red Sea, they realized that the blessing was coming true. Edom was "confounded" by Egypt's defeat and the Jewish nation's "spread[ing] towards the sea."

Moav claimed that the Jewish people was not Avraham's legitimate offspring because it descended from the illegitimate union of Avimelech and Sarah. Our Sages teach: "All *mamzerim* will be washed away by water";[31] the generation of the flood had engaged in sexual promiscuity, leading to the birth of mamzerim, and their world was washed away by water. Seeing the Jewish people's rapid population growth, Pharaoh believed they must be engaged in promiscuous relationships. To demonstrate this he instructed that they be "washed away by water," decreeing that "every son that will be born – into the River you shall throw him."[32] When Hashem miraculously

Blessed be the One Who keeps His promise to Yisrael! Blessed be He! For God calculated the end [of our captivity], in order to fulfill what He had said to our forefather Avraham at the Covenant Between the Pieces, as it says, "And He said to Avraham: 'Know with certainty that your offspring will be strangers in a land not their own. They will be enslaved there and oppressed for four hundred years and also I shall judge the nation whom they will serve, and after that they will go out with great wealth.'" *(Bereishit 15:13-14)*

saved Bnei Yisrael from the waters of the Red Sea and washed the Egyptians away, Moav realized their mistake. "Trembling gripped the powers of Moav," as the Jewish people was established as Avraham's rightful heir.

After leaving Egypt, Bnei Yisrael did not take the direct route to Canaan, through Philistine territory; rather, they took the Red Sea route. The Canaanites interpreted this as a sign of weakness, believing that Bnei Yisrael feared a direct confrontation with them. This convinced the Canaanites that Bnei Yisrael would not inherit Canaan. The "inhabitants of Canaan dissolved" in fear upon realizing that Bnei Yisrael had actually taken the sea route in order to further reveal Hashem's greatness.

Calculating the Years in Exile

ועבדום וענו אותם ארבע מאות שנה Hashem told Avraham that the Jewish people would be oppressed as strangers in a foreign land for four hundred years. Since the Torah does not specify that the oppression will take place in Egypt, some commentators explain that the four hundred years refers to all four exiles that *Kelal Yisrael* will undergo. However this explanation is problematic for after subtracting two hundred and ten years spent in Egypt, only one hundred and ninety years remain for the other three exiles. Our own lengthy exile still carries on at close to the two thousand year mark.

Rav Yehonatan suggests that had the Jewish people been forced to endure three exiles in such a short time, the experience would have been too intense and too taxing for them to bear. Hashem had specified four hundred years of exile, but He demonstrated his mercy for *Kelal Yisrael* by lengthening the number of years. This explanation is problematic because it suggests that Hashem reneged on His word by lengthening the exile.

Rav Yehonatan solves this problem through a closer reading of the words "and also" in the verse: "They will be enslaved there and oppressed for four hundred years and also I shall judge the nation." Hashem told Avraham that the Jewish people would be oppressed for four hundred years. However, He immediately added the words "and also." Usually the words "and also" are read as the beginning of the next phrase, "And also I shall judge the nation"; however, by reading these words as part of the previous phrase, "and oppressed for four hundred years and also," Rav Yehonatan reveals that Hashem had already informed Avraham that if necessary the exile would be extended.

The Jewish People's Rapid Population Increase Facilitated Early Redemption

וגם את הגוי אשר יעבודו Hashem told Avraham in the Covenant Between the Pieces that the Jewish people would be in exile for four hundred years, yet the exile in Egypt lasted only two hundred and ten years. Some commentators explain that four hundred years includes both the Egyptian exile and other exiles as well; however, Rav Yehonatan provides another explanation. The Jews were supposed to suffer exile in Egypt for four hundred years. Rav Yehonatan deduces from the verse "the Children of Israel multiplied"[33] rapidly that Bnei Yisrael's rapid population increase enabled them to fulfill the quota of suffering in fewer years, thus, meriting an early redemption.

Since decreasing the length of enslavement was contingent upon rapid population growth, Avraham was distraught that his descendants were to be exiled in Egypt, for the Egyptians did not practice circumcision. Hashem's promise that Avraham would have many descendants was contingent upon their continuing to perform the rite of circumcision. Avraham was afraid that under the Egyptian influence his descendants would stop performing circumcision, crippling their ability to multiply rapidly, and requiring them to spend a full four hundred years in Egypt. Therefore, Hashem reassured Avraham at the Covenant Between the Pieces that he would become the father of a great nation. Bnei Yisrael would continue to circumcise their children in Egypt; they would multiply, and, therefore, they would spend only two hundred and ten years in Egypt, instead of four hundred.

Hashem Does More for the Jewish People Because of Their Closeness to Him

ואחרי כן יצאו ברכוש גדול The Torah reports that prior to praying to Hashem Moshe left the city limits: "And Moshe went outside the city."[34] Rashi explains that Moshe did this because the cities of Egypt were steeped in the impurity of idolatry and, therefore, were unfit both for prayer and for Hashem's presence. Yet the Torah also tells us that during the plague of slaying of the firstborn, Hashem entered the Egyptian cities, smote the Egyptians, and removed the Jewish people with His mighty hand. Why did Hashem enter the Egyptian cities when He could have sent Moshe or an angel to do the job for Him?

Normally the Torah forbids the ritually pure or the sacred from coming into contact with the ritually impure. For instance, a *kohen* must avoid any physical contact with a corpse; however, there are exceptions. A kohen is permitted close physical proximity to and may even bury several close relatives because of the special relationship he shared with them. An exceptionally close relationship relaxes the ban on coming into contact with impurity. The Torah demonstrates that Hashem had an especially close relationship with the Jewish people and that is why He could personally redeem them from Egypt.

Thus, the Torah reports that "it came to pass, when Pharaoh had let the people go, that God led them not by the way of the land of the Philistines, although that was *near*"(italics added).[35] According to the *Midrash* the word "near" not only refers to a destination but also describes the intimate relationship between Hashem and the Jewish people. Furthermore, the Jewish people are referred to as "Bnei Yisrael, the nation *close* to Him"(italics added).[36] Owing to this special relationship Hashem could expose Himself to Egypt's impurities in order to redeem His close relatives, the Jewish people.

The Role of Egypt and the Nations in the Fulfillment of the Covenant Between the Pieces

וגם את הגוי ... דן אנכי At the Covenant Between the Pieces, Hashem informed Avraham that his descendants would be enslaved in a foreign land. Some commentators explain that Hashem was referring not only to the Egyptian exile but also to the other three exiles the Jewish people would undergo. Rav Yehonatan connects this interpretation with the verse in *Eicha*, "Hashem has done that which He devised; He has carried out His word that He commanded in Kedem [literally, "the days of old," or the name of the place where Abraham dwelled]; He has destroyed without pity; and He has caused the enemy to rejoice over you, He has raised the horn of your adversaries."[37]

Rav Yehonatan explains that Hashem "carried out His word" by informing

Avraham, who was from Kedem, of the four exiles that the Jewish people would be "destroyed [in] without pity." Furthermore, Hashem promised Avraham that He would punish all the other nations who persecuted Bnei Yisrael. This is alluded to in the latter part of the verse from *Eicha*, "He has caused the enemy to rejoice over you." The enemy, Egypt, will rejoice not because it has defeated Bnei Yisrael, but because it shares the burden of punishment with other nations.

Yosef Fulfills the Prophecy of the Covenant Between the Pieces

כי גר יהיה זרעך בארץ לא להם This prophetic statement – cited by the Haggadah from the Covenant Between the Pieces – foretells the first Jewish exile and promises that the Jews will depart from this "alien land" with great wealth. Yosef was instrumental in the Jews moving to Egypt and in ensuring that they would leave with great wealth. The exile was begun with Yosef's brothers selling him into slavery and gained momentum when Yosef invited his father and the rest of the family to join him in Egypt.

When the Jewish people arrived in Egypt, Yosef made certain that they would receive a choice portion of land to settle on and helped them achieve financial security, as he explained to his brothers: "for it was to be a provider that Hashem sent me ahead of you [to Egypt]."[38] In addition to providing his family with its own firm financial basis, Yosef stored Egypt's surplus grain during the years of plenty. When the famine hit, he was able to amass great wealth for Egypt by selling the grain to those in need. When Hashem redeemed the Jewish people, they took the money that Yosef had amassed, leaving Egypt "with great wealth" as Hashem had promised.

The Tribe of Levi's Role

ואחרי כן יצאו ברכוש גדול Hashem promised the Jewish people that having been enslaved and oppressed by the Egyptians, they would be redeemed and leave Egypt with many possessions. The vast majority of the Jewish people were promised material wealth; in contrast, the Levites were promised spiritual wealth, to emphasize that the Jewish people's raison d'etre is the pursuit of spirituality. The Levites were brought out of Egypt solely to serve Hashem and to serve as a role model for the Jewish people, for the *Midrash* teaches that the verse, "do not desecrate My name,"[39] refers to the Levites who would not desecrate the name of Hashem because they serve Him and the Jewish people.[40] The Levite's unique role was revealed when the Jewish people left Egypt, for the Torah states, "I am the Lord Hashem who has sanctified you and taken you out of Egypt."[41] Hashem confirmed the Jewish people's sanctity by taking them out of Egypt and declared that the Levites would be responsible for sustaining their holiness.

AUTHOR'S COMMENTS Two singular mitzvot in *Parshat Shoftim* support the claim that Bnei Yisrael's central purpose is spiritual growth: the commandment not to destroy fruit trees belonging to the enemy during the course of a war, and *egla arufa*. In explaining the logic behind the first mitzva, the Torah writes: "for man [is compared] to the [fruit] tree of the field." What does the Torah's comparison of man to a fruit tree mean? Rabbi Zalman Sorotzkin (1881-1966), who served as a rabbi in Lithuania, explains in his commentary *Oznayim Latora* that the fruit tree provides man with sustenance. This sustenance in turn provides man with the strength necessary to study and grow in Torah. The fruit tree functions as man's partner facilitating his growth towards ever-greater commitment and service to Hashem. Man must treat this benefactor with appropriate gratitude and respect; therefore, he is prohibited from destroying fruit trees, even though this may make it more difficult for him to wage a successful war.

The second mitzva, egla arufa, also stresses the vital place spiritual growth has in the Jew's life. When a corpse is discovered between two cities, and a homicide seems to have been committed, the *beit din* of the city closest to the corpse, must take a heifer and kill it in "*nachal eitan*." According to one interpretation, a "nachal eitan" is a valley that "bares no fruit" (is denuded of vegetation) and has no potential for growth. Rav Yehonatan explains that just as a tree produces fruit for consumption and procreation, man performs mitzvot and raises children for the sake of perpetuating Judaism's future. The corpse found between the cities belongs to an unfortunate individual who can no longer raise a family or fulfill mitzvot and, therefore, he symbolizes someone who "bares no fruit," and sows no seeds to connect himself to Hashem. To symbolize this harsh reality, the egla arufa is killed in a "nachal eitan," a sterile locale: a place representing the absolute inability of this Jew to fulfill his primary spiritual purpose.

Some people believe that peoples' accomplishments and the level of their success can be measured quantitatively by examining their financial success. They are wrong. From a Torah perspective success is measured by the level of one's dedication to Hashem and His Torah: by one's constantly striving to accumulate ever more Torah knowledge, and one's unrelentingly demonstrating, to oneself and others, the importance of passing on this dedication to the next generation as well. When we sit at the Seder with our families, we transmit the message that we left Egypt in order to become servants of Hashem. In doing so, we once again remind ourselves of the Jewish people's purpose, and encourage the younger generations at the Seder to make this message a central element in their lives as well.

Fulfilling a Promise

ואחרי כן יצאו ברכוש גדול Hashem told Moshe to instruct the Jewish people before leaving Egypt: "Please speak in the ears of the people: Let each man request

Cover the matza and then raise the cup.

וְהִיא שֶׁעָמְדָה לַאֲבוֹתֵינוּ וְלָנוּ, שֶׁלֹּא אֶחָד בִּלְבָד עָמַד עָלֵינוּ לְכַלּוֹתֵנוּ, אֶלָּא שֶׁבְּכָל דּוֹר וָדוֹר עוֹמְדִים עָלֵינוּ לְכַלּוֹתֵנוּ, וְהַקָּדוֹשׁ בָּרוּךְ הוּא מַצִּילֵנוּ מִיָּדָם:

Put the cup down and the uncover the matza.

צֵא וּלְמַד מַה בִּקֵּשׁ לָבָן הָאֲרַמִּי לַעֲשׂוֹת לְיַעֲקֹב אָבִינוּ. שֶׁפַּרְעֹה לֹא גָזַר אֶלָּא עַל הַזְּכָרִים, וְלָבָן בִּקֵּשׁ לַעֲקֹר אֶת הַכֹּל. שֶׁנֶּאֱמַר:

אֲרַמִּי אֹבֵד אָבִי, וַיֵּרֶד מִצְרַיְמָה, וַיָּגָר שָׁם בִּמְתֵי מְעָט, וַיְהִי שָׁם לְגוֹי גָּדוֹל עָצוּם וָרָב:

וַיֵּרֶד מִצְרַיְמָה. אָנוּס עַל פִּי הַדִּבּוּר:

of his fellow ... silver vessels and gold vessels."[42]

Rashi explains that Hashem told Moshe to instruct Bnei Yisrael to request valuables from the Egyptians because He had promised Avraham that they would leave Egypt with great wealth. Nevertheless, Hashem used the word "please," which implies that the Jewish people might have been hesitant to fulfill His request. Bnei Yisrael might have hesitated because they feared that if they demanded silver and gold, the Egyptians would realize they planned to escape and would pursue them. Rav Yehonatan explains that Hashem

And it is this that has stood by our fathers and by us! For it is not just one individual who rose against us to annihilate us, but in every single generation people rise up against us to annihilate us, and God saves us from their hands!

Go and see (an illustration of God saving us from annihilation) what Lavan the Aramean wanted to do to our father Jacob. For Pharaoh condemned only the male children, but Lavan sought to obliterate everyone, as it says:

"An Aramean [sought to] destroy my forefather. And he went down to Egypt and sojourned there with a small number of people, and there he became a great, powerful and numerous nation" *(Devarim 26:5)*.

And he went down to Egypt – by force, in response to a Divine decree.

persuaded His people to listen to Him by using the word "please," because He wanted the Egyptians to pursue the Jews, so that He could destroy them at the Red Sea.

Another reason why Bnei Yisrael might have hesitated was that there were righteous Jews anxious to leave Egypt solely in order to serve Hashem. They feared that if they left Egypt with wealth, it would appear that they had ulterior motives. Hashem recognized their sincerity and informed them that He would not misinterpret their motives. Their scruples notwithstanding, He asked them to "please" request

וַיָּגָר שָׁם. מְלַמֵּד שֶׁלֹּא יָרַד יַעֲקֹב אָבִינוּ לְהִשְׁתַּקֵּעַ בְּמִצְרַיִם אֶלָּא לָגוּר שָׁם, שֶׁנֶּאֱמַר: וַיֹּאמְרוּ אֶל פַּרְעֹה: לָגוּר בָּאָרֶץ בָּאנוּ, כִּי אֵין מִרְעֶה לַצֹּאן אֲשֶׁר לַעֲבָדֶיךָ, כִּי כָבֵד הָרָעָב בְּאֶרֶץ כְּנָעַן, וְעַתָּה יֵשְׁבוּ נָא עֲבָדֶיךָ בְּאֶרֶץ גֹּשֶׁן:

בִּמְתֵי מְעָט. כְּמָה שֶׁנֶּאֱמַר: בְּשִׁבְעִים נֶפֶשׁ יָרְדוּ אֲבֹתֶיךָ מִצְרָיְמָה, וְעַתָּה שָׂמְךָ יְיָ אֱלֹהֶיךָ כְּכוֹכְבֵי הַשָּׁמַיִם לָרֹב:

וַיְהִי שָׁם לְגוֹי. מְלַמֵּד שֶׁהָיוּ יִשְׂרָאֵל מְצֻיָּנִים שָׁם:

גָּדוֹל עָצוּם. כְּמָה שֶׁנֶּאֱמַר: וּבְנֵי יִשְׂרָאֵל פָּרוּ וַיִּשְׁרְצוּ וַיִּרְבּוּ וַיַּעַצְמוּ בִּמְאֹד מְאֹד וַתִּמָּלֵא הָאָרֶץ אֹתָם:

silver and gold vessels from the Egyptians, so that He could fulfill His promise to Avraham.

Judaism Declares the Proactive Approach the Only Acceptable Approach

ובני ישראל פרו וישרצו The *Midrash* in *Shir Hashirim Rabba* relates that during one of his sermons Rebbe noticed that his audience was falling asleep. In order to wake the people up, Rebbe offered the following homily: "In Egypt, one woman gave birth to sixty thousand babies at one time. Moshe, our teacher, is equivalent to sixty thousand people."[43]

This *Midrash* raises many questions. Why is it important for us to know that people were falling asleep during Rebbe's *shiur*? Why did Rebbe choose to wake them up with this particular midrash regarding the miraculous birthing abilities of the

And sojourned there – This teaches that our father Jacob did not go down to settle in Egypt permanently, but to (temporarily) sojourn there. Thus it says, "[Jacob's sons] said to Pharaoh: We have come to sojourn in the land, for there is no pasture for your servants' sheep, because the famine is severe in the land of Canaan. So now, let your servants please dwell in the land of Goshen" *(Bereishit 47:4)*.

With a small number of people – as it says: "With seventy souls your forefathers went down to Egypt, and now Hashem your God has made you as numerous as the stars of heaven" *(Devarim 10:22)*.

And there he became a... nation – this teaches that the Israelites were distinguished there.

Great, powerful – as it says: "And the Children of Israel multiplied and proliferated and became very, very powerful, and the land became filled with them" *(Shemot 1:7)*.

Jewish women in Egypt? How can Moshe possibly be equated with sixty thousand people?

Rebbe was distressed when the people in his class began to fall asleep because it demonstrated disregard both for Torah learning and for our vital attempt to gain a better understanding of the mitzvot. Trying to inspire the people, Rebbe reminded them that in Egypt one woman miraculously gave birth to sixty thousand children. This grabbed their attention and Rebbe continued by explaining that one person – such as, a Torah scholar – can

וָרָב. כְּמָה שֶׁנֶּאֱמַר: רְבָבָה כְּצֶמַח הַשָּׂדֶה נְתַתִּיךְ, וַתִּרְבִּי וַתִּגְדְּלִי, וַתָּבֹאִי בַּעֲדִי עֲדָיִים, שָׁדַיִם נָכֹנוּ וּשְׂעָרֵךְ צִמֵּחַ וְאַתְּ עֵרֹם וְעֶרְיָה. וָאֶעֱבֹר עָלַיִךְ וָאֶרְאֵךְ מִתְבּוֹסֶסֶת בְּדָמָיִךְ. וָאֹמַר לָךְ בְּדָמַיִךְ חֲיִי וָאֹמַר לָךְ בְּדָמַיִךְ חֲיִי:

even be equivalent in importance to sixty thousand people. The Talmud in *Yoma* teaches that "anyone who brings merit to the many, will be spared from sin."[44] When a Torah scholar performs mitzvot in public he both demonstrates how to do the mitzvot and strengthens others' commitment to Torah. This in turn enables them to perform many mitzvot and gain the commensurate rewards. Moshe, who led the Jewish people and taught them how to do the mitzvot, sanctified the name of Hashem before an entire nation of people and, therefore, his own personal merit could be compared to that of sixty thousand people. Rebbe taught his listeners that those who choose to become actively involved are far more meritorious than those who choose to remain uninspired and unknowledgeable.

AUTHOR'S COMMENTS My Rebbe, Rabbi Beryl Wein, shlita, often says, "Judaism is not a spectators' sport." Jews are expected to engage their Judaism proactively.

Bnei Yisrael only burst into song after the splitting of the Red Sea, not when they left Egypt. Rav Yosef Dov Soloveitchik explains why: We were delivered from Egypt solely by Hashem, "with His strong hand and outstretched arm";[45] however, at the Red Sea, Bnei Yisrael participated

And numerous – as it says: "I made you abundant like the vegetation in the field; you increased and grew and you came to have great charm, with your breasts developed and your hair sprouting, but you were naked and bare." "I passed by you and saw you wallowing in your blood, and I said to you, By your blood you shall live!' I said to you, By your blood you shall live!''' *(Yechezkel 16:7,6)*.

with Hashem in the miracle by jumping in the sea before it began to split. Bnei Yisrael's special joy resulted from their being invited by Hashem to take an active role in this wondrous miracle. The Jewish people learned that active participation helps to ensure spiritual gratification.

This interpretation helps clarify Hashem's response to Moshe at the sea: "Why do you call upon me? Speak to Bnei Yisrael and move forward."[46] Why did Hashem respond this way to Moshe's desperation and the people's panic? Why did Hashem react to Moshe's helpless cries by challenging him to enter the sea?

When Hashem demanded that Moshe march with Bnei Yisrael into the sea, He was preparing them for a relationship with Him. It was as if Hashem had said, "There is no need to scream, just take action and proceed." To partner with Hashem, we must demonstrate both conviction and the willingness to act. Hashem did not want either Moshe or the Jewish people, His partners, to lose this opportunity to reveal His greatness to the world. Therefore Hashem told Moshe: "Stop yelling (even praying) and seize the moment! Proceed, and, as a people, you will be *mekadesh Shem Shamayim* while the whole world watches."

וַיָּרֵעוּ אוֹתָנוּ הַמִּצְרִים וַיְעַנּוּנוּ, וַיִּתְּנוּ עָלֵינוּ עֲבוֹדָה קָשָׁה:

וַיָּרֵעוּ אוֹתָנוּ הַמִּצְרִים. כְּמָה שֶׁנֶּאֱמַר: הָבָה נִתְחַכְּמָה לוֹ פֶּן יִרְבֶּה, וְהָיָה כִּי תִקְרֶאנָה מִלְחָמָה וְנוֹסַף גַּם הוּא עַל שֹׂנְאֵינוּ, וְנִלְחַם בָּנוּ וְעָלָה מִן הָאָרֶץ:

וַיְעַנּוּנוּ. כְּמָה שֶׁנֶּאֱמַר: וַיָּשִׂימוּ עָלָיו שָׂרֵי מִסִּים לְמַעַן עַנֹּתוֹ בְּסִבְלֹתָם, וַיִּבֶן עָרֵי מִסְכְּנוֹת לְפַרְעֹה, אֶת פִּתֹם וְאֶת רַעַמְסֵס:

וַיִּתְּנוּ עָלֵינוּ עֲבוֹדָה קָשָׁה. כְּמָה שֶׁנֶּאֱמַר: וַיַּעֲבִדוּ מִצְרַיִם אֶת בְּנֵי יִשְׂרָאֵל בְּפָרֶךְ:

וַנִּצְעַק אֶל יְיָ אֱלֹהֵי אֲבוֹתֵינוּ, וַיִּשְׁמַע יְיָ אֶת קוֹלֵנוּ, וַיַּרְא אֶת עָנְיֵנוּ וְאֶת עֲמָלֵנוּ וְאֶת לַחֲצֵנוּ:

The Method to the Madness of Enslaving Bnei Yisrael

וירעו אותנו המצרים While in Egypt, the Jews successfully persuaded many Egyptians to convert. Pharaoh was nervous that the Jewish people's population would increase not only as a result of their high birthrate but also through their conversion efforts. Therefore, says Rav Yehonatan, Pharaoh decided to enslave Bnei Yisrael with hard labor so as to distract them from converting others.

"The Egyptians mistreated us and afflicted us, and forced hard labor upon us" *(Devarim 26:6).*

The Egyptians mistreated us – as it says: "Come, let us deal cunningly with them, lest they multiply and when there is a war they will join our enemies and fight us, and leave the land" *(Shemot 1:10).*

And afflicted us – as it says: "And they placed taskmasters over them to afflict them with their burdens; and they built storage cities for Pharaoh – Pithom and Ra'amses" *(Shemot 1:11).*

And forced hard labor upon us – as it is says: "And the Egyptians forced the Children of Israel to do back-breaking labor" *(Shemot 1:13).*

"And we cried out to Hashem, the God of our fathers, and Hashem heard our voice and saw our suffering, our travail and our pressure" *(Devarim 26:7).*

This insight explains why the Torah introduces the beginning of the Jewish people's enslavement with the verse: "A new king arose over Egypt, who did not know of Yosef."[47] Yosef symbolized the Jewish people's conversion drive because when he first arrived in Egypt he attempted to convince the Egyptians to circumcise themselves and convert. By mentioning Yosef in this context, the verse emphasizes that Pharaoh was intentionally distancing himself from Yosef and his conversion policies.

וַנִּצְעַק אֶל יְיָ אֱלֹהֵי אֲבוֹתֵינוּ. כְּמָה שֶׁנֶּאֱמַר: וַיְהִי בַיָּמִים הָרַבִּים הָהֵם וַיָּמָת מֶלֶךְ מִצְרַיִם, וַיֵּאָנְחוּ בְנֵי יִשְׂרָאֵל מִן הָעֲבֹדָה. וַיִּזְעָקוּ, וַתַּעַל שַׁוְעָתָם אֶל הָאֱלֹהִים מִן הָעֲבֹדָה:

וַיִּשְׁמַע יְיָ אֶת קֹלֵנוּ. כְּמָה שֶׁנֶּאֱמַר, וַיִּשְׁמַע אֱלֹהִים אֶת נַאֲקָתָם, וַיִּזְכֹּר אֱלֹהִים אֶת בְּרִיתוֹ, אֶת אַבְרָהָם אֶת יִצְחָק וְאֶת יַעֲקֹב:

וַיַּרְא אֶת עָנְיֵנוּ. זוֹ פְּרִישׁוּת דֶּרֶךְ אֶרֶץ, כְּמָה שֶׁנֶּאֱמַר: וַיַּרְא אֱלֹהִים אֶת בְּנֵי יִשְׂרָאֵל, וַיֵּדַע אֱלֹהִים:

וְאֶת עֲמָלֵנוּ. אֵלּוּ הַבָּנִים, כְּמָה שֶׁנֶּאֱמַר, כָּל הַבֵּן הַיִּלּוֹד הַיְאֹרָה תַּשְׁלִיכֻהוּ, וְכָל הַבַּת תְּחַיּוּן:

וְאֶת לַחֲצֵנוּ. זוֹ הַדְּחַק, כְּמָה שֶׁנֶּאֱמַר: וְגַם רָאִיתִי אֶת הַלַּחַץ אֲשֶׁר מִצְרַיִם לֹחֲצִים אֹתָם:

וַיּוֹצִאֵנוּ יְיָ מִמִּצְרַיִם בְּיָד חֲזָקָה וּבִזְרֹעַ נְטוּיָה וּבְמֹרָא גָּדֹל וּבְאֹתוֹת וּבְמֹפְתִים:

Why Hashem Performs Miracles with a "Strong Hand and an Outstretched Arm"

ויוציאנו יי ממצרים ביד חזקה ובזרע נטויה Why does the Torah proclaim that Hashem took Bnei Yisrael out of Egypt

And we cried out to Hashem, the God of our fathers – as it says: "It happened during those long days that the king of Egypt died, and the Children of Israel groaned because of the labor, and they cried out. And their plea from their labor ascended to God" *(Shemot 2:23)*.

And Hashem heard our voice – as it says: "And God heard their groaning, and God remembered His covenant with Avraham, Yitzchak and Yaakov" *(ibid. 2:24)*.

And saw our suffering – This refers to their forced abstention from marital relations, as it says: "God saw the children of Israel, and God knew" *(ibid. 2:25)*.

Our travail – This refers to their sons, as it says: "Every boy that is born you shall throw into the river, but spare all the daughters" *(ibid. 1:22)*.

And our pressure – This refers to pushing, as it is said: "And I have also seen the pressure with which the Egyptians press them" *(ibid. 3:9)*.

"And Hashem took us out of Egypt with a strong hand and an outstretched arm, and with great terror, and with signs and with wonders" *(Devarim 26:8)*.

"with a strong hand and an outstretched arm"?[48] Was the task of taking Bnei Yisrael out of Egypt so great that Hashem had to summon up His "strong hand" – a special

וַיּוֹצִאֵנוּ יְיָ מִמִּצְרַיִם. לֹא עַל יְדֵי מַלְאָךְ, וְלֹא עַל יְדֵי שָׂרָף, וְלֹא עַל יְדֵי שָׁלִיחַ, אֶלָּא הַקָּדוֹשׁ בָּרוּךְ הוּא בִּכְבוֹדוֹ וּבְעַצְמוֹ. שֶׁנֶּאֱמַר: וְעָבַרְתִּי בְאֶרֶץ מִצְרַיִם בַּלַּיְלָה הַזֶּה וְהִכֵּיתִי כָל בְּכוֹר בְּאֶרֶץ מִצְרַיִם מֵאָדָם וְעַד בְּהֵמָה וּבְכָל אֱלֹהֵי מִצְרַיִם אֶעֱשֶׂה שְׁפָטִים אֲנִי יְיָ. וְעָבַרְתִּי בְאֶרֶץ מִצְרַיִם

weapon – for the task?

Rav Yehonatan responds that nothing is challenging for Hashem who "in His goodness renews daily, perpetually, the work of creation."[49] Hashem established a world based upon man's exercising his free will, and subsequently receiving his reward or his punishment. When the Torah describes Hashem as employing His "strong hand," this does not mean that the task was difficult for Him; rather, it means that He had to break the rules He had established at the time of Creation. When redeeming the Jews from Egypt, the *Midrash* teaches us that Hashem miraculously overturned the laws of reward and punishment. During the miracle of the splitting of the Red Sea the angels complained to Hashem saying, "Why should You save Bnei Yisrael? They too are idol worshippers just like the Egyptians!" Hashem responded that although Bnei Yisrael worshipped idols in Egypt, nonetheless, as descendants of Avraham, Yitzchak and Yaakov, they deserved to be redeemed. Hashem demonstrated His strong hand and merciful arm by subverting His normal rules of justice to miraculously spare Bnei Yisrael.[50]

The Rambam explains that miraculous phenomena by definition do not continue indefinitely; otherwise, they

And Hashem took us out of Egypt – not through an angel, not through a seraph and not through an agent, but God in His glory, by Himself. Thus it says: "I will pass through the land of Egypt on that night, and I will strike every firstborn in the land of Egypt from man to beast, and against all the gods of Egypt I will mete out judgments, I am Hashem" *(Shemot 12:12)*. *I will*

would become part of the natural process and no longer be miraculous. While Hashem showed Bnei Yisrael His favor at the sea, His miraculous intervention in the natural process of reward and punishment was temporary and certainly did not change the Jewish people's nature. Following the splitting of the Red Sea, nature would resume its normal course and the Jewish people would still have to make tremendous efforts to cleanse themselves of the stench of idolatry.

In this context, Moshe's choice of wording when praying on Bnei Yisrael's behalf after the sin of the golden calf makes sense. Moshe used keywords intended to remind Hashem that Bnei Yisrael were taken out of Egypt with His "great power and a strong hand,"[51] even though they had worshipped idols. Hashem had already overridden His own rules once and performed a miracle, and it would take time for the Jewish people to purify themselves of the weakness for worshipping idols. By recalling Hashem's former mercy, Moshe pleaded that He once again adopt a miraculous path: "Relent from Your flaring anger and reconsider regarding the evil against Your people."[52]

בַּלַּיְלָה הַזֶּה, אֲנִי וְלֹא מַלְאָךְ. וְהִכֵּיתִי כָל בְּכוֹר בְּאֶרֶץ מִצְרַיִם, אֲנִי וְלֹא שָׂרָף. וּבְכָל אֱלֹהֵי מִצְרַיִם אֶעֱשֶׂה שְׁפָטִים אֲנִי יְיָ, אֲנִי הוּא וְלֹא הַשָּׁלִיחַ. אֲנִי יְיָ, אֲנִי הוּא וְלֹא אַחֵר:

Hashem Demonstrated to Pharaoh that He Created the World and Continues to Influence It

אני ולא השליח The Talmud teaches:

> Pharaoh who personally blasphemed Hashem was punished by Hashem Himself. Sennacherib who had his messenger blaspheme Hashem, suffered the indignity of having Hashem punish him through a messenger as it says, 'An angel of Hashem went out and struck down one hundred eighty-five thousand [people] of the Assyrian camp.'[53]

The Talmud demonstrates that Sennacherib, the king of Assyria, and Pharaoh, the ruler of Egypt, took two different approaches to blaspheming Hashem, and, hence, received two different types of punishments. Sennacherib by proclaiming, "Who from all of the gods of all the countries could save you [the Jewish people] from my hand,"[54] declared that no god would come to aid the Jewish people; Sennacherib denied Hashem's existence. Hashem, in turn, destroyed Sennacherib's army by casting "a strange air" over it. This method of destruction was so unusual that Sennacherib would be forced to realize that the mighty hand of Hashem had destroyed his army.

Pharaoh responded to Moshe's plea that he free the Jewish people, by proclaiming, "Who is Hashem that I should heed His voice to send out Yisrael?" Pharaoh believed that there was a God, but he believed that God was no longer actively involved in the world. Hashem Himself delivered Bnei Yisrael from Egypt to prove to Pharaoh *pass through the land of Egypt on that night — I* and not an angel; *and I will strike every firstborn in the land of Egypt — I* and not a seraph; *and against all the gods of Egypt I will mete out judgments — I* and not an agent; *I am Hashem* – it is *I*, and no other.

that not only did He create the world, He also continues to have an effect on it. The hand of Hashem performed the Exodus from Egypt and the splitting of the Red Sea, undeniably miraculous feats. Consequently Hashem could assert: "And Egypt shall know that I am Hashem."[55]

The Effects of Impurity on Sanctity

ועברתי בארץ מצרים בלילה הזה אני ולא מלאך The *Zohar* explains that the holier someone is the greater potential there is for his spiritual downfall. For instance, Yitzchak after being offered as a sacrifice to Hashem was described as a "wholesome sacrifice."[56] Having undergone the *Akeida*, his level of spirituality, like that of an angel's, was extremely high. Therefore, he was instructed to remain in Eretz Yisrael and not go down to Egypt because of the compromising effect this might have had on his pure spirituality. For the same reason, Hashem did not want His angels to enter Egypt. Had an angel entered Egypt, its purity would have been compromised by Egypt's impurity. For this reason Bnei Yisrael had to be redeemed directly by Hashem and not by way of an intermediary.

The Impurity of Egypt Versus the Sanctity of Eretz Yisrael

אני ולא מלאך Before Yehoshua began Bnei Yisrael's war for Eretz Yisrael, with his attack upon Jericho, the *Navi* relates the following story:

> He [Yehoshua] lifted up his eyes and saw, and behold, a man was standing opposite him with his sword drawn in his hand. Yehoshua walked toward him and said, 'Are you for us or for our enemies?' And he said, 'No I am the commander of Hashem's host; now I have come.' Yehoshua fell before him to the ground and prostrated himself and said to him, 'What does my lord say to his servant?' [And] the commander of Hashem's host said to Yehoshua, 'Remove your shoe from your foot, for the place upon which you stand is holy.' And Yehoshua did so.[57]

Yehoshua's conversation with the angel highlights a significant difference between Eretz Yisrael and Egypt. Hashem personally redeemed Bnei Yisrael from Egypt because even an angel could not enter the impure atmosphere there without jeopardizing his spiritual essence. Only Hashem could enter Egypt with impunity, as confirmed by the verse, "I shall go through Egypt on this night."[58] However, as Yehoshua learns from his conversation with the angel, even though the inhabitants of Jericho worshipped the moon (the name Jericho in Hebrew is *Yericho*, stemming from the word for moon, *yare'ach*); the sanctity of Eretz Yisrael is so great that it was not completely displaced by this idolatry, and an angel could enter and conquer Jericho without putting his spiritual essence at great risk. The angel pointed this out to Yehoshua when it told him to remove his shoe implying that even though Jericho was steeped in idolatry, it still retained a certain level of spirituality stemming from the holiness of Eretz Yisrael.

AUTHOR'S COMMENTS In *Parshat Yitro* the Torah records Bnei Yisrael's acceptance of the Torah. *Parshat Mishpatim* follows Parshat Yitro and challenges Bnei Yisrael to incorporate Torah law into their daily lives. The Torah offers a formula for doing so which presents a method for naturally progressing up the ladder of spiritual refinement.

The Torah delineates two basic types of mitzvot: those between man and his fellow man, and those between man and Hashem. Parshat Mishpatim contains both types, but begins with those between man and his fellow man. The parsha begins by teaching us how to treat the indentured servant and the bondswoman. Then it discusses the laws concerning damages, personal injury, and borrowing, and continues with the necessity of acting sensitively towards the unfortunate and dispensing justice. All of the above are mitzvot between man and his fellow man.

Thereafter, the Torah presents mitzvot between man and Hashem. The parsha continues with the laws of the seventh – Sabbatical – year, during which the land is left fallow, and follows with the laws of the seventh day of the week, the Shabbat, during which man is commanded to rest. Both of these mitzvot demonstrate man's faith in Hashem, the provider. For even though man does not work, he believes that Hashem will provide. The laws of the three Festivals immediately follow, demanding thrice-yearly pilgrimages to Hashem's Temple in Jerusalem; these pilgrimages demonstrate the Jew's commitment to Hashem and His Temple.

The Torah teaches us that attaining spirituality is a multi-stepped process. Without first learning to appreciate and establish a rapport with your fellow man, you cannot begin relating to Hashem. The Torah teaches us that only after Bnei Yisrael learned to relate to one another and subsequently to Hashem could they finally reach and sanctify Eretz Yisrael, the land given them by Hashem: "Behold! I send an angel before you to protect you on the way, and to bring you to the place that I have made ready."[59]

Thus, first the Jew learns to relate to his fellow man, then he learns to relate to Hashem, and finally his relationship with the people of Israel and Hashem reaches a spiritual peak in Eretz Yisrael. For this reason, healthy spiritual development requires a combination of time and commitment. Healthy spirituality is not developed by leaps of faith or sudden professions of commitment; rather, it demands that man, step-by-step, naturally progress up the long ladder of spiritual refinement.

Even Moshe Rabbeinu's spirituality developed in a slow but steady fashion. Before Moshe was chosen by Hashem to lead Bnei Yisrael, he learned to be compassionate and to empathize with his fellow man, as the Torah teaches, "It happened in those days that Moshe grew up and went to his brethren and observed their burdens."[60] A simple understanding of this verse teaches us that Moshe left the comfort of Pharaoh's palace and went to witness Bnei Yisrael's enslavement with his own eyes. However, a more profound reading teaches us that Moshe realized that he did not belong amongst the Egyptians. He felt an emotional connection to his Jewish brethren who were enslaved and he wished to empathize with them. Rashi comments upon the words "And observed their burdens," "this was his intention: to see their suffering and grieve with them."[61] First Moshe connected with his people and later Hashem revealed Himself and appointed Moshe His messenger.

Prior to Hashem's revelation to Moshe at the burning bush the Torah relates, "Moshe said to himself: 'I will turn aside now and look at this great sight.'"[62] Moshe was sensitive both to people and to his surroundings. This is why Hashem revealed Himself and chose Moshe as the leader of the Jewish people, as the Torah says, "Hashem saw that he turned aside to see and God called to him."[63] Moshe progressed spiritually and received his spiritual calling because first he related to his fellow man and then he recognized the presence of Hashem. Only after Hashem revealed Himself to Moshe and described His plan, was Moshe informed that Hashem would "bring the nation up from the land to a good and spacious land, to a land flowing with milk and honey."[64]

At the Pesach Seder the Jew both joins with his fellow Jews and bonds with Hashem. To accomplish the former, he chooses a *chavura*, made up of family and friends, with which he eats the Pesach sacrifice and transmits the story of the Exodus. To accomplish the latter, he sincerely rejoices in Hashem's taking the

Jewish people out of Egypt, and he recognizes that in every generation, even though the Jewish people is persecuted, Hashem saves it from destruction, as the Haggadah proclaims: "But the Holy One, blessed be He, rescues us from their hand." Near the end of the Seder, having linked man with his fellow man and man with Hashem, the crescendo of the entire Seder is reached when the participants declare the purpose of the Jewish nation: "Next year in Jerusalem," signifying the Jewish people's service of Hashem as a unified people in the Promised Land, Eretz Yisrael.

Hashem's Mercy Is Beyond Our Comprehension

והכיתי כל בכור בארץ מצרים אני ולא שרף Rav Yehonatan explains that the extent of Hashem's mercy is beyond our comprehension. On the one hand, when Hashem has to annihilate a nation, He cannot bear to do so Himself so he sends an intermediary, an angel, to destroy all in its path, as Hashem tells Moshe: "For my *angel* shall go before you and bring you to the Amorite, the Hittite, the Perizzite, the Canaanite, the Hivvite and the Jebusite, and I will *annihilate* them" (italics added).[65] On the other hand, in Egypt, when Hashem did not wish to annihilate the entire people, He demonstrated His compassion by going Himself. Had He sent an angel, it could not have distinguished between the firstborn and the other Egyptians, and the entire nation would have been wiped out.

A Jew Is Obligated to Recognize that Both Mercy and Retribution Come from Hashem

אני יי. אני הוא ולא אחר The Talmud teaches us that "one is obligated to bless Hashem for the bad, just as one is obligated to bless Hashem for the good."[66] It is difficult to understand why Hashem demands we bless Him for bad things that happen to us.

Rav Yehonatan explains that fully recognizing the extent of Hashem's power

בְּיָד חֲזָקָה. זוֹ הַדֶּבֶר, כְּמָה שֶׁנֶּאֱמַר: הִנֵּה יַד יְיָ הוֹיָה בְּמִקְנְךָ אֲשֶׁר בַּשָּׂדֶה: בַּסּוּסִים, בַּחֲמֹרִים, בַּגְּמַלִּים, בַּבָּקָר וּבַצֹּאן, דֶּבֶר כָּבֵד מְאֹד:

וּבִזְרֹעַ נְטוּיָה. זוֹ הַחֶרֶב, כְּמָה שֶׁנֶּאֱמַר: וְחַרְבּוֹ שְׁלוּפָה בְּיָדוֹ נְטוּיָה עַל יְרוּשָׁלָיִם:

וּבְמֹרָא גָּדוֹל. זוֹ גִּלּוּי שְׁכִינָה, כְּמָה שֶׁנֶּאֱמַר: אוֹ הֲנִסָּה אֱלֹהִים לָבוֹא לָקַחַת לוֹ גוֹי מִקֶּרֶב גּוֹי, בְּמַסֹּת בְּאֹתֹת וּבְמוֹפְתִים וּבְמִלְחָמָה וּבְיָד חֲזָקָה וּבִזְרוֹעַ נְטוּיָה וּבְמוֹרָאִים גְּדֹלִים, כְּכֹל אֲשֶׁר עָשָׂה לָכֶם יְיָ אֱלֹהֵיכֶם בְּמִצְרַיִם לְעֵינֶיךָ:

means realizing that it is all encompassing. On the one hand, Hashem acts with mercy and compassion, and, on the other hand, He dispenses justice and exacts retribution. Pharaoh and his people believed that Hashem existed, but they could not understand a god who exhibited both traits. The *Zohar* relates that when Moshe revealed Hashem's four-letter name (the *Shem Havaya*) to Pharaoh, Pharaoh understood this name to indicate that Hashem was intrinsically benevolent and compassionate, not demanding of retribution. Hashem demonstrated otherwise to Pharaoh and his people throughout the Exodus from Egypt. Hashem performed miracles demonstrating both His merciful nature and His desire to exact retribution, so that the Egyptian nation would know that Hashem is responsible for both. This is why the Torah declares, "And Egypt shall know that I am Hashem, when I stretch out My hand

With a strong hand – This refers to the plague of Pestilence, as it says: "Behold, the hand of Hashem will be upon your livestock in the field, upon the horses, the donkeys, the camels, the cattle and the sheep, [with] a very severe pestilence" *(ibid. 9:3)*.

And with an outstretched arm – This refers to the sword, as it says: "His sword was drawn in his hand, stretched out over Jerusalem" *(I Divrei Hayamim 21:16)*.

And with great terror – This refers to the revelation of the Divine Presence, as it says: "Or has any god ever attempted to go and take for himself a nation from the midst of another nation, with trials, signs and wonders, with wars and with a strong hand and an outstretched arm and with great terrors, like all that Hashem your God did for you in Egypt before your eyes?" *(Devarim 4:34)*.

over Egypt; and I shall take Bnei Yisrael out from among them."[67]

Hashem's declaration that "it is I, and no other," reminds the Jewish people to believe in Hashem both when He acts mercifully and when He exacts punishment. Therefore, Hashem even obligates us to recite a blessing upon painful or sad events because by doing so we acknowledge the all-encompassing presence and power of Hashem.

Seder night is a night of recognition. We describe the persecution we suffered in Egypt and our miraculous exodus. We describe Hashem's putting into practice His attributes of judgment and of mercy. Having retold this story, we are capable of fully recognizing Hashem's magnitude.

וּבְאֹתוֹת. זֶה הַמַּטֶּה, כְּמָה שֶׁנֶּאֱמַר: וְאֶת הַמַּטֶּה הַזֶּה תִּקַּח בְּיָדֶךָ, אֲשֶׁר תַּעֲשֶׂה בּוֹ אֶת הָאֹתֹת:

וּבְמֹפְתִים. זֶה הַדָּם, כְּמָה שֶׁנֶּאֱמַר: וְנָתַתִּי מוֹפְתִים בַּשָּׁמַיִם וּבָאָרֶץ:

The Symbolical Meanings of the Staff and of the Way Moshe Handled It

ובאותות זה המטה The staff symbolized Hashem's attribute of judgment and the punishment that would be meted out to the Egyptians, the beating they would endure through the plagues. The way Moshe used the staff – casting it to the ground – also has great symbolical significance. The Egyptians enslaved Bnei Yisrael and persecuted them even when they reached the forty-ninth level of impurity, the most desperate physical and spiritual state. Moshe cast his staff downwards to symbolize the Egyptian's persecution of a downtrodden people and to demonstrate to Pharaoh that judgment would ensue. Both the staff itself and the way Moshe handled it, revealed Egypt's cruelty and foretold their punishment.

AUTHOR'S COMMENTS There are times when Bnei Yisrael requires a rude awakening from Hashem to help it recognize how far it has strayed from Him. Hashem can send this wake-up call in the guise of persecution at the hands of the Gentiles, as the Talmud says, "Rabbi Yehoshua said [to him]: 'If Bnei Yisrael do not repent, they will not be redeemed?! Impossible. Rather, Hashem appoints a foreign leader, such as Haman, who persecutes the Jewish people, and causes them to awaken and repent.' "[68]

In 1990 during the first Gulf War, as Saddam Hussein threatened Jewish lives by

And with signs – This refers to the staff, as it says: "Take this staff in your hand, with which you shall perform the signs" *(Shemot 4:17)*.

And with wonders – This refers to the blood, as it says: "And I shall place wonders in heaven and on earth:

launching scud missiles at Eretz Yisrael, I was learning in yeshiva. Rav Simcha HaKohen Kook spoke to the students regarding the situation and explained that at times Hashem will strike the Jewish people with a staff in order to provoke better behavior. Rav Kook explained that Haman was the staff Hashem used in the days of Mordechai and Esther, while Saddam Hussein was the staff He was using in our time. When Bnei Yisrael demonstrates insubordination, the staff is wielded against it. Fortunately, on Seder night, the Jewish people has an opportunity to be on its best behavior, to perform many mitzvot and demonstrate its allegiance to the Halacha and Hashem. If the Jewish people does so then rather than being beaten with the staff of foreign persecution, Hashem's staff will protect it from persecution as it did in Egypt.

Hashem Encourages Bnei Yisrael to Repent by Sending Trials and Tribulations

ואת המטה הזה תקח בידך The Torah records the following conversation between Moshe and Hashem at the burning bush:

> Moshe said, 'But they will not believe me and they will not heed my voice, for they will say Hashem did not appear to you.' Hashem said to him, 'What is that in your hand?' and he said, 'A staff.' He [Hashem] said, 'Cast it on the ground,' and he cast it on the ground and it became a snake. Moshe fled from it. Hashem said to Moshe,

> 'Stretch out your hand and grasp its tail.' He stretched out his hand and grasped it tightly, and it became a staff in his palm.[69]

While the events described in these verses are easy to picture, they also raise many questions. Why did Moshe question Bnei Yisrael's faith? Why did Hashem respond to Moshe's question by ordering him to throw his staff on the ground, instead of directly addressing his concerns? Why did Hashem change the staff into a snake, an animal cursed since man's stay in the Garden of Eden? Why did Moshe flee from the snake? Why did Hashem tell Moshe to grab the snake by its tail in order to transform it back into a staff? In answering these questions we will recognize the deep symbolism inherent in this conversation.

Bnei Yisrael, steeped in idolatry, had descended to the forty-ninth level of ritual impurity in Egypt. The Torah reports that when Moshe informed Bnei Yisrael of their impending redemption, "they did not heed Moshe because of shortness of breath and hard work."[70] The *Midrash* explains that the phrase "shortness of breath" refers to Bnei Yisrael's waning spirituality and their lack of faith in Hashem.[71] So it is not surprising that Moshe was certain that Bnei Yisrael was neither worthy of redemption nor interested in listening to his message saying, "they will not believe me and they will not heed my voice."

The Talmud teaches us that the hind has difficulty giving birth because she has a narrow womb. Hashem sends a snake to bite her, thus opening the womb and facilitating the birthing process.[72] This text speaks symbolically. The hind is Bnei Yisrael, and its birthing pains represent the difficulties Bnei Yisrael sometimes has in serving Hashem. When the nation strays, Hashem responds by sending a snake, a foreign nation, to persecute it and encourage it to do *teshuva*. Hashem, metaphorically speaking, sends a snake to bite Bnei Yisrael, causing its womb to open and the repentance process to begin. Rabbi Yehoshua expresses a similar sentiment elsewhere in the Talmud: "Rabbi Yehoshua said (to him): 'If Bnei Yisrael do not repent they, will not be redeemed?! Impossible. Rather, Hashem appoints a foreign leader such as Haman, who persecutes the Jewish people and causes them to awaken and repent.' "[73]

Responding to Moshe's doubts about Bnei Yisrael, Hashem alluded to the metaphor of the hind by transforming Moshe's staff into a snake. Moshe fled from the snake because he was frightened that it was a sign that Hashem would judge Bnei Yisrael harshly. Hashem wanted Moshe to understand that Egypt – the snake – was only summoned to enslave Bnei Yisrael so that it would abandon idolatry and embrace Hashem. When people are downtrodden and desperate to better their situation, their desire to improve themselves is greater. Hashem told Moshe to cast the staff on the ground as a sign of the Jewish people's spiritual decline. He then turned the staff into a snake signaling that Bnei Yisrael needed to repent. Finally Moshe was instructed to grab the snake by the tail. The tail is located behind and underneath the animal, as such it symbolizes that Bnei Yisrael were broken and humbled by their exile and were ready to return to Hashem, as the Torah says, "and Bnei Yisrael groaned because of the work and they cried out. Their outcry because of the work went up to Hashem."[74]

Hashem expects us to recognize His role in all of our experiences, regardless of how difficult they are. When we do so, nothing can impede our willingness to serve Him.

(For a different interpretation of this verse, see "Moshe's Ascent to Leadership," found in the essay section following the text of the Haggadah.)

It is customary to spill out some wine with a finger from the cup sixteen times while saying the following words:

1 2 3

דָּם וָאֵשׁ וְתִמְרוֹת עָשָׁן:

דָּבָר אַחֵר:

בְּיָד חֲזָקָה. שְׁתַּיִם. וּבִזְרֹעַ נְטוּיָה. שְׁתַּיִם.

וּבְמֹרָא גָּדֹל. שְׁתַּיִם.

וּבְאֹתוֹת. שְׁתַּיִם. וּבְמֹפְתִים. שְׁתַּיִם:

אֵלּוּ עֶשֶׂר מַכּוֹת שֶׁהֵבִיא הַקָּדוֹשׁ בָּרוּךְ הוּא עַל הַמִּצְרִים בְּמִצְרַיִם, וְאֵלּוּ הֵן:

4 דָּם	5 צְפַרְדֵּעַ	6 כִּנִּים
7 עָרוֹב	8 דֶּבֶר	9 שְׁחִין
10 בָּרָד	11 אַרְבֶּה	12 חֹשֶׁךְ

13

מַכַּת בְּכוֹרוֹת:

Blood and **Fire** and **Pillars of Smoke**

(Yoel 3:3).

Another explanation of the verse is:

With a strong hand indicates two plagues;

With an outstretched arm indicates two plagues;

With great terrors indicates two plagues;

With signs indicates two plagues;

And with wonders indicates two plagues.

This makes altogether ten plagues, which God inflicted upon the Egyptians:

Blood Frogs Lice

Mixed Beasts Pestilence Boils

Hail Locusts Darkness

The Plague of the Firstborn

רַבִּי יְהוּדָה הָיָה נוֹתֵן בָּהֶם סִמָּנִים:

14 15 16

דְּצַ"ךְ עֲדַ"שׁ בְּאַחַ"ב:

A Miracle Within a Miracle

ערוב Hashem told Moshe that "the houses of Egypt shall be filled with the swarm (of wild beasts), and even the ground upon which they are."[75] Why does the Torah tell us that "even the ground which they are [upon]" would swarm with wild beasts? If "the houses of Egypt would be filled with the wild beasts," wouldn't the ground swarm with the wild beasts as well?

Ridiculed and taunted by children, Elisha, the prophet, reacted by cursing them. Miraculously "two bears then came out of the forest and tore apart forty-two of the children."[76] The Talmud discusses the exact nature of this miracle. Rav contends that the bears miraculously appeared. Shmuel maintains that before Elisha cursed the children neither a forest nor bears had been there; miraculously, both a forest and bears appeared. The Talmud explains that, according to Shmuel, Hashem had to create both the bears and the forest because, by nature, bears will only attack when they feel the security of being near their natural habitat. Therefore, Hashem had to perform "a miracle within a miracle," creating both the bears and their habitat, so that the bears would ferociously attack the children.[77]

This insight explains why the Torah teaches us that the wild beasts were upon "the ground." Pharaoh doubted that the wild beasts, distant from their natural habitats, would attack people in his cities. Hashem miraculously brought both the wild beasts and their habitats – "the ground upon which they are" – to the cities in order to facilitate a merciless attack. Hence the verse confirms that the miracle of the wild beasts

Rabbi Yehudah used to combine their initials into an acronym:

D.Tza.Ch. (Blood, Frogs, Lice);

A.Da.Sh. (Mixed Beasts, Pestilence, Boils);

Be.A.Cha.B. (Hail, Locusts, Darkness, Firstborn).

was twofold: the houses were filled with "the swarm of wild beasts," and the beasts appeared with "the ground upon which they" were.

Often Hashem reveals His greatness through nature. Here, as Rav Yehonatan demonstrates, Hashem performed a miracle within a miracle to proclaim His greatness. If we look closely at Hashem's creations and the world around us we are bound to notice His omnipresence, His all-pervasive influences on the world. As we recite in our daily prayers, "Holy, holy, holy is Hashem, Master of Legions; the whole world is filled with His glory."[78]

The Extraordinary Miracle of the Locusts

ארבהAll of the plagues ruined Egypt, but miraculously left Goshen, where Bnei Yisrael resided, unscathed. This was all the more extraordinary in the plague of locusts because a swarm of locusts naturally searches for food, and, if the food is scarce, it immediately searches for another food source. The Torah describes the plague of locusts: "It [the swarm of locusts] covered the surface of the entire land, and the land was darkened; it ate all the grass of the land and all the fruit of the tree that the hail left over. No greenery remained on the trees or the grass of the field in the entire land of Egypt."[79] The Torah not only describes a massive swarm of locust but also confirms that there was *no greenery or grass of the field* in all of Egypt for the locusts to eat and yet, miraculously, they did not enter the neighboring land of Goshen in their search for food.

All Egyptians Were Held Accountable

ארבה וחשך Before afflicting Egypt with locusts and darkness, Hashem explained to Moshe why he was hardening Pharaoh's heart: "So that you may relate in the ears of your son and your son's son that I made a mockery of Egypt and My signs that I placed among them – that you may know that I am Hashem."[80] Why did Hashem preface these particular plagues with this message? In addition, why did the Egyptians suffer for Pharaoh's refusal to free the Jewish people? After all, Moshe only asked Pharaoh to free the Jews; the Egyptians were not responsible for Pharaoh's stubbornness.

The Torah hints at an answer to the second question in Moshe's angry retort to Pharaoh: "Then all these servants of yours will come down to me and bow to me saying, 'Leave – you and the entire people [Bnei Yisrael] that follows you.' After that I will leave."[81] This verse demonstrates that the Egyptians could have freed the Jewish people, yet they acted cruelly towards them, reaping the benefits of slavery. Therefore, they deserved to share the blame with Pharaoh. For example, during the plague of darkness when Bnei Yisrael had light and the Egyptians did not, the Egyptians should have attempted to argue with Pharaoh, pointing out that Hashem miraculously protected Bnei Yisrael, and, therefore, the Jews should be freed. Their acquiescence to Pharaoh's decisions during the plague of darkness demonstrated that they had no desire to release the Jewish people.

Hashem wanted all future generations to understand that Egypt received its just deserts, so Hashem stressed before the plague of darkness that its purpose was to reveal that He rules the world with absolute justice. This plague clarified the Egyptian people's complicity, and verified Hashem's absolute integrity. Hashem "made a mockery of Egypt [of all Egyptians]" through "the signs ... placed among them" because they subscribed to Pharaoh's authority, and not

His. Hashem explained that Egypt would be subjected to these plagues, so "that you may know that I am Hashem."

Double Darkness and Its Dual Meaning

חשך The *Midrash* commenting upon the verse "and there was a thick darkness (*choshech afela*)"[82] asks: "What is meant by a thick darkness? Rav Avdimi said, 'A type of covering, this darkness was doubled.' "[83] What does the midrash mean by a "darkness that was doubled?" One interpretation offered is that the miracle of the darkness was doubled. The Egyptians were covered in darkness day and night, while Bnei Yisrael enjoyed light, day and night.

The *Midrash*, in interpreting the opening verses of the Torah, offers another, more profound explanation. The Torah reports that "the earth was astonishingly empty (*tohu*) ... And God said: 'Let there be light,' ... And Hashem saw that the light was good, and Hashem separated between the light and the darkness. Hashem called to the light: 'Day,' and to the darkness He called: 'Night.' And there was evening and there was morning, one day."[84]

The *Midrash* commenting upon these verses writes:

> Rabbi Yannai said: 'From the very beginning of creation, the Holy One, blessed be He, observed the deeds of the righteous and of the wicked. "And the earth was astonishingly empty," these are the deeds of the wicked. "And God said: 'Let there be light,'" these are the deeds of the righteous. And "God separated between the light and the darkness," between the deeds of the righteous and the deeds of the wicked. "And God called to the light: 'Day,'" these are the deeds of the righteous; "And to the darkness He called: 'Night,'" these are the deeds of the wicked.'[85]

Rashi explains that according to the midrash the

original light was of an intense spiritual quality. When Hashem realized that the wicked people were unworthy of it, he set it aside for the use of the righteous in the World to Come. According to Rashi's interpretation, light represents positive traits, while darkness represents negative, or, even, evil traits. The Egyptians, who were wicked people, were enveloped by darkness, representing their negative traits and destructive behavior.

The *Midrash* even relates that during the plague of darkness the wicked amongst Bnei Yisrael – those who doubted Hashem – were killed. After these wicked people were killed, only the righteous Jews were left alive. This is why the verse says, "for all Bnei Yisrael there was light in their dwellings."[86] In Bnei Yisrael's dwellings only light, representing the positive attributes and righteousness, remained.

Consequently the effect of the plague of darkness was doubled because it punished both the Egyptians and the wicked Jewish people, while simultaneously preserving the light of the righteous Jews.

The Extraordinary Miracle of the Darkness

חשך The Torah repeatedly emphasizes that Hashem's greatness was further revealed to the Egyptians by the contrast between the plagues' devastating effect upon them and their passing over the land of Goshen, leaving its Jewish inhabitants unscathed. Yet, the Torah reports that during the plague of darkness, "No man could see his brother nor could anyone rise from his place."[87] How could the Egyptians know that Bnei Yisrael were not affected by the darkness, when they themselves could neither see nor move?

The Torah alludes to an answer in the continuation of this same verse, "but for all Bnei Yisrael there was light in their dwellings." Based upon the *Midrash,* Rashi explains that this verse teaches us that during the plague, Bnei Yisrael entered the Egyptians' houses to look for treasures, so that when Hashem freed them, they could demand the

Egyptians' possessions for themselves. The phrase, "for all Bnei Yisrael there was light in their dwellings," means that light accompanied them wherever they went, even when they left Goshen, and entered plague-stricken Egypt. When the moment of the Exodus arrived, the Jewish people told their persecutors exactly where their possessions were kept. Consequently, the Egyptians recognized that indeed Bnei Yisrael had light during the plague of darkness that enabled them to tell the Egyptian's where their treasures were kept.

The Final Three Plagues

ארבה חשך מכת בכורות While Hashem battered the Egyptians with plagues, they must have wondered why Hashem insisted on Bnei Yisrael leaving with Pharaoh's consent. Why didn't He just instruct Bnei Yisrael to get up and leave while their taskmasters were incapacitated? During the first few plagues the Egyptians may have explained to themselves that the Jewish people had been enslaved for so many years that they were emotionally battered and spiritually broken. They had become so psychologically dependant upon being slaves that notwithstanding how easily they could escape, they were afraid to leave.

Hashem Himself recognized this psychological weakness, and instructed the Jews after leaving Egypt not to travel by way of the land of the Philistines because "Perhaps the people [Bnei Yisrael] will reconsider when they see a war, and they will return to Egypt."[88] Therefore, it was reasonable for the Egyptians to also conclude that Bnei Yisrael needed Pharaoh's permission to leave and his assurance that they would not be pursued.

However, applying this rationale to the last three plagues is difficult, particularly concerning the plague of darkness when Bnei Yisrael could easily have left unnoticed, guided by the light Hashem provided for them. The Egyptians viewed this hesitation as a sign of weakness and they concluded that Hashem lacked the power to free Bnei Yisrael without Pharaoh's consent. The harshness of the last plagues also caused Pharaoh to reach this conclusion and harden his heart even more. Thus, when Hashem told Moshe about these plagues, He explained that He was sending them, "so that I can put these signs of Mine in his midst."[89] Hashem placed these signs – Locusts, Darkness and the Slaying of the Firstborn – in the midst of Egypt knowing that they would harden the hearts of Pharaoh and his servants even more than the previous plagues had.

The Slaying of the Firstborn, The Redemption of the Firstborn – Destroying Impurity, Enhancing Sanctity

מכת בכורות Judaism obligates us to instill sanctity and purity where impurity – potentially obstructive to spiritual growth – is found. The firstborn child, a prime example of this, is the first fruit of intense desire. Conceived at the peak of a new lust, this child has the potential for great impurity. Thus, Kayin, Adam's firstborn, was overcome by his potential to sin because he did not incorporate purity into his life; he murdered his brother. Within the Jewish nation, the firstborn were also overcome by sin, worshipping the golden calf and, consequently, losing their claim to leadership.

During the slaying of the firstborn, Hashem cleansed Egypt of an enormous amount of impurity as all of Egypt's firstborn sons and animals were killed. Hashem legislated the mitzva of *pidyon haben* immediately following this plague because He wanted Bnei Yisrael to recognize that in order to eliminate spiritual impurity one must enhance purity and further the cause of spirituality. For this reason, the annual mitzva of redeeming the first fruit in the Temple is called *bikkurim*, from the word *bechor* – firstborn. Sanctifying the fruit transforms the corporeal into the spiritual.

AUTHOR'S COMMENTS The Torah introduces Shabbat observance by saying, "Six days shall you accomplish your activities, and on the seventh day you shall desist."[90] Why is it necessary for the Torah to preface the commandment to rest on Shabbat, the seventh day, with a directive to work for six days? Observing the Shabbat on the seventh day is not contingent upon working six days before, is it? Rav Moshe Feinstein, in the *Drash Moshe*, explains that a Jew is expected to sanctify this world by harnessing the mundane to a higher cause. Therefore, the Torah encourages us to work for six days with the explicit intention of sanctifying the seventh day of Shabbat. The six workdays are themselves elevated by the sanctification of Shabbat.[91]

This same concept also applies to the *Shemitta* year. The Torah introduces the *Shemitta* by stating, "Six years shall you sow your land and gather in its produce. And in the seventh you shall leave it untended and unharvested."[92] We toil and work our fields for six years, and, in the seventh year, we observe the Sabbatical year. The Torah instructs us to elevate the six years of hard labor by sanctifying the seventh. When we do so, the mundane toil of maintaining and working the land for six years attains a greater purpose and significance. The six days prior to Shabbat and the six years prior to *Shemitta* demonstrate that spirituality is not attained instantaneously but rather through gradual, unrelenting effort.

רַבִּי יוֹסֵי הַגְּלִילִי אוֹמֵר: מִנַּיִן אַתָּה אוֹמֵר, שֶׁלָּקוּ הַמִּצְרִים בְּמִצְרַיִם עֶשֶׂר מַכּוֹת, וְעַל הַיָּם לָקוּ חֲמִשִּׁים מַכּוֹת? בְּמִצְרַיִם מַה הוּא אוֹמֵר: וַיֹּאמְרוּ הַחַרְטֻמִּם אֶל פַּרְעֹה אֶצְבַּע אֱלֹהִים הִיא. וְעַל הַיָּם מַה הוּא אוֹמֵר: וַיַּרְא יִשְׂרָאֵל אֶת הַיָּד הַגְּדֹלָה אֲשֶׁר עָשָׂה יְיָ בְּמִצְרַיִם, וַיִּירְאוּ הָעָם אֶת יְיָ, וַיַּאֲמִינוּ בַּייָ וּבְמֹשֶׁה עַבְדּוֹ. כַּמָּה לָקוּ בְּאֶצְבַּע? עֶשֶׂר מַכּוֹת. אֱמֹר מֵעַתָּה:

בְּמִצְרַיִם לָקוּ עֶשֶׂר מַכּוֹת, וְעַל הַיָּם לָקוּ חֲמִשִּׁים מַכּוֹת:

רַבִּי אֱלִיעֶזֶר אוֹמֵר: מִנַּיִן שֶׁכָּל מַכָּה וּמַכָּה שֶׁהֵבִיא הַקָּדוֹשׁ בָּרוּךְ הוּא עַל הַמִּצְרִים בְּמִצְרַיִם הָיְתָה שֶׁל אַרְבַּע מַכּוֹת? שֶׁנֶּאֱמַר: יְשַׁלַּח בָּם חֲרוֹן אַפּוֹ, עֶבְרָה וָזַעַם וְצָרָה, מִשְׁלַחַת מַלְאֲכֵי רָעִים. **עֶבְרָה** אַחַת. **וָזַעַם** שְׁתַּיִם. **וְצָרָה** שָׁלֹשׁ. **מִשְׁלַחַת מַלְאֲכֵי רָעִים** אַרְבַּע. אֱמֹר מֵעַתָּה:

בְּמִצְרַיִם לָקוּ אַרְבָּעִים מַכּוֹת, וְעַל הַיָּם לָקוּ מָאתַיִם מַכּוֹת:

רַבִּי עֲקִיבָא אוֹמֵר: מִנַּיִן שֶׁכָּל מַכָּה וּמַכָּה שֶׁהֵבִיא הַקָּדוֹשׁ בָּרוּךְ הוּא עַל הַמִּצְרִים בְּמִצְרַיִם הָיְתָה שֶׁל חָמֵשׁ מַכּוֹת. שֶׁנֶּאֱמַר: יְשַׁלַּח בָּם חֲרוֹן אַפּוֹ, עֶבְרָה וָזַעַם וְצָרָה,

Rabbi Yosi Haglili said: How can it be shown that the Egyptians suffered ten plagues in Egypt, and then suffered fifty plagues at the sea? What does it say about [the plagues of] Egypt? "The magicians said to Pharaoh: This is the *finger* of God" *(Shemot 8:15)*. But when it comes to [the plagues of] the sea it says, "Israel saw the great *hand that Hashem wielded against Egypt, and the people feared Hashem, and they believed in Hashem and in His servant Moshe"* *(ibid. 14:31)*. Now, how many plagues did they suffer by God's "finger"? Ten plagues!

Hence, you may infer that in Egypt they suffered ten plagues, while at the sea they suffered fifty plagues (for a hand has five fingers)!

Rabbi Eliezer said: How can it be shown that each plague that God inflicted upon the Egyptians in Egypt actually consisted of *four* plagues? Because it says: "He sent against them the heat of His anger, wrath and fury and calamity, a delegation of agents of evil" *(Tehillim 78:49)*: *Wrath* – one, *fury* – two, *calamity* – three, *a delegation of agents of evil* – four.

Hence, you may infer that in Egypt they suffered *forty* plagues, while at the sea they suffered *two hundred* plagues.

Rabbi Akiva said: How can it be shown that each plague that God inflicted upon the Egyptians in Egypt

מִשְׁלַחַת מַלְאֲכֵי רָעִים. חֲרוֹן אַפּוֹ אַחַת. עֶבְרָה שְׁתַּיִם. וָזַעַם שָׁלֹשׁ. וְצָרָה אַרְבַּע. מִשְׁלַחַת מַלְאֲכֵי רָעִים חָמֵשׁ. אֱמֹר מֵעַתָּה:

בְּמִצְרַיִם לָקוּ חֲמִשִּׁים מַכּוֹת, וְעַל הַיָּם לָקוּ חֲמִשִּׁים וּמָאתַיִם מַכּוֹת:

כַּמָּה מַעֲלוֹת טוֹבוֹת לַמָּקוֹם עָלֵינוּ:

אִלּוּ הוֹצִיאָנוּ מִמִּצְרַיִם, וְלֹא עָשָׂה בָהֶם שְׁפָטִים דַּיֵּנוּ:

אִלּוּ עָשָׂה בָהֶם שְׁפָטִים, וְלֹא עָשָׂה בֵאלֹהֵיהֶם דַּיֵּנוּ:

Hashem Can Act Mercifully and Exact Judgment Simultaneously

אלו העבירנו בתוכו בחרבה, ולא שקע צרינו בתוכו, דינו During the splitting of the Red Sea, Hashem exhibited mercy as He miraculously saved Bnei Yisrael. At the same time Hashem exacted judgment by killing the Egyptians. Only Hashem is capable of displaying attributes of mercy and judgment simultaneously in such a glorious fashion. This is what the Torah celebrates when it says:

Hashem shall reign for all eternity! When Pharaoh's cavalry came with his chariots and horsemen into the sea and Hashem turned back the waters of the sea upon them, Bnei Yisrael walked on the dry land amid the sea.[93]

When Pharaoh's cavalry came with his chariots and horsemen into the sea, Hashem, the King, exacted actually consisted of *five* plagues? Because it says: "He sent against them the heat of His anger, wrath and fury and calamity, a delegation of agents of evil": *The heat of His anger* – one, *wrath* – two, *fury* – three, *calamity* – four, *a delegation of agents of evil* – five.

Hence, you may infer that in Egypt they suffered *fifty* plagues, while at the sea they suffered *two hundred fifty* plagues.

How grateful we must be to God for all the different acts of kindness He has done for us!

If He had brought us out of Egypt, but not meted out judgments against them – *it would have been sufficient for us!*

If He had meted out judgments against them, but not against their gods – *it would have been sufficient for us!*

judgment, turning back "the waters of the sea upon them"; as the verse in *Mishlei* teaches: "Through *justice a king establishes* a land" (italics added).[94] At the same time as He punished the Egyptians, Hashem saved Bnei Yisrael by allowing them to walk on dry land in the depths of the sea.

On Seder night we commemorate Hashem's supremacy, as only He could have led us through dry land and simultaneously drowned our oppressors in the sea. For this, we, indeed, say *dayyenu*, "it would have been sufficient for us."

אִלּוּ עָשָׂה בֵאלֹהֵיהֶם, וְלֹא הָרַג אֶת בְּכוֹרֵיהֶם דַּיֵּנוּ:

אִלּוּ הָרַג אֶת בְּכוֹרֵיהֶם, וְלֹא נָתַן לָנוּ אֶת מָמוֹנָם דַּיֵּנוּ:

אִלּוּ נָתַן לָנוּ אֶת מָמוֹנָם, וְלֹא קָרַע לָנוּ אֶת הַיָּם דַּיֵּנוּ:

אִלּוּ קָרַע לָנוּ אֶת הַיָּם, וְלֹא הֶעֱבִירָנוּ בְתוֹכוֹ בֶּחָרָבָה דַּיֵּנוּ:

אִלּוּ הֶעֱבִירָנוּ בְתוֹכוֹ בֶּחָרָבָה, וְלֹא שִׁקַּע צָרֵינוּ בְּתוֹכוֹ דַּיֵּנוּ:

אִלּוּ שִׁקַּע צָרֵינוּ בְּתוֹכוֹ, וְלֹא סִפֵּק צָרְכֵּנוּ בַּמִּדְבָּר אַרְבָּעִים שָׁנָה דַּיֵּנוּ:

The Women Rejoiced Because Hashem Destroyed Their Oppressors, Not Because Their Lives Were Saved

After the Egyptians drowned, Miriam and the Jewish women burst into song: "Miriam spoke up to them, 'Sing to Hashem for He is exalted above the arrogant, having hurled horse with its rider into the sea.'"[95] Why did Miriam and the women praise Hashem for destroying the Egyptian horses and riders as opposed to explicitly thanking Hashem for saving their lives?

One answer may be found in the history of the Jewish people's persecution in Egypt. Pharaoh initially instructed the Egyptians to destroy only the newborn sons: "Every son that will be born, into the river shall you throw him. And every daughter shall you keep alive!"[96] Rashi (on this verse) explains

If He had done so against their gods, but not smitten their firstborn – *it would have been sufficient for us!*

If He had smitten their firstborn, but not given us their money – *it would have been sufficient for us!*

If He had given us their money, but not split the sea for us – *it would have been sufficient for us!*

If He had split the sea for us, but had not led us through it on dry land – *it would have been sufficient for us!*

If He had led us through the sea on dry land, but not submerged our enemies in it – *it would have been sufficient for us!*

If He had submerged our enemies in it, but not supplied our needs in the desert for forty years – *it would have been sufficient for us!*

that Pharaoh acted upon his astrologers' advice, for they warned him that the savior of the Jewish people would be a man, whose downfall would be through water. Therefore, Pharaoh pragmatically decided to have all the newborn boys thrown into the Nile; he did not wish to kill the girls, only to enslave them. Thus, Miriam and the women sang specifically about their oppressors' deaths, because, at least, initially their lives had not been threatened.

A second answer derives from the Rabbis' teaching that "the merit of outstandingly righteous women caused Bnei Yisrael to be saved."[97] The women merited redemption in their own right, and so they did not have to praise Hashem for saving their lives; rather, they could praise Him for destroying the Egyptians.

אִלּוּ סִפֵּק צָרְכֵּנוּ בַּמִּדְבָּר אַרְבָּעִים שָׁנָה, וְלֹא הֶאֱכִילָנוּ אֶת הַמָּן דַּיֵּנוּ:

אִלּוּ הֶאֱכִילָנוּ אֶת הַמָּן, וְלֹא נָתַן לָנוּ אֶת הַשַּׁבָּת דַּיֵּנוּ:

אִלּוּ נָתַן לָנוּ אֶת הַשַּׁבָּת, וְלֹא קֵרְבָנוּ לִפְנֵי הַר סִינַי דַּיֵּנוּ:

אִלּוּ קֵרְבָנוּ לִפְנֵי הַר סִינַי, וְלֹא נָתַן לָנוּ אֶת הַתּוֹרָה דַּיֵּנוּ:

אִלּוּ נָתַן לָנוּ אֶת הַתּוֹרָה, וְלֹא הִכְנִיסָנוּ לְאֶרֶץ יִשְׂרָאֵל דַּיֵּנוּ:

אִלּוּ הִכְנִיסָנוּ לְאֶרֶץ יִשְׂרָאֵל, וְלֹא בָנָה לָנוּ אֶת בֵּית הַבְּחִירָה דַּיֵּנוּ:

The Extraordinary Care Hashem Provided Bnei Yisrael with During Their Sojourn in the Desert

אילו ספק צרכינו במדבר ארבעים שנה Hashem provided for all of Bnei Yisrael's physical needs during their sojourn in the desert, as it says, "Your garment did not wear out upon you and your feet did not swell, these forty years."[98] Bnei Yisrael did not have to make new garments or craft new shoes during their forty years in the desert; however, they were obligated to go out into the fields and collect the manna every day (except for Shabbat). Why didn't Hashem provide Bnei Yisrael with a substantial supply of manna all at once? Doing so would not have been an act of kindness. While clothing and shoes are worn and, therefore,

If He had supplied our needs in the desert for forty years, but not fed us manna – *it would have been sufficient for us!*

If He had fed us manna, but not given us the Sabbath – *it would have been sufficient for us!*

If He had given us the Sabbath, but not brought us before Mount Sinai – *it would have been sufficient for us!*

If He had brought us before Mount Sinai, but not given us the Torah – *it would have been sufficient for us!*

If He had given us the Torah, but not taken us into the Land of Israel – *it would have been sufficient for us!*

If He had taken us into the Land of Israel, but not built the Temple for us – *it would have been sufficient for us!*

easily transported, it would have been very difficult to transport a large supply of food while traveling in the desert. Therefore Hashem mercifully provided Bnei Yisrael with a new food supply on a daily basis.

Shabbat Testifies to Bnei Yisrael's Uniqueness

אילו נתן לנו את השבת... דיינו The *Midrash* teaches that "Shabbat testifies to Bnei Yisrael's unique status among the nations."[99] How is this so? Rav Yehonatan explains that Shabbat was given to Bnei Yisrael as a special gift from Hashem; the merit from its observance would protect Bnei Yisrael from the attacks of hostile nations. Thus, we can surmise that when Bnei Yisrael does not observe

עַל אַחַת כַּמָּה וְכַמָּה, טוֹבָה כְפוּלָה וּמְכֻפֶּלֶת לַמָּקוֹם עָלֵינוּ.

שֶׁהוֹצִיאָנוּ מִמִּצְרַיִם, וְעָשָׂה בָהֶם שְׁפָטִים.
וְעָשָׂה בֵאלֹהֵיהֶם, וְהָרַג אֶת בְּכוֹרֵיהֶם.
וְנָתַן לָנוּ אֶת מָמוֹנָם, וְקָרַע לָנוּ אֶת הַיָּם.
וְהֶעֱבִירָנוּ בְתוֹכוֹ בֶּחָרָבָה, וְשִׁקַּע צָרֵינוּ בְּתוֹכוֹ.
וְסִפֵּק צָרְכֵּנוּ בַּמִּדְבָּר אַרְבָּעִים שָׁנָה, וְהֶאֱכִילָנוּ אֶת הַמָּן.
וְנָתַן לָנוּ אֶת הַשַּׁבָּת, וְקֵרְבָנוּ לִפְנֵי הַר סִינַי.
וְנָתַן לָנוּ אֶת הַתּוֹרָה, וְהִכְנִיסָנוּ לְאֶרֶץ יִשְׂרָאֵל.
וּבָנָה לָנוּ אֶת בֵּית הַבְּחִירָה לְכַפֵּר עַל כָּל עֲוֹנוֹתֵינוּ:

Shabbat it is open to attack, and, indeed, the Talmud explains that Bnei Yisrael was threatened by Amalek because they did not observe Shabbat.[100]

The Talmud states that only Jews are allowed to observe Shabbat.[101] If Hashem permitted other nations to also do so, they too could claim special treatment from Hashem. Hashem wanted to reserve that exclusive right for His chosen people. Thus, the Halacha ensures that Shabbat observance "testifies to Bnei Yisrael's unique status among the nations."

Torah and Eretz Yisrael – The Perfect Partnership

אלו נתן לנו את התורה ולא הכניסנו לארץ ישראל דיינו The author of the Haggadah places Torah and Eretz Yisrael next to each other in this paragraph because they are intrinsically connected. How so? King David wrote in *Tehillim*,

How much more so, then, must we be grateful to God for the manifold, repeated beneficence that He has bestowed upon us:

For He brought us out of Egypt, meted out judgments against them, did so also against their gods, smote their firstborn, gave us their money, split the sea for us, led us through it on dry land, submerged our enemies in it, supplied our needs in the desert for forty years, fed us manna, gave us the Sabbath, brought us before Mount Sinai, gave us the Torah, took us into the Land of Israel, and built the Temple for us, to atone for all our sins.

"The Torah of Hashem is perfect ... making the simple one wise."[102] Similarly the Talmud teaches, "the air of Eretz Yisrael enhances one's wisdom."[103] Both Torah and Eretz Yisrael promote knowledge and wisdom.

AUTHOR'S COMMENTS Torah and Eretz Yisrael are also similar because of the way in which they are obtained. The Talmud teaches:

> Rabbi Yitzchak said: 'If someone tells you, "I have studied [Torah] laboriously, but have not succeeded," do not believe him; If he tells you "I did not study [Torah] laboriously, but I have succeeded in learning it," do not believe him; If however he tells you, "I have labored in the study of Torah and I have succeeded," believe him.'[104]

The Talmud declares that there are no shortcuts to becoming a Torah scholar. To succeed in Torah learning and accumulate Torah knowledge, you must be prepared to invest much time and effort. Only by doing so, will you gain a true appreciation of the Torah's worth, and eventually become a Torah scholar.

The same lesson applies to Eretz Yisrael. The Midrash relates the story of Rav Chananya ben Teradyon who, though poor and destitute, desperately wanted to make a donation to the Temple in Jerusalem. Rav Chananya, who lived in northern Eretz Yisrael, went out to the fields and found a large boulder that he vowed to dedicate as a cornerstone for the Temple, on condition that he could transport it to Jerusalem. The Midrash recounts that five angels suddenly appeared, to miraculously transport the boulder to Jerusalem for him. However, they had one condition: Rav Chananya would have to place his hand on the stone together with them. Rav Chananya did so and he miraculously found himself in Jerusalem with the boulder.[105]

Rav Yissaschar Shlomo Teichtel questions why Rav Chananya had to place his hand on the boulder for the miracle to occur. He answers that miracles do not just happen. Man must take the initiative by placing his hand on the stone. Rav Teichtel explains that the same is true regarding Eretz Yisrael. We cannot sit idly by and wait for Eretz Yisrael to develop by itself. We must build up Eretz Yisrael, actively enhancing both its physical and spiritual realms. We must touch the stone in order to hasten our redemption.[106]

The Intrinsic Connection Between Shabbat, Torah and Eretz Yisrael

נתן לנו את השבת, וקרבנו לפני הר סיני, ונתן לנו את התורה, והכניסנו לארץ ישראל What is the intrinsic connection between Shabbat, Torah and Eretz Yisrael? Eretz Yisrael is called "the land of the deer"[107] because even though the land appears small in size, miraculously it expands like a deerskin and holds as many people as it must. This is also why Eretz Yisrael is referred to as "the portion of Yaakov,"[108] for when Yaakov left his father's home, fleeing from Esav, Hashem folded-up all of

Eretz Yisrael and placed it under his head to sleep on. Eretz Yisrael is truly a land without boundaries for it can contract and expand as needed. Hashem did not divulge the special nature of Eretz Yisrael, for had the other nations known about this special country they would have accepted the Torah in order to receive the Land. Instead, they rejected the Torah, and Eretz Yisrael was left exclusively for those who embraced the Torah: Hashem's people, the Jewish people. The Talmud declares that any Jew who observes the Shabbat is equated with someone who has observed the entire Torah, and, therefore, he will receive a "portion without boundaries."[109] This portion refers to the land that is compared to deerskin, Eretz Yisrael. Hashem offered Bnei Yisrael the gift of Eretz Yisrael because it accepted the Shabbat and the Torah wholeheartedly.

(For a more detailed discussion of this concept, see "The Intrinsic Connection Between Shabbat, Torah and Eretz Yisrael" found in the essay section following the text of the Haggadah.)

The Angelic Level of Bnei Yisrael at Mount Sinai

וקרבנו לפני הר סיני While it is true that learning Torah enhances our performance of the mitzvot, performing the mitzvot enhances our Torah learning to a far greater degree. For the more we observe the mitzvot, the greater our commitment to Hashem, and the greater our commitment to Hashem, the greater success we will have in learning Torah and obtaining Torah knowledge. The optimal path to serving Hashem begins with blind observance because this entails a willingness to perform without understanding. As a reward for such commitment, Hashem grants us Torah knowledge and understanding. Attaining this level of mitzva performance, however, is difficult because most of us have difficulty committing to doing something we do not understand. Additionally, the evil inclination works hard to deter us from performing mitzvot. Recognizing these obstacles the Rabbis suggested in the Talmud, "If you stumble upon the evil inclination lure him into the house of [Torah] study";[110] study Torah first and then perform the mitzvot.

Angels are exceptionally close to Hashem because they have no evil inclinations; they serve Hashem without even fully comprehending the import of their actions. At Mount Sinai, the Jewish people had no evil inclinations; they attained the ideal level of serving Hashem. When they accepted the Torah and were willing to perform the mitzvot without knowing why, Hashem compared them to angels as the Talmud relates: "At Mount Sinai Bnei Yisrael proclaimed: 'First, we will do and then we will listen.' Hashem responded by saying, 'Who revealed this secret of the angels to My children?' "[111]

Why Bnei Yisrael Received the Torah Instead of the Angels

ונתן לנו את התורה According to the Halacha, anyone selling a field must offer the owner of the adjacent field the first option to buy it. This is referred to as the law of *Bar Mitzra*. This law was formulated to enable individuals to conveniently expand their own holdings by buying fields adjoining their own. An exception to this law occurs when the seller already has a partner or a relative. In such a case the relative or partner has the right of first refusal in purchasing the field.[112]

The Talmud relates that the angels attempted to apply the law of Bar Mitzra to the giving of the Torah. They argued that since they reside in heaven and the Torah comes from the heavens, they should have the right of first refusal, and, therefore, they should receive the Torah, not Bnei Yisrael.[113]

The *Midrash* explains that before Hashem gave Bnei Yisrael the Torah at Mount Sinai, he taught them the concept of Jewish law. He did this so that the Jews would understand the importance of law and order before receiving the Torah. In doing so, Hashem made Bnei Yisrael partners with Him in enforcing the law, and, by extension, partners in Creation. As partners with Hashem, Bnei Yisrael were exempt from the law of Bar Mitzra. Bnei Yisrael could claim the right of first refusal, when Hashem wanted to give away the Torah, and so they did, affirming their partnership with Hashem.

The Torah Was Given to Be Studied by Every Single Jew

ונתן לנו את התורה The Haggadah stresses that Hashem gave the Torah to "us," to every single Jew. The Torah teaches us that not only those who stood at Mount Sinai are capable of comprehending the Torah, for "It [the Torah] is not in heaven...-rather the matter is very near to you."[114] The Rabbis teach us that even though "the simple handmaiden [at the splitting of the Red Sea] witnessed greater heights of spirituality than Yechezkel,"[115] not only those who walked on dry land in the Red Sea are holy enough to appreciate the Torah, for the Torah says, "nor is it [the Torah] across the sea ... rather it is in your mouth and heart."

Is it possible that attaining high levels of Torah scholarship depends upon the constellations and stars in the sky, one's astrological sign, what is written in the stars? Are only those living in Israel's wisdom-enhancing air capable of growing in learning, but those living in the Diaspora prevented from doing so? The Torah rejects all of these excuses and stipulates that anyone can attain and cherish its wisdom, as it says, "It is not hidden from you and it is not distant."[116]

At the Seder we proclaim, "He gave us the Torah." We negate any arguments that discourage the individual Jew from delving into Torah study, and we demonstrate that Hashem gave the Torah to us so that we can grow and develop through its study.

רַבָּן גַּמְלִיאֵל הָיָה אוֹמֵר: כָּל שֶׁלֹּא אָמַר שְׁלשָׁה דְבָרִים אֵלּוּ בַּפֶּסַח, לֹא יָצָא יְדֵי חוֹבָתוֹ, וְאֵלּוּ הֵן:

פֶּסַח מַצָּה וּמָרוֹר:

פֶּסַח שֶׁהָיוּ אֲבוֹתֵינוּ אוֹכְלִים בִּזְמַן שֶׁבֵּית הַמִּקְדָּשׁ הָיָה קַיָּם, עַל שׁוּם מָה. עַל שׁוּם שֶׁפָּסַח הַקָּדוֹשׁ בָּרוּךְ הוּא עַל בָּתֵּי אֲבוֹתֵינוּ בְּמִצְרַיִם. שֶׁנֶּאֱמַר: וַאֲמַרְתֶּם זֶבַח פֶּסַח הוּא לַיְיָ, אֲשֶׁר פָּסַח עַל בָּתֵּי בְנֵי יִשְׂרָאֵל בְּמִצְרַיִם בְּנָגְפּוֹ אֶת מִצְרַיִם, וְאֶת בָּתֵּינוּ הִצִּיל, וַיִּקֹּד הָעָם וַיִּשְׁתַּחֲווּ:

Clarifying Rabban Gamliel's Opinion

רבן גמליאל היה אומר Rabban Gamliel emphasizes that we eat the Pesach offering to commemorate Hashem's passing over the Jewish people's houses in Egypt during the slaying of the firstborn, and we eat matza to commemorate the unleavened bread that the Jewish people had to eat as they hastily left Egypt. However, as Rav Yehonatan notes, there is an additional event that we should commemorate while consuming the Pesach offering and eating the matza – the angels' visit to Avraham, described by the Torah in the following verses: "So Avraham hastened to the tent to Sarah and said ... knead and make cakes ... then Avraham ran to the cattle and took a calf."[117] According to the *Midrash*, the angels arrived on Pesach eve, and Avraham intended to use the cakes that he told Sarah to prepare, as matzot, and the calf that he took to be served alongside the Pesach sacrifice.[118]

Rabban Gamliel used to say: Whoever does not talk about the [symbolism of] the following three things on Pesach has not fulfilled his obligation:

the Pesach sacrifice, matza and maror.

The Pesach sacrifice, which our ancestors ate when the Temple was still standing – what does it represent? It represents the fact that God passed over our ancestors' houses in Egypt, as it says: "You shall say, It is a Pesach sacrifice to Hashem, offered because He passed over the houses of the Children of Israel in Egypt when He smote the Egyptians, and He saved our houses. And the people bowed and prostrated themselves" *(Shemot 12:27)*.

Why did Rabban Gamliel fail to mention the connection between our forefather Avraham and Seder night (the Pesach sacrifice and the matzot)? One might explain that Rabban Gamliel simply wanted to emphasize the reasons for the mitzvot mentioned explicitly in the Torah, as opposed to reasons recorded in the *Midrash*. However, there is also a deeper significance to his rejection of this explanation.

According to the Torah, Avraham instructed Sarah to "knead [dough] and make cakes";[119] however, when Avraham fed the angels, the Torah reports: "He took cream and milk and the calf which he had prepared, and placed these before them."[120] The cakes that Sarah had prepared are not mentioned. Why were these cakes never served?

The *Midrash* relates that while Sarah was kneading the dough her body began menstruating in preparation for Yitzchak's birth.[121] Rabbi Meir explains that even though Sarah began menstruating while kneading the dough, because she used fruit juice the dough could not become ritually impure and it could not become chametz. Therefore, according to Rabbi Meir, Sarah could have been baking kosher for Passover cakes;[122] it is unclear why these cakes were not served to the angels.

Rabban Gamliel, apparently, agrees with Rabbi Meir that kneading dough with fruit juice prevents it from becoming ritually impure; however, according to Rabban Gamliel any dough kneaded with wine, oil or honey (substances similar to fruit juice) is considered chametz and must be burned immediately on Pesach.[123] Therefore, according to Rabban Gamliel, Sarah could not have prepared these cakes on Pesach because even if she kneaded them with "wine, oil or honey" to avoid impurity, they still would have been chametz. Hence, Rabban Gamliel concludes that Sarah could not have been baking matzot, and the angels did not visit Avraham on Pesach.

However, lest we still contend that it was Pesach eve and Avraham only served the angels the calf, the Torah teaches us that the Pesach sacrifice has to be consumed with matza, as it says, "and the matzot with the bitter herbs shall they eat";[124] thus, the calf given to the angels to eat (without the matza) could not have been the Pesach offering. Consequently, Rabban Gamliel stressed the reasons written in the Torah because in his opinion there are no other reasons for consuming these foods on Seder night.

Hashem's Extraordinary Love for Bnei Yisrael

ואמרתם זבח פסח הוא לה' When Bnei Yisrael arrived in the land of Edom during their sojourn in the desert, Moshe sent messengers ahead to the king of Edom. Moshe, wanting to impress the king, reminded him of the ordeal that Bnei Yisrael underwent in Egypt: "We cried out to Hashem and he heard our voice. He sent an emissary and took us out of Egypt."[125] Why was it important for Moshe to mention in his message to the king of Edom that an emissary was sent to take Bnei Yisrael out of Egypt?

In *Tehillim,* King David writes: "But they sought to beguile Him with their mouths and they deceived Him with their tongues."[126] This verse reveals how deceitfully the Jewish people acted towards Hashem when they were slaves in Egypt. Had Hashem entered Bnei Yisrael's homes during the slaying of the firstborn, He would have punished them too. To avoid doing so, Hashem sent an emissary to protect Bnei Yisrael during the slaying of the firstborn, thus signifying that they were His chosen people.

Based on this interpretation, we can explain Moshe's message to the king of Edom. Moshe informed the king that Bnei Yisrael cried out to Hashem in despair, not as a demonstration of their loyalty. Bnei Yisrael were not expressing their desire to commit to Hashem; they were making a desperate plea for salvation. Nonetheless, Hashem heard their cry and in order to avoid exacting judgment, He sent an emissary to take Bnei Yisrael out of Egypt. Moshe wanted to impress upon the king of Edom how much Hashem cherished the Jewish people. Even though they did not deserve to be freed, and even though they should have been punished, Hashem not only spared them but also out of His love for them, sent an emissary to redeem them. Moshe hinted to the king that the smart course of action would be to allow Bnei Yisrael to pass through his land.

Raise the matza and say:

מַצָּה זוֹ שֶׁאָנוּ אוֹכְלִים, עַל שׁוּם מָה. עַל שׁוּם שֶׁלֹּא הִסְפִּיק בְּצֵקָם שֶׁל אֲבוֹתֵינוּ לְהַחֲמִיץ, עַד שֶׁנִּגְלָה עֲלֵיהֶם מֶלֶךְ מַלְכֵי הַמְּלָכִים הַקָּדוֹשׁ בָּרוּךְ הוּא וּגְאָלָם. שֶׁנֶּאֱמַר, וַיֹּאפוּ אֶת הַבָּצֵק אֲשֶׁר הוֹצִיאוּ מִמִּצְרַיִם עֻגֹת מַצּוֹת, כִּי לֹא חָמֵץ, כִּי גֹרְשׁוּ מִמִּצְרַיִם וְלֹא יָכְלוּ לְהִתְמַהְמֵהַּ, וְגַם צֵדָה לֹא עָשׂוּ לָהֶם:

We Eat Matza on Seder Night for One Reason Only; In Order to Fulfill the Mitzva of Eating Matza, We Must Keep This Reason in Mind

מצה זו שאנו אוכלים על שום מה? Why does the author of the Haggadah introduce the section dealing with matza by proclaiming, "Matza - This is what we eat," and then asking, "Why do we eat [this unleavened bread]"? He could have skipped his brief proclamation and his opening question by beginning with the reason we eat matza: to commemorate that "the dough of our forefathers did not have time to become leavened." Rav Yehonatan explains that this complex opening recalls the two different reasons why matza is eaten: to commemorate the Exodus from Egypt and to commemorate Avraham's serving the three angels matza on Pesach.

Whether we choose to commemorate the unleavened bread of the Exodus or Avraham's hosting of the angels has halachic ramifications. The Torah dictates: "You shall not eat leavened bread with it, for seven days you shall eat matzot."[127] The Talmud explains that only dough with the potential to become leavened bread can be used to make matza.[128] This is especially true of the matza eaten by biblical injunction upon Seder night.

This matza that we eat – why do we eat [this unleavened bread]? It represents the fact that the dough of our ancestors did not have a chance to become leavened before God – the King of the kings of kings – appeared to them and redeemed them, as it says: "And they baked the dough that they had brought out of Egypt into unleavened cakes, for it had not become leavened; for they were driven out of Egypt and were unable to delay, nor had they prepared any food for themselves" *(ibid. 12:39)*.

The Talmud concludes that matza consumed to fulfill the biblical injunction cannot be made out of rice or millet because dough made from these grains cannot become leavened bread.

Why is it so important that the dough possess the potential to become leavened bread? If the reason for eating matza is to remember the dough of our forefathers, which could have potentially become leavened bread, but did not, than the Halacha's insistence upon dough that could potentially leaven makes sense. Since rice and millet cannot become leavened bread, they do not help us recall what happened to our forefathers as they left Egypt, and, therefore, cannot be used to make matza for the Seder. However, if we eat matza on Seder night to commemorate the story of Avraham and his guests then there is no connection between the consumption of matza and leavened or unleavened bread. Therefore, there would be no obligation to make matza from dough that could potentially leaven, and it would be permissible to make matza from rice or millet.

Now, we can understand the Haggadah's complex opening to this section

Return the matza, and then raise the maror and say:

מָרוֹר זֶה שֶׁאָנוּ אוֹכְלִים, עַל שׁוּם מָה. עַל שׁוּם שֶׁמֵּרְרוּ הַמִּצְרִים אֶת חַיֵּי אֲבוֹתֵינוּ בְּמִצְרַיִם. שֶׁנֶּאֱמַר: וַיְמָרְרוּ אֶת חַיֵּיהֶם בַּעֲבֹדָה קָשָׁה, בְּחֹמֶר וּבִלְבֵנִים וּבְכָל עֲבֹדָה בַּשָּׂדֶה, אֵת כָּל עֲבֹדָתָם אֲשֶׁר עָבְדוּ בָהֶם בְּפָרֶךְ:

Return the maror.

dealing with matza. Rav Yehonatan explains that the author of the Haggadah begins by proclaiming, "*this* is what we eat," to emphasize that we eat only *this*, matza made from these grains which can potentially leaven. Then the author continues by asking, "Why do we eat this unleavened bread?" Aware that there are two reasons why we eat matza, he wishes to emphasize that only one of the reasons explains the halachic requirement to use dough that can potentially become leavened bread. Subsequently, the author explains that on Seder night we eat matza made from this type of dough to commemorate the dough of our forefathers that did not have time to become leavened bread.

The Reason We Eat Matza and Offer the Pesach Sacrifice Stems from the Time of Creation

פסח ומצה Both Kayin and Hevel offered sacrifices to Hashem. Kayin, a farmer, offered produce from his fields, and Hevel, a shepherd, offered a lamb from his flock. Kayin's sacrifice did not find favor in Hashem's eyes, while Hevel's did. Envy and a lack of harmony were introduced into the brother's relationship. In a burst of jealous rage, Kayin murdered his brother in cold blood.

Eating the matza and consuming the Pesach sacrifice atones for this gargantuan sin, as matza is made from wheat, a product that

This *maror* that we eat – what does it represent? It represents the fact that the Egyptians embittered the lives of our ancestors in Egypt, as it says: "And they embittered their lives with hard labor, with mortar and bricks, and with all sorts of work in the field; all their work with which they enslaved them with backbreaking labor" *(ibid. 1:14)*.

grows from the ground, and the Pesach sacrifice is a lamb. On Pesach we demonstrate that both the produce of the land and the lamb can be offered together to the "Source of all Blessings," Hashem. The joint offering demonstrates a harmonious relationship between the two and atones for the discord highlighted by Kayin and Hevel's sacrifices.

The Three Main Mitzvot of Seder Night Correspond to the Three Categories of Mitzvot in the Torah

פסח, מצה ומרור Bnei Yisrael performed three mitzvot the night they left Egypt: offering the Pesach sacrifice, eating matza and consuming maror. Each of these mitzvot corresponds to one of the three categories of mitzvot given to the Jewish people: *mitzvot*, *edot* and *chukim*. The *Haftorah* portion read on the second day of Pesach explains that Hashem wants us to "observe His *mitzvot* [commandments], His *edot* [testimonies], and His *chukot* [decrees]."[129] *Mitzvot* has a similar meaning to the Hebrew word *mishpat*, judgment; eating the bitter herbs is a *mitzva* because it reminds us that we were judged and bitterly enslaved in Egypt. Eating matza at the Seder is an *eda*, a testimonial (a commandment whose purpose is clear); we eat it to commemorate our hasty departure from Egypt. Consuming the Pesach sacrifice is the fulfillment of a *chok*, a commandment with clearly delineated halachic guidelines, since the verse itself labels the Pesach sacrifice as a *chok*: "Hashem said to Moshe and Aharon, 'This is the decree of [*chukat*] the Pesach-offering.'"[130] When we commemorate our Exodus from Egypt by fulfilling a mitzva from each of these categories, we demonstrate our dedication to Hashem and His entire Torah.

The wise son also refers to the three mitzva categories and their respective representatives at the Pesach Seder when he asks: "What are the testimonies, decrees, and commandments which Hashem, our God, has commanded you?"[131] Clearly, he longs to comprehend what each one of these mitzvot represents. In answering him, the Haggadah emphasizes the faith demonstrated by Bnei Yisrael in Hashem, in performing these mitzvot at the time of the Exodus. Bnei Yisrael followed Hashem into the desert with virtually no food. They eagerly fled Egypt with only half-baked crackers, the matzot, to sustain them. Furthermore, they followed Hashem's instructions to eat bitter herbs that cause food to digest quickly, and His command to consume roasted meat, which digests rapidly, clearly demonstrating their faith that Hashem would provide sustenance in the desert.

However, if Bnei Yisrael knew that Hashem was going to provide them with manna in the desert, then leaving Egypt without proper rations and consuming all of these foods would not have been such an exceptional expression of faith. After all if they were expecting manna to fall from the heavens it would not matter how quickly they needed more food. The wise son's question, on a more profound level, raises this issue. He understands that Bnei Yisrael performed the testimonies (matza), the commandments (bitter herbs), and the decrees (Pesach sacrifice), at the time of the Exodus; however, in asking, "What are the testimonies...?" Rav Yehonatan believes that he is also questioning the depth of Bnei Yisrael's faith statement: Did they know the manna would fall?

The response the Haggadah offers the wise son reveals that the Jewish people did not know about the manna when they left Egypt: "Therefore explain to him the laws of the Pesach offering: that one may not eat dessert – the afikoman, after the final taste of the Pesach offering." The Greek word for dessert, afikoman, is actually a combination of two words, *afik* and *man*, which together mean "no manna." The Haggadah teaches the wise son that when Bnei Yisrael offered the Pesach sacrifice, they had no inkling that "a taste of manna" would follow it. So they demonstrated complete faith when they performed the three mitzvot on Seder night and left Egypt without sufficient provender.

Yirmiyahu, the prophet, refers to this faith: "Thus said Hashem: 'I recall for you the kindness of your youth, the love of your nuptials, your following Me into the wilderness, into an unsown land.'"[132] Hashem promises to have mercy on Bnei Yisrael because of the faith they demonstrated in their youth, as a newborn nation, just redeemed from slavery. The Jewish people followed Hashem into the wilderness, into an unsown land. They did not know Hashem would rain down manna but they had faith in Him.

The Rabbis wanted to prolong our recollection of the Exodus. Therefore, they prohibited eating after the afikoman because they wanted its taste – symbolically the taste of the Pesach sacrifice – to remain in our mouths. The Torah designated three mitzvot to act as Pesach symbols, so that Jewish memory of the Exodus would be strengthened, as the Rabbis say, "People remember questions asked twice (or more)."[133]

בְּכָל דּוֹר וָדוֹר חַיָּב אָדָם לִרְאוֹת אֶת עַצְמוֹ כְּאִלּוּ הוּא יָצָא מִמִּצְרָיִם. שֶׁנֶּאֱמַר: וְהִגַּדְתָּ לְבִנְךָ בַּיּוֹם הַהוּא לֵאמֹר בַּעֲבוּר זֶה עָשָׂה יְיָ לִי בְּצֵאתִי מִמִּצְרָיִם. לֹא אֶת אֲבוֹתֵינוּ בִּלְבַד גָּאַל הַקָּדוֹשׁ בָּרוּךְ הוּא, אֶלָּא אַף אוֹתָנוּ גָּאַל עִמָּהֶם. שֶׁנֶּאֱמַר: וְאוֹתָנוּ הוֹצִיא מִשָּׁם לְמַעַן הָבִיא אֹתָנוּ לָתֶת לָנוּ אֶת הָאָרֶץ אֲשֶׁר נִשְׁבַּע לַאֲבֹתֵינוּ:

Raise the cup and cover the matza until you finish drinking the wine.

לְפִיכָךְ אֲנַחְנוּ חַיָּבִים לְהוֹדוֹת, לְהַלֵּל, לְשַׁבֵּחַ, לְפָאֵר, לְרוֹמֵם, לְהַדֵּר, לְבָרֵךְ, לְעַלֵּה וּלְקַלֵּס לְמִי שֶׁעָשָׂה לַאֲבוֹתֵינוּ וְלָנוּ אֶת כָּל הַנִּסִּים הָאֵלּוּ. הוֹצִיאָנוּ מֵעַבְדוּת לְחֵרוּת, מִיָּגוֹן לְשִׂמְחָה, וּמֵאֵבֶל לְיוֹם טוֹב, וּמֵאֲפֵלָה לְאוֹר גָּדוֹל, וּמִשִּׁעְבּוּד לִגְאֻלָּה, וְנֹאמַר לְפָנָיו שִׁירָה חֲדָשָׁה, הַלְלוּיָהּ:

הַלְלוּיָהּ הַלְלוּ עַבְדֵי יְיָ, הַלְלוּ אֶת שֵׁם יְיָ. יְהִי שֵׁם יְיָ מְבֹרָךְ מֵעַתָּה וְעַד עוֹלָם. מִמִּזְרַח שֶׁמֶשׁ עַד מְבוֹאוֹ, מְהֻלָּל שֵׁם יְיָ. רָם עַל כָּל גּוֹיִם יְיָ, עַל הַשָּׁמַיִם כְּבוֹדוֹ. מִי כַּיְיָ אֱלֹהֵינוּ, הַמַּגְבִּיהִי לָשָׁבֶת. הַמַּשְׁפִּילִי לִרְאוֹת בַּשָּׁמַיִם

In each and every generation a person is obligated to regard himself as if he himself had left Egypt, as it says, "You shall tell your son on that day (in the distant future): Because of this Hashem did for *me when I left Egypt" (Shemot 13:8)*. It was not only our ancestors that God redeemed from Egypt; rather, He redeemed us with them as well, as it is says, "[And you shall tell your son (in the distant future): We were slaves to Pharaoh...] and [Hashem] brought *us out from there, in order to bring us* [here] to give us the land that He swore to our forefathers" *(Devarim 6:21-3)*.

Therefore, we are obligated to thank, to praise, to laud, to glorify, to exalt, to honor, to bless, to elevate and to extol the One who performed all these miracles for our ancestors – *and for us*. He took us out from enslavement to freedom, from sadness to joy, from mourning to celebration, from darkness to great light, and from subjugation to redemption. And we will recite before Him a new song of praise – Halleluyah!

Halleluyah! Praise, you servants of Hashem, praise the name of Hashem! May Hashem's name be blessed from now to eternity. From the place of the rising of the sun to the place of its setting Hashem's name is praised. Hashem is supreme over all nations, His glory is over the heavens. Who is like

וּבָאָרֶץ. מְקִימִי מֵעָפָר דָּל, מֵאַשְׁפֹּת יָרִים אֶבְיוֹן. לְהוֹשִׁיבִי עִם נְדִיבִים, עִם נְדִיבֵי עַמּוֹ. מוֹשִׁיבִי עֲקֶרֶת הַבַּיִת, אֵם הַבָּנִים שְׂמֵחָה, הַלְלוּיָהּ:

Continue holding the cup upraised.

בְּצֵאת יִשְׂרָאֵל מִמִּצְרָיִם, בֵּית יַעֲקֹב מֵעַם לֹעֵז, הָיְתָה יְהוּדָה לְקָדְשׁוֹ, יִשְׂרָאֵל מַמְשְׁלוֹתָיו. הַיָּם רָאָה וַיָּנֹס, הַיַּרְדֵּן יִסֹּב לְאָחוֹר. הֶהָרִים רָקְדוּ כְאֵילִים, גְּבָעוֹת כִּבְנֵי צֹאן. מַה לְּךָ הַיָּם כִּי תָנוּס, הַיַּרְדֵּן תִּסֹּב לְאָחוֹר, הֶהָרִים תִּרְקְדוּ כְאֵילִים, גְּבָעוֹת כִּבְנֵי צֹאן. מִלִּפְנֵי אָדוֹן חוּלִי אָרֶץ, מִלִּפְנֵי אֱלוֹהַּ יַעֲקֹב. הַהֹפְכִי הַצּוּר אֲגַם מָיִם חַלָּמִישׁ לְמַעְיְנוֹ מָיִם:

From Darkness to Light, From Rags to Riches

מקימי מעפר דל, מאשפת ירים אביון: להושיבי עם נדיבים עם נדיבי עמו
Why must the "destitute wallow in the dust and the trash heaps" before being raised up by Hashem to sit "with the nobles"? Why doesn't Hashem seat the poor with the nobles before they have sunken to this level? Before describing the creation of the world, the Torah records the disturbing presence of a void: "When the earth was astonishingly empty, with darkness upon the surface of the deep."[134] The Torah did this so that we could truly appreciate the created world. When all is empty and dark, and then suddenly Hashem creates light, His impact upon Creation is crystal clear. Hashem uses a similar technique to highlight man's achievements. Hashem wants the poor to appreciate

Hashem our God, Who dwells on high, and lowers Himself to look upon heaven and earth! He raises up the destitute from the dust, He lifts the needy from the trash heaps – to seat them with nobles, with the nobles of His people. He causes the barren woman to be established with a family, a joyful mother of children. Halleluyah! *(Tehillim 113)*.

When Israel went out of Egypt, the House of Jacob from a people of a foreign language, Judah became His sanctified one, Israel His dominion. The sea saw and fled, the Jordan turned back. The mountains danced like rams, the hills like young sheep. What is with you, O sea, that you flee, O Jordan, that you turn back? You mountains, why do you dance like rams; you hills, like young sheep? Tremble, O earth, from before Hashem, from before the God of Jacob, Who transforms a rock into a pond of water, a hard stone into a spring of water! *(Tehillim 114)*.

their newly elevated status. Therefore, He first impresses upon them what it means to wallow in the dust and the trash. This way upon being granted salvation, they appreciate the stark contrast between living in despair and sitting at the table with the nobles.

AUTHOR'S COMMENTS The Talmud records an argument between Rabbi Abbahu and Rabbi Yochanan comparing the level of the *tzaddik* – the wholly righteous person – with that of the *ba'al teshuva*, the man who has sinned and repented. Rabbi Abbahu suggests that the ba'al teshuva actually attains a higher spiritual level than the tzaddik.[135] How can this be? Rav Chaim Shmulevitz provides the following answer. When a person sitting in the darkness suddenly moves into the light, he is enthralled by the new world he has entered. Metaphorically speaking, a person who sinned sat in darkness. When he begins to repent, he suddenly moves from the darkness into the light; the impact upon his persona is tremendous. Often he becomes intensely committed to observing the mitzvot in the best way possible. In contrast, a righteous individual – accustomed to sitting in the light – does not experience the same intense revelation when he moves towards more light, so he never reaches as high a level as the ba'al teshuva.[136]

The Sea Had to Convince Itself to Split for the Egyptian Converts

הים ראה וינס The *Midrash* explains that when "the sea saw" that it was supposed to split to enable the Jewish people's miraculous escape, it "fled," turned to Hashem and asked, "Why should I split apart to save Bnei Yisrael and drown the Egyptian idol worshippers? Many Egyptians joined Bnei Yisrael before it left, so there are many idol worshippers amongst Bnei Yisrael as well!" Hashem replied that the Egyptians who joined Bnei Yisrael during the Exodus repented, while the Egyptian nation did not.[137]

Hashem's response to the Sea proves that He considers a non-Jew's repentance valid. The Talmud's understanding of the following verse from *Mishlei* also proves this point: "Remembrance of a righteous one brings blessing, but the name of the wicked will rot."[138] The Talmud explains that the names of the wicked will rot because the Jewish people will not use their names.[139] Given this premise, it is surprising that the name Yishmael was given to a great Torah scholar. Logic forces us to conclude that "Yishmael" repented, hence even one of the greatest Talmudic scholars was given the name, Rabbi Yishmael. This helped to assure that the name would not fall into disuse by the

Jewish people. Thus, a non-Jew's repentance is clearly valid.

This insight explains another *Midrash* which recounts, "'The sea saw' – What did the sea see? [The Midrash answers] It observed the teachings of Rabbi Yishmael."[140] Why would the Sea have seen the particular teachings of a certain Talmudic sage and why would this be important? Perhaps, the Sea originally believed that some of the people leaving Egypt – particularly, those Egyptians who had just converted – did not deserve miraculous salvation at the Sea. However, when the Sea saw that in the future a great sage called Rabbi Yishmael would teach Torah, it realized that if the name "Yishmael" was used by the Jewish nation, even a non-Jew could repent, and it should even split for those Egyptians who had just converted.

Bnei Yisrael Were Convinced of Hashem's Greatness by the Miracles They Personally Witnessed

מה לך הים כי תנוס הירדן תסב לאחור

Watching the Sea flee, the Jordan turn backward, the mountains skip like rams and the hills dance like young lambs, Bnei Yisrael were convinced of Hashem's awesome power over nature. When the Jewish people needed water in the desert, Hashem caused water to flow from solid rock twice, as the Torah attests: "Behold! I shall stand before you by the rock in Horeb; you shall strike the rock and water will come forth from it and the people will drink";[141] and again, "abundant water came forth [from the rock] and the assembly and their animals drank."[142] Bnei Yisrael were privileged to witness Hashem, "the God of Yaakov," overturn the laws of nature, turning "the rock into a pond of water, [and] the flint into a flowing fountain."

Continue holding the cup upraised.

בָּרוּךְ אַתָּה יְיָ, אֱלֹהֵינוּ מֶלֶךְ הָעוֹלָם, אֲשֶׁר גְּאָלָנוּ וְגָאַל אֶת אֲבוֹתֵינוּ מִמִּצְרַיִם, וְהִגִּיעָנוּ הַלַּיְלָה הַזֶּה לֶאֱכָל בּוֹ מַצָּה וּמָרוֹר. כֵּן יְיָ אֱלֹהֵינוּ וֵאלֹהֵי אֲבוֹתֵינוּ יַגִּיעֵנוּ לְמוֹעֲדִים וְלִרְגָלִים אֲחֵרִים הַבָּאִים לִקְרָאתֵנוּ לְשָׁלוֹם, שְׂמֵחִים בְּבִנְיַן עִירֶךָ וְשָׂשִׂים בַּעֲבוֹדָתֶךָ, וְנֹאכַל שָׁם מִן הַזְּבָחִים וּמִן הַפְּסָחִים אֲשֶׁר יַגִּיעַ דָּמָם עַל קִיר מִזְבַּחֲךָ לְרָצוֹן, וְנוֹדֶה לְךָ שִׁיר חָדָשׁ עַל גְּאֻלָּתֵנוּ וְעַל פְּדוּת נַפְשֵׁנוּ. בָּרוּךְ אַתָּה יְיָ, גָּאַל יִשְׂרָאֵל:

בָּרוּךְ אַתָּה יְיָ, אֱלֹהֵינוּ מֶלֶךְ הָעוֹלָם, בּוֹרֵא פְּרִי הַגָּפֶן:

Drink the wine, while reclining on your left side.

רָחְצָה

Wash your hands and recite the following blessing. From this point on there should be no speaking or interruption until after Korech.

בָּרוּךְ אַתָּה יְיָ, אֱלֹהֵינוּ מֶלֶךְ הָעוֹלָם, אֲשֶׁר קִדְּשָׁנוּ בְּמִצְוֹתָיו וְצִוָּנוּ עַל נְטִילַת יָדָיִם:

מוֹצִיא מַצָּה

Recite the first blessing while holding all three matzot:

בָּרוּךְ אַתָּה יְיָ, אֱלֹהֵינוּ מֶלֶךְ הָעוֹלָם, הַמּוֹצִיא לֶחֶם מִן הָאָרֶץ:

Blessed are You, Lord, our God, King of the universe, who has redeemed us and redeemed our ancestors from Egypt, and allowed us to reach this night, to eat matza and maror on it. So too, Lord, our God and the God of our fathers, allow us to reach in peace other holidays and festivals in the future, rejoicing in the rebuilding of Your city, and delighting in Your Temple service. And there we will partake of sacrifices and Pesach offerings, whose blood will be sprinkled on the wall of Your altar for Your acceptance, and we will give thanks to You with a new song for our redemption and the salvation of our souls. Blessed are You, Lord, Who redeemed Israel.

Blessed are You, Lord, our God, King of the universe, Who creates the fruit of the vine.

Rachtzah

Blessed are You, Lord, our God, King of the universe, Who has sanctified us through His commandments, and commanded us concerning the washing of the hands.

Motzi Matza

Blessed are You, Lord, our God, King of the universe, Who brings forth bread from the earth.

Recite the second blessing while holding only the top and broken middle matzot. While reciting the blessing, bear in mind the afikoman to be eaten later:

בָּרוּךְ אַתָּה יְיָ, אֱלֹהֵינוּ מֶלֶךְ הָעוֹלָם, אֲשֶׁר קִדְּשָׁנוּ בְּמִצְוֹתָיו וְצִוָּנוּ עַל אֲכִילַת מַצָּה:

Eat a kezayit from each of the two matzot, while reclining on your left side. If you only eat one kezayit, you have still fulfilled the minimum requirement for the mitzva.

מָרוֹר

Dip the maror in charoset. Shake the charoset off, and recite the following blessing:

בָּרוּךְ אַתָּה יְיָ, אֱלֹהֵינוּ מֶלֶךְ הָעוֹלָם, אֲשֶׁר קִדְּשָׁנוּ בְּמִצְוֹתָיו וְצִוָּנוּ עַל אֲכִילַת מָרוֹר:

Eat a kezayit of maror without reclining.

We Do Not Eat the Matza and Maror for Their Symbolic Value, But Rather Because the Torah Commands Us To

מצה ומרור The Haggadah's description of why we eat the matza and maror sandwich is quite surprising. Firstly, why does the Haggadah's author inform us that we do so in commemoration of Hillel's custom "in the time of the Beit Hamikdash"; why do we need to know this? Secondly, why does the Haggadah stipulate that Hillel performed this act in order "to fulfill that which it

Blessed are You, Lord, our God, King of the universe, Who has sanctified us through His commandments, and commanded us concerning the eating of matza.

Maror

Blessed are You, Lord, our God, King of the universe, Who has sanctified us through His commandments, and commanded us concerning the eating of maror.

says in the Torah"? Presumably, every mitzva Hillel performed complied with the Torah's instructions.

As a prelude to answering these questions, Rav Yehonatan suggests that an even more fundamental question needs to be addressed: Why do we eat the matza before the maror? Since the maror commemorates the bitterness of enslavement and the matza commemorates the exhilarating feeling of leaving Egypt, logic dictates that the maror should have been consumed first. To answer this question we must turn our attention to the main reason we eat matza and maror, respectively, on Seder night: the Torah commands us to in two verses: "For a seven day period shall you eat matzot"[143]; "They shall eat it [i.e., the Pesach sacrifice on Seder night] together with matza and maror."[144] Even today, after the Destruction of the Temple, and the subsequent discontinuation of the

כּוֹרֵךְ

Take a kezayit of the bottom matza and a kezayit of maror dipped in charoset, and shake the charoset off. Combine them in a sandwich and then recite the following:

זֵכֶר לְמִקְדָּשׁ כְּהִלֵּל:

כֵּן עָשָׂה הִלֵּל בִּזְמַן שֶׁבֵּית הַמִּקְדָּשׁ הָיָה קַיָּם. הָיָה כּוֹרֵךְ (פֶּסַח וּ)מַצָּה וּמָרוֹר וְאוֹכְלָם בְּיַחַד, לְקַיֵּם מַה שֶּׁנֶּאֱמַר: עַל מַצּוֹת וּמְרֹרִים יֹאכְלֻהוּ: (במדבר ט יא)

Eat the matzah-and-maror combination, while reclining on your left side.

Pesach sacrifice, when we eat the matza on Pesach, we fulfill a biblical commandment; as the verse cited above clearly states, the commandment to eat matza (for seven days) is independent of the commandment to eat the Pesach sacrifice. However, there is no independent commandment to eat maror; we are only commanded to eat it with the Pesach sacrifice. Therefore, today when the Pesach sacrifice is no longer brought, we only eat maror to fulfill the rabbinic injunction commanding us to commemorate the bitter enslavement we experienced in Egypt. We eat the matza before the bitter herbs because fulfilling a biblical commandment takes precedence over a rabbinic one.

Another reason we eat the matza and maror is recalled by Yirmiyahu's lament in *Eicha*, "He filled me with bitterness, sated me with wormwood."[145] The *Midrash* explains that the first half of the verse, "He filled me with

Korech

A remembrance of the Temple in accordance with the custom of Hillel: This is what Hillel did, when the Temple was still standing. He would combine matza and maror and eat them together, in fulfillment of what it says: "They shall eat it together with matza and bitter herbs" *(Bamidbar 9:11)*.

bitterness," refers to the first night of Pesach when we are obligated to eat the maror. The second half, "[He] sated me with wormwood," refers to the evening of the Ninth of Av when we mourn the Destruction of the Temple.[146] Seder night and the night of the Ninth of Av are intrinsically connected because they always fall out on the same night of the week. Therefore, maror commemorates both holidays. Maror reminds the Jewish people of the slavery in Egypt, as well as of the Temple's destruction in Jerusalem and the bitter exile following. Chronologically speaking, according to the *Midrash* it makes sense to eat the matza before the maror because the matza reminds us of our redemption from Egypt, while the maror reminds us of the Temple's destruction and of our exile from Israel, events which occurred far later in our history.

Explaining why we eat the matza before the maror based upon this *Midrash* seems problematic because it presumes an eternal connection between Seder night and the Ninth of Av. However,

שֻׁלְחָן עוֹרֵךְ

Eat the festive meal.

צָפוּן

Eat at least a kezayit of the matza set aside at the beginning of the Seder for use as the afikoman. You should try to eat two kezaytim.

when the Jewish people are redeemed from exile and the Temple is rebuilt, we will no longer commemorate the Ninth of Av. Our time of exile will be forgotten, so half the reason for eating the maror would disappear. It is difficult to imagine the Jewish people exempted from fulfilling the explicit biblical commandment of eating maror with the Pesach sacrifice when the Temple is rebuilt.

Thus, we are lead to realize that the main reason we eat the matza and the maror is because the Torah instructs us to commemorate our bitter enslavement and redemption from Egypt. The author of the Haggadah informed us that Hillel ate the matza and maror sandwich even "in the time of the Beit Hamikdash," to emphasize that even in a period when the Jews lived in their own land, matza and maror were eaten because that is what the Torah commands. Indeed, the author explicitly states that Hillel ate the matza and bitter herbs "to fulfill what is written in the Torah; 'they shall eat it together with matza and maror.'"

Shulchan Orech

Eat the festive meal.

Tzafun

Eat at least a kezayit of the matza set aside at the beginning of the Seder for use as the afikoman. You should try to eat two kezaytim.

Why the Pesach Sacrifice Must Be Offered "Between the Evenings"

קרבן פסח There is a reason why the Torah commands that the Pesach sacrifice be offered *bein ha'arbayim*, "between the evenings"[147] (at twilight), a period neither clearly night nor clearly day.[148] The Egyptians worshipped the sun and the moon. Had Bnei Yisrael offered the sacrifice during the day, the Egyptian worshippers of the moon would have claimed that the Jews were afraid of the moon god. Had Bnei Yisrael offered the sacrifice at night, the Egyptian worshippers of the sun would have claimed that the Jews were afraid of the sun god. Therefore, Hashem instructed His people to offer the Pesach sacrifice at twilight when both the sun and the moon appear in the sky. This would demonstrate to everyone that Bnei Yisrael did not fear either the sun or the moon; Bnei Yisrael feared only Hashem.

Upon entering Eretz Yisrael, Bnei Yisrael offered the Pesach sacrifice for the second time. (During the forty

בָּרֵךְ

Pour the third cup of wine (the cup must be washed if it is not clean). It is customary to recite or sing the following psalm before reciting Birkat Hamazon:

שִׁיר הַמַּעֲלוֹת, בְּשׁוּב יְיָ אֶת שִׁיבַת צִיּוֹן, הָיִינוּ כְּחֹלְמִים: אָז יִמָּלֵא שְׂחוֹק פִּינוּ וּלְשׁוֹנֵנוּ רִנָּה, אָז יֹאמְרוּ בַגּוֹיִם, הִגְדִּיל יְיָ לַעֲשׂוֹת עִם אֵלֶּה: הִגְדִּיל יְיָ לַעֲשׂוֹת עִמָּנוּ, הָיִינוּ שְׂמֵחִים: שׁוּבָה יְיָ אֶת שְׁבִיתֵנוּ, כַּאֲפִיקִים בַּנֶּגֶב: הַזֹּרְעִים בְּדִמְעָה בְּרִנָּה יִקְצֹרוּ: הָלוֹךְ יֵלֵךְ וּבָכֹה, נֹשֵׂא מֶשֶׁךְ הַזָּרַע, בֹּא יָבֹא בְרִנָּה, נֹשֵׂא אֲלֻמֹּתָיו:

years in the desert, the Jews did not practice circumcision, so the Pesach sacrifice was not offered.) At this time, the same guidelines applied. Bnei Yisrael underwent circumcision in Gilgal, and then offered the Pesach sacrifice "on the eve" of the fourteenth day, just as the day was coming to an end and the evening approached. In one of its first acts taken as a people upon entering Eretz Yisrael, Bnei Yisrael reaffirmed its belief in Hashem by offering the sacrifice "between the evenings."

The Pursuit of True Happiness

שיר המעלות King David described how during their redemption the Jewish people would "sing to Hashem a

Barech

A Song of Ascents. When Hashem will return the exiles of Zion, we will be like dreamers. Then our mouth will be filled with laughter, and our tongue with glad song. Then will they say among the nations, "Hashem has done great things for these people." Hashem has done great things for us; we were gladdened. Hashem, return our exiles, like streams in parched land. Those who sow in tears will reap with shouts of joy. He keeps going along weeping, carrying the load of seed; but he will surely come back with shouts of joy, carrying his sheaves.

(Tehillim 126)

new song."[149] The greatness of the Jewish people is revealed in their understanding of true happiness. The Jewish people achieves true happiness when the Jews attain greater spirituality by "fill[ing] their mouths with laughter and their tongues with glad songs" of praise to Hashem. In the future, the nations of the world will recognize the difference between their happiness and Bnei Yisrael's when they hear these glad songs. They define the search for happiness as the search for physical pleasure. When they see Bnei Yisrael pursuing happiness by singing praises to Hashem in the quest for spirituality, they will declare that the Jewish people deserves to be the chosen nation: "Hashem has done great things for these people." The nations will acknowledge that they are not worthy of such a relationship with Hashem because their goals are different than the Jews, as they proclaim, "[had] Hashem done great things for us, we were gladdened" – we would have been happy had He just satisfied our physical needs; we do not need Him to fulfill our spiritual ones.

AUTHOR'S COMMENTS Many people spend their lives pursuing happiness. Judaism teaches us that happiness is not enough; we must strive for the higher level of "*simcha.*" The Torah provides clear physical and spiritual guidelines for reaching this level. Thus, the Talmud offers physical pleasures as a means of reaching simcha: "in the Temple period, simcha was achieved by [eating] meat [from the sacrifices], but now that the Temple has been destroyed, simcha can only be obtained by [drinking] wine."[150] Additionally, the Talmud instructs Bnei Yisrael to attain simcha by the spiritual means of reciting *Hallel* while preparing the Pesach offering.[151]

On Rosh Hashana and Yom Kippur, the Talmud instructs the Jewish people to refrain from reciting Hallel:

> From this we learn that one does not recite Hallel on Rosh Hashana. Why not? Rabbi Abbahu explained that the angels asked Hashem: 'Master of the Universe, why don't the Jewish people recite the song of Hallel before You on Rosh Hashana and Yom Kippur?' Hashem answered them: 'Can we expect someone who is being judged – with the Book of Life and the Book of Death open in front of him – to sing?'[152]

The Rabbis presume that people cannot be both fearful and happy at the same time; on Rosh Hashana and Yom Kippur when one's fate is being sealed it is improper, if not impossible, to rejoice. Surprisingly, the Rambam lists Rosh Hashana as a *Yom Tov*, along with the three Festivals of Pesach, Shavuot and Sukkot.[153] On these three

Festivals, the Jew is commanded to rejoice – to be *sameach*. Could the Rambam possibly mean that Rosh Hashana also requires simcha, after the Talmud suggested otherwise?

Interestingly enough, elsewhere in the *Mishneh Torah*, the Rambam rules, in keeping with the Talmud, that we do not recite Hallel on Rosh Hashana and Yom Kippur; however, he explains that we omit Hallel because "they [i.e., these days] are days of fear and awe and not days of extra happiness."[154] Thus, on the one hand, the Rambam seems to expect the Jew to be happy on Rosh Hashana and Yom Kippur, but, on the other hand, he does not expect him to be "extra happy." Deducing from the Rambam's use of the phrase "extra happiness," the commentaries explain that while Rosh Hashana and Yom Kippur are not days of "extra happiness," they do warrant some level of simcha. How is this simcha attained?

My Rebbe, Rav Aharon Lichtenstein, explained that before answering this question one must first define the precise nature of simcha. The Talmud declares: "There is no sadness before the Holy One, blessed be He, as it says, 'Glory and majesty are before Him; might and joy are in His place.'"[155] The Talmud also states: "The Divine Presence does rest upon one who is lazy or sad, or one engaged in idle laughter, light-headed [pursuits], or idle conversations, but upon one imbued with the simcha of performing mitzvot."[156] These citations from the Talmud describe simcha as a state entered when an individual surrounds himself or herself with the Divine Presence. Simcha is to be found *lifnei Hashem*, in the presence of Hashem's divine glory. This is the state the high priest enters while serving Hashem in the Temple, as the Rambam writes: "his glory and honor will derive from his sitting in the Holy Temple all day."[157] The high priest is privileged to bask in Hashem's glory while in the Temple, and, in the midst of performing the service on Yom Kippur, he would sing: "Happy is the people for whom this is so; happy is the people whose God is Hashem."[158] For the high priest and Bnei Yisrael, the simcha on Yom Kippur stemmed not only from Hashem's forgiveness of their sins, but also from the opportunity to bask in Hashem's glory and engage in dialogue with Him for a whole day. Thus, Rav Aharon continues, one is supposed to eat meat at the fast-breaking meal following Yom Kippur. Meat, a sign of simcha, is the central component of a festive meal. We rejoice after Yom Kippur not only because we are confident of having been forgiven but because of the rapture achieved in having stood before Hashem for an entire day.

Based upon this conception of simcha, we can distinguish between regular simcha and the Rambam's notion of "extra happiness." The Talmud describes two methods of attaining simcha: one, basically physical, drinking wine and eating meat, and the other, wholly spiritual, praying and offering sacrifices. On the High Holidays, one is expected to refrain from attaining the "extra happiness" arrived at through physical pleasures. It is highly inappropriate to drink wine and eat sumptuous meat meals upon the days of awe and judgment. However, the simcha of being "lifnei Hashem" is something that every individual should yearn for constantly, particularly on the days of awe and penitence.

To reach this level on Rosh Hashana and Yom Kippur, the Jew does not need external stimuli. Even Hallel, a prayer that expresses simcha, and, thus provides the necessary atmosphere for standing before Hashem, is omitted. On Rosh Hashana and Yom Kippur this prayer can be left out, for carried away by the holiness of the days, the Jew is enveloped by the glory of Hashem's Divine Presence.

The Path to the Final Redemption

The Jews raise their voices in "the glad song" of Torah learning, because for them happiness is realized through spiritual fulfillment. The verse "to hear the song [of Torah learning] and the prayer"[159] testifies to the fact that Jewish learning and prayer is intimately related to joyous singing. Bnei Yisrael automatically rejoices when it can sing glad songs of Torah learning and offer prayers. When the nations of the world see Bnei Yisrael's joyous celebration of spiritual fulfillment, they concede and declare: "Hashem has done great things for His people." For they admit that "[had] Hashem done great things for us" it would have been a waste of His energies because we "were gladdened" by materialism and physical pleasures that are ultimately meaningless. This aspect of Bnei Yisrael's uniqueness is also attested to by the prophet Yeshayahu who exclaimed, "Exult and shout for joy, O inhabitant of Zion, for the Holy One of Yisrael is great in your midst."[160] Yeshayahu described the time of the ultimate redemption. He explained that when the Jewish people "exult and shout for joy" in pursuit of holiness, then Hashem will inhabit Zion and be "great in their midst."

Recite the following invitation to say Birkat Hamazon when three adult males are present. When ten or more adult males are present the words in parentheses are also added:

Leader:

רַבּוֹתַי, נְבָרֵךְ:

The participants respond, followed by the leader:

יְהִי שֵׁם יְיָ מְבֹרָךְ מֵעַתָּה וְעַד עוֹלָם:

Leader:

בִּרְשׁוּת מָרָנָן וְרַבָּנָן וְרַבּוֹתַי נְבָרֵךְ (בעשרה: אֱלֹהֵינוּ) שֶׁאָכַלְנוּ מִשֶּׁלּוֹ:

The participants respond, followed by the leader:

בָּרוּךְ (בעשרה: אֱלֹהֵינוּ) שֶׁאָכַלְנוּ מִשֶּׁלּוֹ וּבְטוּבוֹ חָיִינוּ:

Leader:

בָּרוּךְ הוּא וּבָרוּךְ שְׁמוֹ:

ברכת המזון

בָּרוּךְ אַתָּה יְיָ, אֱלֹהֵינוּ מֶלֶךְ הָעוֹלָם, הַזָּן אֶת הָעוֹלָם כֻּלּוֹ בְּטוּבוֹ, בְּחֵן בְּחֶסֶד וּבְרַחֲמִים, הוּא נוֹתֵן לֶחֶם לְכָל בָּשָׂר, כִּי לְעוֹלָם חַסְדּוֹ. וּבְטוּבוֹ הַגָּדוֹל תָּמִיד לֹא חָסַר לָנוּ, וְאַל יֶחְסַר לָנוּ מָזוֹן לְעוֹלָם וָעֶד. בַּעֲבוּר שְׁמוֹ הַגָּדוֹל, כִּי הוּא אֵל זָן וּמְפַרְנֵס לַכֹּל, וּמֵטִיב לַכֹּל, וּמֵכִין מָזוֹן לְכָל בְּרִיּוֹתָיו אֲשֶׁר בָּרָא. (כָּאָמוּר פּוֹתֵחַ אֶת יָדֶךָ וּמַשְׂבִּיעַ לְכָל חַי רָצוֹן.) בָּרוּךְ אַתָּה יְיָ, הַזָּן אֶת הַכֹּל:

Leader: Gentlemen, let us say Grace!

The participants respond, followed by the leader: "May the Name of Hashem be blessed from now to eternity" *(Tehillim 113:2)*.

Leader: With the permission of my masters, teachers and gentlemen –

Let us bless Him (*our God*), of whose [bounty] we have eaten.

The participants respond, followed by the leader: Blessed be He *(our God)* of whose [bounty] we have eaten, and by Whose grace we live.

Leader: Blessed be He and Blessed be His Name.

Blessed are You, Lord, our God, King of the universe, Who feeds the whole world in His benevolence, with graciousness, with kindness and with compassion. He "gives food to all flesh, for His kindness is forever" *(Tehillim 136:25)*. And in His great benevolence, we have never lacked food, nor will we ever lack food, for the sake of His great Name, for He is God, Who feeds and sustains all, is benevolent to all, and prepares food for all His creatures that He created, {as it says: "[You] open up Your hand and satisfy the desire of every living thing" *(Tehillim 145:16)*}. Blessed are You, Lord, Who provides food for all.

נוֹדֶה לְּךָ יְיָ אֱלֹהֵינוּ, עַל שֶׁהִנְחַלְתָּ לַאֲבוֹתֵינוּ, אֶרֶץ חֶמְדָּה טוֹבָה וּרְחָבָה, וְעַל שֶׁהוֹצֵאתָנוּ, יְיָ אֱלֹהֵינוּ, מֵאֶרֶץ מִצְרַיִם, וּפְדִיתָנוּ מִבֵּית עֲבָדִים, וְעַל בְּרִיתְךָ שֶׁחָתַמְתָּ בִּבְשָׂרֵנוּ, וְעַל תּוֹרָתְךָ שֶׁלִּמַּדְתָּנוּ, וְעַל חֻקֶּיךָ שֶׁהוֹדַעְתָּנוּ, וְעַל חַיִּים חֵן וָחֶסֶד שֶׁחוֹנַנְתָּנוּ, וְעַל אֲכִילַת מָזוֹן שָׁאַתָּה זָן וּמְפַרְנֵס אוֹתָנוּ תָּמִיד, בְּכָל יוֹם וּבְכָל עֵת וּבְכָל שָׁעָה:

וְעַל הַכֹּל יְיָ אֱלֹהֵינוּ אֲנַחְנוּ מוֹדִים לָךְ וּמְבָרְכִים אוֹתָךְ, יִתְבָּרַךְ שִׁמְךָ בְּפִי כָּל חַי תָּמִיד לְעוֹלָם וָעֶד. כַּכָּתוּב: וְאָכַלְתָּ וְשָׂבָעְתָּ, וּבֵרַכְתָּ אֶת יְיָ אֱלֹהֶיךָ עַל הָאָרֶץ הַטֹּבָה אֲשֶׁר נָתַן לָךְ: בָּרוּךְ אַתָּה יְיָ, עַל הָאָרֶץ וְעַל הַמָּזוֹן:

רַחֵם נָא, יְיָ אֱלֹהֵינוּ, עַל יִשְׂרָאֵל עַמֶּךָ, וְעַל יְרוּשָׁלַיִם עִירֶךָ, וְעַל צִיּוֹן מִשְׁכַּן כְּבוֹדֶךָ, וְעַל מַלְכוּת בֵּית דָּוִד מְשִׁיחֶךָ, וְעַל הַבַּיִת הַגָּדוֹל וְהַקָּדוֹשׁ שֶׁנִּקְרָא שִׁמְךָ עָלָיו. אֱלֹהֵינוּ, אָבִינוּ, רְעֵנוּ, זוּנֵנוּ, פַּרְנְסֵנוּ וְכַלְכְּלֵנוּ וְהַרְוִיחֵנוּ, וְהַרְוַח לָנוּ, יְיָ אֱלֹהֵינוּ, מְהֵרָה מִכָּל צָרוֹתֵינוּ: וְנָא אַל תַּצְרִיכֵנוּ, יְיָ אֱלֹהֵינוּ, לֹא לִידֵי מַתְּנַת בָּשָׂר וָדָם, וְלֹא לִידֵי

We thank You, Lord, our God, for having bestowed upon our ancestors a precious, good and spacious land; for having brought us out, Lord our God, from the land of Egypt and redeeming us from the house of bondage; for Your covenant, which You have sealed in our flesh; for Your Torah, which You have taught us; for Your statutes, which You have made known to us; for life, grace and kindness which You have graciously granted us; and for our eating of the food that You provide and sustain us with constantly, every day, at all times, and at every hour.

For everything, Lord our God, we are thankful to You and bless You. May Your Name always be blessed in the mouth of every living being, forever. Thus it is written: "And you will eat and become sated, and you shall bless Hashem your God for the fine land that He has given you" (*Devarim 8:10*). Blessed are You, Lord, for the land and for the food.

Have mercy, Lord our God, upon Israel Your people, upon Jerusalem Your city, upon Zion the abode of Your glory, upon the kingship of the House of David Your anointed one, and upon the great and holy Temple with which Your name is associated. Our God, our Father! Provide for us, feed us, sustain us, nourish us and relieve us; and speedily grant us relief, Lord our God, from all our troubles.

הַלְוָאָתָם, כִּי אִם לְיָדְךָ הַמְּלֵאָה, הַפְּתוּחָה, הַקְּדוֹשָׁה
וְהָרְחָבָה, שֶׁלֹּא נֵבוֹשׁ וְלֹא נִכָּלֵם לְעוֹלָם וָעֶד:

On Shabbat recite the following paragraph:

רְצֵה וְהַחֲלִיצֵנוּ יְיָ אֱלֹהֵינוּ בְּמִצְוֹתֶיךָ וּבְמִצְוַת יוֹם הַשְּׁבִיעִי, הַשַּׁבָּת הַגָּדוֹל וְהַקָּדוֹשׁ הַזֶּה. כִּי יוֹם זֶה גָּדוֹל וְקָדוֹשׁ הוּא לְפָנֶיךָ, לִשְׁבָּת בּוֹ וְלָנוּחַ בּוֹ בְּאַהֲבָה כְּמִצְוַת רְצוֹנֶךָ. וּבִרְצוֹנְךָ הָנִיחַ לָנוּ, יְיָ אֱלֹהֵינוּ, שֶׁלֹּא תְהֵא צָרָה וְיָגוֹן וַאֲנָחָה בְּיוֹם מְנוּחָתֵנוּ. וְהַרְאֵנוּ, יְיָ אֱלֹהֵינוּ, בְּנֶחָמַת צִיּוֹן עִירֶךָ, וּבְבִנְיַן יְרוּשָׁלַיִם עִיר קָדְשֶׁךָ, כִּי אַתָּה הוּא בַּעַל הַיְשׁוּעוֹת וּבַעַל הַנֶּחָמוֹת:

אֱלֹהֵינוּ וֵאלֹהֵי אֲבוֹתֵינוּ, יַעֲלֶה וְיָבֹא וְיַגִּיעַ, וְיֵרָאֶה וְיֵרָצֶה וְיִשָּׁמַע, וְיִפָּקֵד וְיִזָּכֵר זִכְרוֹנֵנוּ וּפִקְדוֹנֵנוּ וְזִכְרוֹן אֲבוֹתֵינוּ, וְזִכְרוֹן מָשִׁיחַ בֶּן דָּוִד עַבְדֶּךָ, וְזִכְרוֹן יְרוּשָׁלַיִם עִיר קָדְשֶׁךָ, וְזִכְרוֹן כָּל עַמְּךָ בֵּית יִשְׂרָאֵל לְפָנֶיךָ, לִפְלֵיטָה, לְטוֹבָה, לְחֵן וּלְחֶסֶד וּלְרַחֲמִים, לְחַיִּים וּלְשָׁלוֹם, בְּיוֹם חַג הַמַּצּוֹת הַזֶּה. זָכְרֵנוּ יְיָ אֱלֹהֵינוּ בּוֹ לְטוֹבָה, וּפָקְדֵנוּ בוֹ לִבְרָכָה, וְהוֹשִׁיעֵנוּ בוֹ לְחַיִּים. וּבִדְבַר יְשׁוּעָה וְרַחֲמִים חוּס

And do not make us dependent, Lord our God, upon gifts of mortal men nor upon their loans – but only upon Your full, open, holy and bountiful hand, that we may never be ashamed or embarrassed.

May it please You, Lord our God, to grant us strength through Your commandments, and through the commandment of the seventh day – this great and holy Sabbath. For this day is a great and holy one before You, to refrain from work and to rest on it with love, in accordance with the commandment of Your will. And may it be Your will, Lord, our God, to grant us tranquillity, that there should be no misfortune, sorrow or anguish on our day of our rest. And allow us to behold, Lord our God, the solace of Zion Your city and the rebuilding of Jerusalem Your holy city, for You are the Master of salvations and the Master of consolations.

Our God and God of our fathers! May they ascend, come and reach, be seen and accepted, heard, recalled and remembered before You – the remembrance and recollection of us, the remembrance of our fathers, the remembrance of the Messiah, the descendant of David Your servant, the remembrance of Jerusalem Your holy city, and the remembrance of all Your people the House of Israel, for deliverance, welfare, grace, kindness, mercy, life and peace, on this day of the Festival of Matzot. Remember us on it, Lord, our God, for good; recall us on it for a blessing; and spare us on it for life. And with a word of

וְחָנֵּנוּ, וְרַחֵם עָלֵינוּ וְהוֹשִׁיעֵנוּ, כִּי אֵלֶיךָ עֵינֵינוּ, כִּי אֵל (מֶלֶךְ) חַנּוּן וְרַחוּם אָתָּה:

וּבְנֵה יְרוּשָׁלַיִם עִיר הַקֹּדֶשׁ בִּמְהֵרָה בְיָמֵינוּ. בָּרוּךְ אַתָּה יְיָ, בּוֹנֵה בְרַחֲמָיו יְרוּשָׁלָיִם. אָמֵן:

בָּרוּךְ אַתָּה יְיָ, אֱלֹהֵינוּ מֶלֶךְ הָעוֹלָם, הָאֵל אָבִינוּ, מַלְכֵּנוּ, אַדִּירֵנוּ, בּוֹרְאֵנוּ, גּוֹאֲלֵנוּ, יוֹצְרֵנוּ, קְדוֹשֵׁנוּ, קְדוֹשׁ יַעֲקֹב, רוֹעֵנוּ רוֹעֵה יִשְׂרָאֵל, הַמֶּלֶךְ הַטּוֹב וְהַמֵּטִיב לַכֹּל, שֶׁבְּכָל יוֹם וָיוֹם הוּא הֵטִיב, הוּא מֵטִיב, הוּא יֵטִיב לָנוּ, הוּא גְמָלָנוּ, הוּא גוֹמְלֵנוּ, הוּא יִגְמְלֵנוּ לָעַד, לְחֵן וּלְחֶסֶד וּלְרַחֲמִים וּלְרֶוַח, הַצָּלָה וְהַצְלָחָה, בְּרָכָה וִישׁוּעָה, נֶחָמָה, פַּרְנָסָה וְכַלְכָּלָה וְרַחֲמִים וְחַיִּים וְשָׁלוֹם וְכָל טוֹב, וּמִכָּל טוּב לְעוֹלָם אַל יְחַסְּרֵנוּ:

Guests should recite the following prayer at this point:

יְהִי רָצוֹן שֶׁלֹּא יֵבוֹשׁ וְלֹא יִכָּלֵם בַּעַל הַבַּיִת הַזֶּה לֹא בָּעוֹלָם הַזֶּה וְלֹא בָּעוֹלָם הַבָּא. וְיַצְלִיחַ בְּכָל נְכָסָיו, וְיִהְיוּ נְכָסָיו מוּצְלָחִים וּקְרוֹבִים לָעִיר, וְלֹא יִשְׁלוֹט שָׂטָן בְּמַעֲשֵׂה יָדָיו וְאַל יִזְדַּקֵּק לְפָנָיו שׁוּם דְּבַר חֵטְא וְהִרְהוּר עָוֹן מֵעַתָּה וְעַד עוֹלָם:

salvation and compassion, pity us and be gracious to us, and have mercy upon us and save us; for our eyes are [lifted] towards You, for You are a gracious and merciful God and King.

Rebuild Jerusalem the holy city speedily in our days. Blessed are You, Lord, Who rebuilds Jerusalem in His mercy. Amen.

Blessed are You, Lord, our God, King of the universe, the God, our Father, our Mighty One, our Creator, our Redeemer, our Maker, our Holy One, the Holy One of Yaakov, our Shepherd, the Shepherd of Israel, the King who is benevolent and bestows benevolence upon all, Who each and every day has done good for us, does good for us and will do good for us; He has bestowed upon us, bestows upon us and will forever bestow upon us grace, kindness and mercy, relief, salvation, success, blessing, deliverance, consolation, sustenance and nourishment, mercy, life, peace and all goodness; and may He never allow us any lack of bounty.

May it be [Your] will that the master of this house should not be embarrassed or ashamed in This World or in the Next World. May he have success with all his property, and may his property be successful and close to the city. May the Accuser not hold any influence over his work, and may there not occur to him any manner of transgression or sinful thoughts, from now and forever!)

Birkat Hamazon continues:

הָרַחֲמָן הוּא יִמְלוֹךְ עָלֵינוּ לְעוֹלָם וָעֶד. הָרַחֲמָן הוּא יִתְבָּרַךְ בַּשָּׁמַיִם וּבָאָרֶץ. הָרַחֲמָן הוּא יִשְׁתַּבַּח לְדוֹר דּוֹרִים, וְיִתְפָּאַר בָּנוּ לָעַד וּלְנֵצַח נְצָחִים, וְיִתְהַדַּר בָּנוּ לָעַד וּלְעוֹלְמֵי עוֹלָמִים. הָרַחֲמָן הוּא יְפַרְנְסֵנוּ בְּכָבוֹד. הָרַחֲמָן הוּא יִשְׁבֹּר עֻלֵּנוּ מֵעַל צַוָּארֵנוּ וְהוּא יוֹלִיכֵנוּ קוֹמְמִיּוּת לְאַרְצֵנוּ. הָרַחֲמָן הוּא יִשְׁלַח לָנוּ בְּרָכָה מְרֻבָּה בַּבַּיִת הַזֶּה וְעַל שֻׁלְחָן זֶה שֶׁאָכַלְנוּ עָלָיו. הָרַחֲמָן הוּא יִשְׁלַח לָנוּ אֶת אֵלִיָּהוּ הַנָּבִיא זָכוּר לַטּוֹב וִיבַשֶּׂר לָנוּ בְּשׂוֹרוֹת טוֹבוֹת יְשׁוּעוֹת וְנֶחָמוֹת:

הָרַחֲמָן הוּא יְבָרֵךְ אֶת אָבִי מוֹרִי בַּעַל הַבַּיִת הַזֶּה, וְאֶת אִמִּי מוֹרָתִי בַּעֲלַת הַבַּיִת הַזֶּה, אוֹתָם וְאֶת בֵּיתָם וְאֶת זַרְעָם וְאֶת כָּל אֲשֶׁר לָהֶם, (ואם הוא נשוי אומר) הָרַחֲמָן הוּא יְבָרֵךְ אוֹתִי וְאֶת אִשְׁתִּי וְאֶת זַרְעִי וְאֶת כָּל אֲשֶׁר לִי. אוֹתָנוּ וְאֶת כָּל אֲשֶׁר לָנוּ, כְּמוֹ שֶׁנִּתְבָּרְכוּ אֲבוֹתֵינוּ אַבְרָהָם יִצְחָק וְיַעֲקֹב, בַּכֹּל מִכֹּל כֹּל, כֵּן יְבָרֵךְ אוֹתָנוּ, כֻּלָּנוּ יַחַד בִּבְרָכָה שְׁלֵמָה, וְנֹאמַר אָמֵן:

May the Merciful One reign over us forever and ever. May the Merciful One be blessed in heaven and on earth. May the Merciful One be praised for all generations, and may He be glorified among us forever and ever, and may He be honored among us for all eternity. May the Merciful One grant us honorable sustenance. May the Merciful One break off our yoke from our necks and lead us upright to our land. May the Merciful One send us abundant blessing into this house, and upon this table at which we have eaten. May the Merciful One send us Elijah the Prophet – may he be remembered for a blessing – to proclaim good tidings of salvation and consolation to us.

May the Merciful One bless my father /my teacher /the master of this house /(and) my mother /my teacher /the mistress of this house – them, their household, their offspring, and all that is theirs, as well as us and all that is ours. Just as our forefathers Avraham, Yitzchak and Yaakov, were blessed "with everything" *(Bereishit 24:1)*, "from everything" *(ibid. 27:33)* and "everything" *(ibid. 33:11)*, so may He bless all of us together, with a complete blessing. And let us say, Amen.

בַּמָּרוֹם יְלַמְּדוּ עֲלֵיהֶם וְעָלֵינוּ זְכוּת, שֶׁתְּהֵא לְמִשְׁמֶרֶת שָׁלוֹם, וְנִשָּׂא בְרָכָה מֵאֵת יְיָ וּצְדָקָה מֵאֱלֹהֵי יִשְׁעֵנוּ, וְנִמְצָא חֵן וְשֵׂכֶל טוֹב בְּעֵינֵי אֱלֹהִים וְאָדָם:

On Shabbat add the following segment:

הָרַחֲמָן, הוּא יַנְחִילֵנוּ יוֹם שֶׁכֻּלּוֹ שַׁבָּת וּמְנוּחָה לְחַיֵּי הָעוֹלָמִים:

הָרַחֲמָן, הוּא יַנְחִילֵנוּ יוֹם שֶׁכֻּלּוֹ טוֹב, יוֹם שֶׁכֻּלּוֹ אָרוֹךְ, יוֹם שֶׁצַּדִּיקִים יוֹשְׁבִים וְעַטְרוֹתֵיהֶם בְּרָאשֵׁיהֶם וְנֶהֱנִים מִזִּיו הַשְּׁכִינָה, וִיהִי חֶלְקֵנוּ עִמָּהֶם:

הָרַחֲמָן, הוּא יְזַכֵּנוּ לִימוֹת הַמָּשִׁיחַ וּלְחַיֵּי הָעוֹלָם הַבָּא. מִגְדּוֹל יְשׁוּעוֹת מַלְכּוֹ וְעֹשֶׂה חֶסֶד לִמְשִׁיחוֹ, לְדָוִד וּלְזַרְעוֹ עַד עוֹלָם: עֹשֶׂה שָׁלוֹם בִּמְרוֹמָיו הוּא יַעֲשֶׂה שָׁלוֹם עָלֵינוּ וְעַל כָּל יִשְׂרָאֵל, וְאִמְרוּ אָמֵן:

Patience is Crucial in Waiting for the Moshiach

מגדול ישועות מלכו, ועושה חסד למשיחו לדוד ולזרעו עד עולם Shmuel, the prophet, first spoke these words (now incorporated in Birkat Hamazon) in a conversation with King David. Before officially ascending the throne, David fought countless wars against many foreign nations. At one point, he pessimistically wondered where his salvation would come from and whether he would ever sit on his throne. Shmuel comforted David and gave

On High, may there be invoked merit for them and for us, which will serve them as a safeguard for peace. And may we receive blessing from the Lord and kindness from the God of our salvation, and may we "find grace and good repute in the eyes of God and man" *(Mishlei 3:4)*.

May the Merciful One allow us to enjoy that day that will be a complete Sabbath and rest, for eternal life.

May the Merciful One allow us to enjoy that day that will be total goodness, a day that is infinitely long, a day on which the righteous sit with their crowns [of glory] on their heads, benefiting from the Splendor of God's Presence, and may our lot be with them!

May the Merciful One grant us the privilege of experiencing the Messianic era and the life of the Next World. "He is a tower of salvation to His king, and does kindness for His anointed one, for David and his descendants forever" *(II Shmuel 22:51)*. "He Who makes peace in His heights" *(Iyov 25:2)* – may He make peace over us and over all Israel. And say, Amen.

him strength by reminding him that by remaining patient and faithful, he would eventually reign. Shmuel told David that Hashem is "a tower of salvation to His king"; He performed "acts of kindness on behalf of [David] His anointed one" even though,

יְראוּ אֶת יְיָ קְדֹשָׁיו כִּי אֵין מַחְסוֹר לִירֵאָיו: כְּפִירִים רָשׁוּ וְרָעֵבוּ, וְדֹרְשֵׁי יְיָ לֹא יַחְסְרוּ כָל טוֹב. הוֹדוּ לַייָ כִּי טוֹב כִּי לְעוֹלָם חַסְדּוֹ: פּוֹתֵחַ אֶת יָדֶךָ וּמַשְׂבִּיעַ לְכָל חַי רָצוֹן: בָּרוּךְ הַגֶּבֶר אֲשֶׁר יִבְטַח בַּייָ וְהָיָה יְיָ מִבְטַחוֹ: נַעַר הָיִיתִי גַּם זָקַנְתִּי, וְלֹא רָאִיתִי צַדִּיק נֶעֱזָב וְזַרְעוֹ מְבַקֶּשׁ לָחֶם: יְיָ עֹז לְעַמּוֹ יִתֵּן, יְיָ יְבָרֵךְ אֶת עַמּוֹ בַשָּׁלוֹם:

בָּרוּךְ אַתָּה יְיָ, אֱלֹהֵינוּ מֶלֶךְ הָעוֹלָם, בּוֹרֵא פְּרִי הַגָּפֶן:

Drink the third cup of wine while reclining on your left side.

just anointed, David had not yet sat on the throne. Hashem's salvation and acts of kindness may not always be clear to us nor take place when we expect them to, but Shmuel advised David to be patient, for Hashem would provide support and salvation for both himself and his descendants "for evermore."

David learned Shmuel's lesson well, for he wrote in *Tehillim*, "Why do the nations assemble, and the peoples talk in vain? The kings of the earth take their stand and the princes conspire secretly against Hashem and against His anointed."[161] The nations of the world were impatient, and attempted to prod the Jewish people into rebelling against Hashem by urging them to "cast off their ropes."[162] The nations argued that if Hashem was really the father of the Jewish people He could not leave it languishing in exile; surely, a father would never abandon his child for such a long period of time? Criticizing the Jewish people's stubbornness, the nations invited the Jews to join them in eating non-kosher foods. Finally, the nations questioned whether Moshiach will ever come. If the Moshiach has been chosen

Fear Hashem, you, His holy ones, for those who fear Him want for nothing. Young lions may be deprived and go hungry, but those who seek out Hashem shall not lack any goodness" *(Tehillim 34:10-11)*. "Give thanks to Hashem, for He is good, for His kindness is forever" *(ibid. 118:1)*. "[You] open Your hand and satisfy the desire of every living thing" *(ibid. 145:16)*. "Blessed be the man who trusts in Hashem and makes Hashem his security" *(Yirmiyahu 16:7)*. "I was once a boy, and have also grown old, and I have never seen a righteous man forsaken or his offspring begging for bread" *(Tehillim 37:25)*. "Hashem will give strength to His people; Hashem will bless His people with peace" *(ibid. 29:11)*.

Blessed are You, Lord, our God, King of the universe, who creates the fruit of the vine.

to redeem the Jewish people, then why hasn't he arrived yet and ended the Jewish people's suffering?

David himself faced similar questions when he fought abroad against foreign nations. Rav Yehonatan explains that having already considered these questions, David was able to explain to Bnei Yisrael that foreign nations demand and live for instant gratification. They do not understand the values of patience and of endurance. Bnei Yisrael had to be taught that the redemptive process is a lengthy one, taking time and requiring enormous effort. This was King David's response in the psalm's continuation: "I must tell of the decree that Hashem said to me, 'You are my son, I have begotten you this day. Ask it of me and I will make nations your inheritance, and the ends of the earth your possession.'"[163]

King David was confident that these events, marking the redemption, would come to pass even though he would not necessarily live to witness them. He served as a model for the Jewish nation of patience and loyalty, carefully nurturing his relationship with Hashem, because he knew that, ultimately, he and the Jewish people would be redeemed, and Shmuel's prophetic words would become reality.

AUTHOR'S COMMENTS The *Mishkan* and its utensils were *hekdesh*. Any use of hekdesh for a purpose unrelated to the Mishkan or *Mikdash* violates a prohibition called *me'ila*. The Talmud asks how Bnei Yisrael could avoid committing me'ilah during the construction of the Mishkan? Inevitably, during construction someone would sit on one of the beams or sit under a beam to be shaded from the sun. While unintentional, these acts would constitute me'ilah, benefiting illicitly from hekdesh. [164]

The Talmud explains that during its construction, neither the Mishkan nor its materials were holy: "Construct with the mundane and only afterwards sanctify." Only upon its completion was the Mishkan dedicated to serving Hashem, only then did it become holy. Therefore, during the construction process, there was no prohibition of me'ila. Only after the arduous, physical labor was completed did the Mishkan's spiritual attributes manifest themselves. At this point, the Mishkan became Hashem's dwelling place, as the Torah attests, "They shall make a sanctuary for Me, so that I may dwell among them."[165]

Rav Shlomo Aviner, Rosh Yeshiva of Ateret Kohanim, and one of the foremost Religious Zionist leaders in Israel, explains that the injunction to "construct with the mundane and only afterwards sanctify" teaches that attaining holiness is a gradual process, often preceded by a mundane one. Sometimes one cannot recognize what spirituality has to offer without first engaging in the physical world. After investing one's energies to ensure that a project comes to fruition, one appreciates the final product and the benefits derived from it all the more.

On a conceptual level, explains Rav Aviner, this lesson applies to Eretz Yisrael as well. At times we have trouble recognizing the spirituality inherent in today's Eretz Yisrael, for the religious and spiritual components of this land are far from realized. However, we must not forget that the *Shechina* dwells in Eretz Yisrael and any developments, including physical ones, ultimately, have a spiritual impact. In Eretz Yisrael, the Jew may contribute to the physical infrastructure of the country and reap spiritual benefits.[166]

Experiencing the challenges of building Eretz Yisrael, we may become discouraged. However, we must recognize that the mundane country we appear to be constructing is in reality a permanent dwelling place for Hashem and His people. Attaining this level of spiritual awareness is particularly appropriate on Seder night, when we spend the evening performing mitzvot leading to our enthusiastic proclamation, "Next year in Jerusalem."

Peace Is Not Merely a Matter of Diplomacy; Rather, It Is Achieved by Building a Relationship of Friendship and Respect

עושה שלום במרומיו, הוא יעשה שלום עלינו ועל כל ישראל Peace seems to be an ideal worth striving for; however, we must distinguish between two types of peace: false peace and true peace. When two parties, who in reality still hate each other, agree not to fight, as long as both sides meet certain conditions, this is essentially a false peace, for both sides only conform when it serves their own interests. True peace is based upon respect and friendship. Regardless of their initial differences, when true peace is achieved, both parties eventually become emotionally attached to one another, to the point where each has a sincere interest in the other's well-being, and even strives to take on certain characteristics of the other.

The complicated relationship between fire and water in the natural world illustrates the difficulty in achieving true peace. Fire and water appear to embody opposing roles: fire heats and water cools; fire rises upwards and water flows downwards; fire burns causing much damage, while water extinguishes fire, preventing excessive damage. However, regardless of their differences, fire and water manage to coexist and complement each other in the physical world.

The Midrash argues that this coexistence is not enough, fire and water can take the further step of achieving a true peace in the heavens: "For water and fire despise one another, but in the heavenly realm they experience comradeship and are at peace with one another."[167] Rav Yehonatan notes that this midrash is difficult to comprehend because science attests that nature is comprised of the four elements: earth, air, fire and water.[168] Water and fire are able to work together successfully in the physical world too, not only in the heavenly realm as the midrash suggests. For example, a flint stone oozing water, when struck, creates sparks. Likewise, at the center of the Earth, fire and water combine to create enervating mineral baths visible upon the Earth's surface, including, many contend, the hot springs of Tiberius.

The midrash, however, describes an idyllic relationship between the forces, one far surpassing their complementary nature on earth. In the heavens there is true harmony between these elements. In the heavenly realm, fire and water share an authentic peace, as it says in Daniel: "A river of fire streamed forth before Him."[169] This verse describes fire flowing downward, a characteristic typical of water, not fire. Likewise "the waters that are above,"[170] in the heavens, also betray their typical characteristic of flowing downward by staying in place. In the heavens, the ideal harmony between fire and water, where one takes on the characteristics of the other, is achieved. This is the type of reconciliation that the Jewish people seek in the above prayer. The Jewish people ask that Hashem, "who makes peace in His heights [in the heavens]," bestow this same eternal peace upon all of Yisrael.

Peace Will Only Be Reached When the Temple and Its Services Are Restored

ה' עז לעמו יתן, ה' יברך את עמו בשלום *Sefer Tehillim* describes Hashem as "You who places Your majesty on the heavens."[171] The *Midrash* comments that when Hashem decided to give the Torah to the Jewish people, the heavenly angels protested. They demanded that Hashem "place His majesty [the Torah] on the heavens" by giving the Torah to them. Hashem responded that there were many commandments in the Torah that the angels could never fulfill, and, therefore, the Torah was not meant for them.[172] The angels challenged Hashem insisting that there were many commandments that Bnei Yisrael also could not fulfill, such as the laws pertaining to the priests and the Levites, during a period when there is no Temple. Hashem responded that, nonetheless, He will "give might to His people" by providing them with the Torah, and He will "bless His people with peace," because when there is peace, the Temple will be rebuilt enabling them to fulfill all of His commandments.

Pour the fourth cup of wine. In addition, pour an extra cup of wine, and place it on the table (for Eliyahu). Then open the door and recite the following verses before resuming the recitation of Hallel:

שְׁפֹךְ חֲמָתְךָ אֶל הַגּוֹיִם אֲשֶׁר לֹא יְדָעוּךָ וְעַל מַמְלָכוֹת אֲשֶׁר בְּשִׁמְךָ לֹא קָרָאוּ. כִּי אָכַל אֶת יַעֲקֹב וְאֶת נָוֵהוּ הֵשַׁמּוּ. שְׁפָךְ עֲלֵיהֶם זַעְמֶךָ וַחֲרוֹן אַפְּךָ יַשִּׂיגֵם. תִּרְדֹּף בְּאַף וְתַשְׁמִידֵם מִתַּחַת שְׁמֵי יְיָ:

הַלֵּל

The remaining part of Hallel is now recited:

לֹא לָנוּ, יְיָ, לֹא לָנוּ, כִּי לְשִׁמְךָ תֵּן כָּבוֹד, עַל חַסְדְּךָ, עַל אֲמִתֶּךָ. לָמָּה יֹאמְרוּ הַגּוֹיִם, אַיֵּה נָא אֱלֹהֵיהֶם. וֵאלֹהֵינוּ בַשָּׁמָיִם, כֹּל אֲשֶׁר חָפֵץ עָשָׂה. עֲצַבֵּיהֶם כֶּסֶף וְזָהָב, מַעֲשֵׂה יְדֵי אָדָם. פֶּה לָהֶם וְלֹא יְדַבֵּרוּ, עֵינַיִם לָהֶם וְלֹא יִרְאוּ. אָזְנַיִם לָהֶם וְלֹא יִשְׁמָעוּ, אַף לָהֶם וְלֹא יְרִיחוּן. יְדֵיהֶם וְלֹא יְמִישׁוּן, רַגְלֵיהֶם וְלֹא יְהַלֵּכוּ, לֹא יֶהְגּוּ בִּגְרוֹנָם. כְּמוֹהֶם יִהְיוּ עֹשֵׂיהֶם, כֹּל אֲשֶׁר בֹּטֵחַ בָּהֶם. יִשְׂרָאֵל, בְּטַח בַּייָ עֶזְרָם וּמָגִנָּם הוּא. בֵּית אַהֲרֹן, בִּטְחוּ בַייָ עֶזְרָם וּמָגִנָּם הוּא. יִרְאֵי יְיָ, בִּטְחוּ בַייָ עֶזְרָם וּמָגִנָּם הוּא:

"Pour out Your wrath upon the nations that do not acknowledge You and upon the kingdoms that do not call upon Your Name. For they have devoured Yaakov and laid waste his abode" *(Tehillim 79:6-7)*. "Pour out Your fury upon them, and let the heat of Your anger overtake them" *(ibid. 69:25)*. "Pursue [them] with anger, and destroy them from beneath the heavens of Hashem" *(Eichah 3:66)*.

Hallel

The remaining part of Hallel is now recited:

Not for us, Hashem, not for us, but for Your Name give glory, for the sake of Your kindness and Your truth. Why should the nations say, "Where, now, is their God?" But our God is in heaven; He does whatever He desires. Their idols are silver and gold, the product of human hands. They have a mouth but cannot speak; they have eyes but cannot see; they have ears but cannot hear; they have a nose but cannot smell; they have hands but cannot feel; they have feet but cannot walk; they can utter no sound with their throat. May those who make them be like them – all those who trust in them! Israel, trust in Hashem; He is their help and their shield. House of Aaron, trust in Hashem; He is their help and their shield. You who fear Hashem, trust in Hashem; He is their help and their shield *(Tehillim 115)*.

יְיָ זְכָרָנוּ יְבָרֵךְ, יְבָרֵךְ אֶת בֵּית יִשְׂרָאֵל, יְבָרֵךְ אֶת בֵּית
אַהֲרֹן. יְבָרֵךְ יִרְאֵי יְיָ, הַקְּטַנִּים עִם הַגְּדֹלִים. יֹסֵף יְיָ עֲלֵיכֶם,
עֲלֵיכֶם וְעַל בְּנֵיכֶם. בְּרוּכִים אַתֶּם לַייָ, עֹשֵׂה שָׁמַיִם וָאָרֶץ.
הַשָּׁמַיִם שָׁמַיִם לַייָ, וְהָאָרֶץ נָתַן לִבְנֵי אָדָם. לֹא הַמֵּתִים
יְהַלְלוּ יָהּ, וְלֹא כָּל יֹרְדֵי דוּמָה. וַאֲנַחְנוּ נְבָרֵךְ יָהּ, מֵעַתָּה
וְעַד עוֹלָם הַלְלוּיָהּ:

אָהַבְתִּי כִּי יִשְׁמַע יְיָ אֶת קוֹלִי, תַּחֲנוּנָי. כִּי הִטָּה אָזְנוֹ
לִי, וּבְיָמַי אֶקְרָא. אֲפָפוּנִי חֶבְלֵי מָוֶת, וּמְצָרֵי שְׁאוֹל מְצָאוּנִי,
צָרָה וְיָגוֹן אֶמְצָא. וּבְשֵׁם יְיָ אֶקְרָא, אָנָּה יְיָ מַלְּטָה נַפְשִׁי.
חַנּוּן יְיָ וְצַדִּיק, וֵאלֹהֵינוּ מְרַחֵם. שֹׁמֵר פְּתָאִים יְיָ, דַּלּוֹתִי וְלִי
יְהוֹשִׁיעַ. שׁוּבִי נַפְשִׁי לִמְנוּחָיְכִי, כִּי יְיָ גָּמַל עָלָיְכִי. כִּי חִלַּצְתָּ
נַפְשִׁי מִמָּוֶת, אֶת עֵינִי מִן דִּמְעָה, אֶת רַגְלִי מִדֶּחִי. אֶתְהַלֵּךְ
לִפְנֵי יְיָ, בְּאַרְצוֹת הַחַיִּים. הֶאֱמַנְתִּי כִּי אֲדַבֵּר, אֲנִי עָנִיתִי
מְאֹד. אֲנִי אָמַרְתִּי בְחָפְזִי, כָּל הָאָדָם כֹּזֵב:

King David Versus Yeravam and Seizing the Opportunity to Walk with Hashem

אתהלך לפני ה' בארצות החיים Yeravam ben Nevat served as the first king of the Kingdom of Israel after the Jewish kingdom split in two. Yeravam ruled over Northern Israel, while Rechavam, the son of Shlomo, ruled over Yehuda; most significantly, Rechavam governed the territory encompassing Yerushalayim and the Temple.

Hashem, Who has always remembered us, will bless – He will bless the House of Israel, He will bless the House of Aaron, He will bless those who fear Hashem, the smaller ones along with the greater ones. Hashem will increase you – you and your children. You are blessed unto Hashem, the Maker of heaven and earth. The heavens are the heavens of Hashem, but the earth He gave to mankind. The dead do not praise God, nor do those who go down to the grave. But we will bless God, from now to eternity. Halleluyah!

I loved that Hashem hears my voice, my prayers. For He turned His ear to me, so all my days I will call [Him]. The pains of death encompassed me, and the anguish of dying came upon me, I encounter misfortune and sorrow – and I call out in the name of Hashem, "Please, Hashem, rescue my life!" Hashem is gracious and righteous; and our God shows compassion. Hashem watches over simple people; when I sink low He will save me. Return, my soul, to your rest, for Hashem has dealt kindly with you. For You have released my soul from death, my eyes from tears, my foot from stumbling. I will walk before Hashem in the lands of the living. I had faith when I said, "I am greatly distressed"; I said in my haste, "All men are deceitful" *(Tehillim 116)*.

Yeravam realized that if his subjects continued offering sacrifices in the Temple in Jerusalem, this would weaken his control over them. So Yeravam threatened to kill anyone who attempted to worship Hashem in Jerusalem, and he placed idols on the way to Jerusalem so as to discourage access to the holy city. Furthermore, within his own kingdom, Yeravam promoted idolatry and was a wicked and ruthless leader. The Talmud relates that, nonetheless, Hashem invited Yeravam to repent:

> Hashem grabbed Yeravam's garment and said: 'Repent and I, you and the son of Yishai [King David] will stroll together in the Garden of Eden.' Yeravam responded: 'Who [will walk] at the head [of the line]?' Hashem answered: 'The son of Yishai will be at the head.' Yeravam replied: 'If so then I am not interested.'[173]

This exchange is difficult to understand. Why did Yeravam reject Hashem's personal invitation to repent? Was walking ahead of King David so important to him that he was willing to forgo the opportunity of basking in Hashem's glory?

Hashem instructs Avraham: "Walk before Me and be perfect (*tamim*)."[174] The *Zohar* explains this verse in the following manner: before being circumcised, man walks in front of Hashem, because it would be inappropriate for him to see Hashem's glory directly yet; having undergone circumcision and achieved "perfection," man merits having Hashem walk in front of him, so he can benefit directly from Hashem's glory, as it says, "Hashem, your God, shall you follow."[175]

The *Zohar*'s explanation also sheds light upon the difference between the holiness of Eretz Yisrael and the holiness of the Temple. In Eretz Yisrael one may be surrounded by Hashem's divinity, but one walks in front of Him, as King David writes, "I shall walk before Hashem in the land of the living."[176] (As Rav Yehonatan notes, "the land of the living" where man walks before Hashem, is Eretz Yisrael.) In Hashem's home, the Temple, man walks behind Hashem, and thus benefits more directly from His glory. This distinction helps explain Yeravam's warped calculations. When Hashem informed Yeravam that He, Yeravam and David would walk in the Garden of Eden, Yeravam assumed that either he would walk before or after Hashem. When Hashem told Yeravam that David would be ahead of him and directly behind Hashem, full of self-pride, he thought that he would not benefit from Hashem's glory as someone of his standing deserved, so he rejected the invitation. David was different. He would certainly not dismiss any opportunity to be close to Hashem, to be in the presence of His holy spirit.

AUTHOR'S COMMENTS The *Mishna* rules that one is forbidden from using the Temple Mount as a *kapandriya* to reach one's desired destination.[177] However, discussing this mishna, the Talmud rules that one can use a synagogue as a shortcut, as long as one enters the synagogue first to pray. (There are other opinions in the Talmud permitting the synagogue's use as a shortcut under other circumstances as well; however, the opinion cited here was codified by the Rambam and universally accepted.) The Talmud emphasizes that this leniency applies only to a synagogue, but not to the Temple Mount; the Temple Mount may never be used as a shortcut.

Rav Yosef Dov Soloveitchik explains that this practical ramification reflects the profound ontological difference between a synagogue and the Temple Mount. In the synagogue, man invites Hashem to "join" him for prayers because he hopes to benefit from Hashem's presence. On the Temple Mount, Hashem invites man to enter His house for prayers. On the Temple Mount, man is bound by the restrictions and rules that Hashem places on the use of His own home and, therefore, needless to say, the Temple Mount can never be used as a shortcut.

מָה אָשִׁיב לַייָ, כָּל תַּגְמוּלוֹהִי עָלָי. כּוֹס יְשׁוּעוֹת אֶשָּׂא, וּבְשֵׁם יְיָ אֶקְרָא. נְדָרַי לַייָ אֲשַׁלֵּם, נֶגְדָה נָּא לְכָל עַמּוֹ. יָקָר בְּעֵינֵי יְיָ, הַמָּוְתָה לַחֲסִידָיו. אָנָּה יְיָ, כִּי אֲנִי עַבְדֶּךָ, אֲנִי עַבְדְּךָ בֶּן אֲמָתֶךָ, פִּתַּחְתָּ לְמוֹסֵרָי. לְךָ אֶזְבַּח זֶבַח תּוֹדָה, וּבְשֵׁם יְיָ אֶקְרָא. נְדָרַי לַייָ אֲשַׁלֵּם, נֶגְדָה נָּא לְכָל עַמּוֹ. בְּחַצְרוֹת בֵּית יְיָ, בְּתוֹכֵכִי יְרוּשָׁלָיִם, הַלְלוּיָהּ:

הַלְלוּ אֶת יְיָ כָּל גּוֹיִם, שַׁבְּחוּהוּ כָּל הָאֻמִּים. כִּי גָבַר עָלֵינוּ חַסְדּוֹ, וֶאֱמֶת יְיָ לְעוֹלָם, הַלְלוּיָהּ:

Our Three Forefathers and King David – The Four Legs of the Chair that the Moshiach Will Sit Upon

כוס ישועות אשא, ובשם ה' אקרא Hashem made four promises to Avraham when he left his homeland at Hashem's request: "I will make of you a great nation; I will bless you, and make your name great and you shall be a blessing."[178] The *Midrash* relates that each of the forefathers received one of the blessings. Avraham received the first blessing, Yitzchak the second and Yaakov the third. Therefore, every time we recite the *Amida* prayer we refer to Hashem as "God of Avraham, God of Yitzchak and God of Yaakov." However, the Talmud asks who received the fourth blessing, "and you shall be a

With what can I repay Hashem for all His kindness to me? I will raise a cup of salvation and call the name of Hashem. I will pay my vows to Hashem now, in the presence of all His people. The death of His pious ones is difficult in the eyes of Hashem. I thank you, Hashem, for I am Your servant; I am Your servant, the son of Your maidservant, and You have broken open my bonds. I will sacrifice a thanksgiving-offering to You, and I will call the name of Hashem. I will pay my vows to Hashem now, in the presence of all His people, in the courtyards of the Temple of Hashem, in the midst of Jerusalem. Halleluyah!

Praise Hashem, all nations! Laud Him, all peoples! For His kindness overwhelms us, and the truth of Hashem is forever. Halleluyah! *(Tehillim 117).*

blessing"? The Talmud explains that Avraham received this blessing as well, which is why the first blessing in the Amida prayer begins "God of Avraham, God of Yitzchak and God of Yaakov," but in closing mentions only Avraham's name: "Blessed are You, Hashem, Shield of Avraham."[179]

The *Zohar* explains that the first three promises – referring to the three forefathers – are like three chair legs. The last promise, which seems to refer to a period far in the future, "and you shall be a blessing," alludes to the future redemption of Bnei Yisrael. Therefore, this last promise refers to King David, who "shall be a blessing," as the Moshiach will descend from him. David is the fourth leg of the chair upon which the

הוֹדוּ לַייָ כִּי טוֹב, כִּי לְעוֹלָם חַסְדּוֹ:
יֹאמַר נָא יִשְׂרָאֵל, כִּי לְעוֹלָם חַסְדּוֹ:
יֹאמְרוּ נָא בֵית אַהֲרֹן, כִּי לְעוֹלָם חַסְדּוֹ:
יֹאמְרוּ נָא יִרְאֵי יְיָ, כִּי לְעוֹלָם חַסְדּוֹ:

מִן הַמֵּצַר קָרָאתִי יָּהּ, עָנָנִי בַמֶּרְחַב יָהּ. יְיָ לִי לֹא אִירָא, מַה יַּעֲשֶׂה לִי אָדָם. יְיָ לִי בְּעֹזְרָי, וַאֲנִי אֶרְאֶה בְשֹׂנְאָי. טוֹב לַחֲסוֹת בַּייָ, מִבְּטֹחַ בָּאָדָם. טוֹב לַחֲסוֹת בַּייָ, מִבְּטֹחַ בִּנְדִיבִים. כָּל גּוֹיִם סְבָבוּנִי, בְּשֵׁם יְיָ כִּי אֲמִילַם. סַבּוּנִי גַם סְבָבוּנִי, בְּשֵׁם יְיָ כִּי אֲמִילַם. סַבּוּנִי כִדְבֹרִים, דֹּעֲכוּ כְּאֵשׁ קוֹצִים, בְּשֵׁם יְיָ כִּי אֲמִילַם. דָּחֹה דְחִיתַנִי לִנְפֹּל, וַייָ עֲזָרָנִי. עָזִּי וְזִמְרָת יָהּ, וַיְהִי לִי לִישׁוּעָה. קוֹל רִנָּה וִישׁוּעָה בְּאָהֳלֵי צַדִּיקִים, יְמִין יְיָ עֹשָׂה חָיִל. יְמִין יְיָ רוֹמֵמָה, יְמִין יְיָ עֹשָׂה

Moshiach will sit. This elevation of David's status is also based upon a midrash found in the Talmud:

> In the future, Hashem will make a feast for the righteous. On the day that He bestows His kindness upon the progeny of Yitzchak, after they eat and drink, they will give the cup of blessing to Avraham, our forefather, to recite the blessing of Birkat Hamazon. Avraham will respond to them: 'I cannot recite the

Give thanks to Hashem, for He is good, for His kindness is forever. Let Israel say: For His kindness is forever. Let the House of Aaron say: For His kindness is forever. Let those who fear Hashem say: For His kindness is forever.

Out of the narrow straits I called to God; God answered me by [granting me] spaciousness. Hashem is with me, I shall not fear; what can man do to me? Hashem is with me among those who help me, and I will see my enemies' [downfall]. It is better to seek shelter with Hashem than to trust in man; it is better to seek shelter in Hashem than to trust in nobles. If all the nations surround me, I will cut them down in the name of Hashem. If they surround me and they encompass me, I will cut them down in the name of Hashem. If they surround me like bees, they are extinguished like a fire of thorns; I will cut them down in the Name of Hashem. You may push me repeatedly to make me fall, but Hashem helps me. God is my strength and my song, and He has always been my salvation. The sound of shouts of joy and salvation is in the tents of the righteous: "The right hand of Hashem acts valiantly. The right hand of

blessing, for Yishmael issued from me'...He will say to David: 'Take the cup and recite the Birkat Hamazon.' David will reply: 'I will recite the blessing, because it is fitting that I recite it.' [180]

חָיִל. לֹא אָמוּת כִּי אֶחְיֶה, וַאֲסַפֵּר מַעֲשֵׂי יָהּ. יַסֹּר יִסְּרַנִּי יָּהּ, וְלַמָּוֶת לֹא נְתָנָנִי. פִּתְחוּ לִי שַׁעֲרֵי צֶדֶק, אָבֹא בָם אוֹדֶה יָהּ. זֶה הַשַּׁעַר לַיְיָ, צַדִּיקִים יָבֹאוּ בוֹ:

Recite each of the following four verses twice before continuing with the next one:

אוֹדְךָ כִּי עֲנִיתָנִי, וַתְּהִי לִי לִישׁוּעָה. אֶבֶן מָאֲסוּ הַבּוֹנִים, הָיְתָה לְרֹאשׁ פִּנָּה.

The Righteous Are Those Who Protect Torah Law by Enacting and Performing Rabbinic Decrees

זה השער לי״י צדיקים יבואו בו In *Eicha*, the prophet wrote another verse about gates: "Her gates have sunk into the earth, He has destroyed and broken her bars."[181] This verse is speaking metaphorically. The Jews allowed the gates of the Halacha to sink into the ground by failing to establish rabbinic edicts – bars or barriers – to prevent a breach of Torah law. Hashem therefore destroyed the Temple – its gates and its bars – because the Jewish people did not preserve the Torah properly. In contrast, the righteous protect these gates and will merit entering the World to Come through them.

Why Chava Was Excluded from the List of the World's Four Most Beautiful Women

אבן מאסו הבונים היתה לראש פנה. מאת יי היתה זאת, היא נפלאת בעינינו The Talmud states that the four most beautiful women in history were Sara, Rachav, Avigayil and Esther. (Some who believe that Esther had a greenish complexion replace her with Vashti on this list.)[182] Tosafot explains that even

Hashem is exalted; the right hand of Hashem acts valiantly!" I shall not die, but I shall live, and I shall relate the deeds of God. God may chastise me, but He has not given me over to death. Open for me the gates of righteousness; I will enter them and give thanks to God. This is the gate of Hashem; the righteous will enter it.

I give thanks to You for You have answered me, and You have been my salvation. The stone despised by the builders has become the cornerstone.

though the Talmud in *Bava Batra* contended that Chava was so gorgeous that next to her Sara looked like a monkey, only women born in the natural way – having gestated in their mothers' wombs – belonged on this list. Chava, created by Hashem, was not included.

This reasoning helps explain an additional portion of Talmud in *Megilla* which claims that the verse, "The stone the builders despised has become the cornerstone," depicts Chava in the role of the stone, and the Talmudic scholars, as the builders who despised her by not including her in this list.[183] According to Tosafot's explanation this interpretation of the verse makes sense. Chava, an exquisitely beautiful woman, should have been listed among these women; however, the scholars excluded her. The second verse cited above reassures us that Chava was actually excluded because she was created directly by Hashem. She is "the cornerstone" of all womankind; as the second verse states, she "emanated from Hashem" and was created in a manner truly "wondrous in our eyes."

מֵאֵת יְיָ הָיְתָה זֹּאת, הִיא נִפְלָאת בְּעֵינֵינוּ.
זֶה הַיּוֹם עָשָׂה יְיָ, נָגִילָה וְנִשְׂמְחָה בוֹ.

Recite each of the following two phrases responsively:

אָנָּא יְיָ הוֹשִׁיעָה נָּא:
אָנָּא יְיָ הַצְלִיחָה נָא:

Recite each of the following four verses twice before continuing with the next one:

בָּרוּךְ הַבָּא בְּשֵׁם יְיָ, בֵּרַכְנוּכֶם מִבֵּית יְיָ.
אֵל יְיָ וַיָּאֶר לָנוּ, אִסְרוּ חַג בַּעֲבֹתִים, עַד קַרְנוֹת הַמִּזְבֵּחַ.
אֵלִי אַתָּה וְאוֹדֶךָּ, אֱלֹהַי אֲרוֹמְמֶךָּ.
הוֹדוּ לַייָ כִּי טוֹב, כִּי לְעוֹלָם חַסְדּוֹ.

Even the Most Righteous Tzaddik Cannot Compare with the Ba'al Teshuva

מאת יי היתה זאת, היא נפלאת בעינינו The *Talmud* records Rabbi Abbahu's opinion that even a completely righteous individual – a tzaddik – cannot compare with a person immersed in teshuva. Rabbi Abbahu proves this by citing the verses: "The stone the builders despised has become the cornerstone. This emanated from Hashem; it is wondrous in our eyes."[184] The ba'al teshuva sinned

This took place because of Hashem; it is wondrous in our eyes. This is the day that Hashem has made, let us be glad and rejoice on it.

Please, Hashem, save us, please!

Please, Hashem, grant us success, please!

Blessed is he who comes in the name of Hashem; we bless you from the House of Hashem. Hashem is God, and He made light shine for us; bind the festival-offering up to the corners of the altar. You are my God and I will give thanks to You; my God, I will exalt You. Give thanks to Hashem, for He is good, for His kindness is forever.

because he despised the stone that represented Torah and mitzvot. However, he became "a builder" and as he constructed a relationship with Hashem, he evolved into "a cornerstone" of Hashem's kingdom. Lest one question how Hashem could embrace someone who was a sinner; the verse reminds us that this acceptance "emanated from Hashem"; even though, such acceptance "is wondrous in our eyes."

Some say the following paragraph at this point; others say it later:

יְהַלְלוּךָ יְיָ אֱלֹהֵינוּ כָּל מַעֲשֶׂיךָ וַחֲסִידֶיךָ צַדִּיקִים עוֹשֵׂי רְצוֹנֶךָ וְכָל עַמְּךָ בֵּית יִשְׂרָאֵל בְּרִנָּה יוֹדוּ וִיבָרְכוּ וִישַׁבְּחוּ וִיפָאֲרוּ וִירוֹמְמוּ וְיַעֲרִיצוּ וְיַקְדִּישׁוּ וְיַמְלִיכוּ אֶת שִׁמְךָ מַלְכֵּנוּ. כִּי לְךָ טוֹב לְהוֹדוֹת וּלְשִׁמְךָ נָאֶה לְזַמֵּר כִּי מֵעוֹלָם וְעַד עוֹלָם אַתָּה אֵל:

הוֹדוּ לַייָ כִּי טוֹב,

כִּי לְעוֹלָם חַסְדּוֹ:

הוֹדוּ לֵאלֹהֵי הָאֱלֹהִים,

כִּי לְעוֹלָם חַסְדּוֹ:

הוֹדוּ לַאֲדֹנֵי הָאֲדֹנִים,

כִּי לְעוֹלָם חַסְדּוֹ:

לְעֹשֵׂה נִפְלָאוֹת גְּדֹלוֹת לְבַדּוֹ,

כִּי לְעוֹלָם חַסְדּוֹ:

לְעֹשֵׂה הַשָּׁמַיִם בִּתְבוּנָה,

כִּי לְעוֹלָם חַסְדּוֹ:

לְרֹקַע הָאָרֶץ עַל הַמָּיִם,

כִּי לְעוֹלָם חַסְדּוֹ:

לְעֹשֵׂה אוֹרִים גְּדֹלִים,

כִּי לְעוֹלָם חַסְדּוֹ:

All Your works shall praise You, Hashem, our God, along with Your pious ones, the righteous who do Your will. And all Your people, the House of Israel, with shouts of joy, will give thanks, bless, laud, glorify, exalt, acclaim, sanctify and proclaim the sovereignty of Your Name, our King. For it is good to give thanks to You, and it is befitting to sing to Your Name, for You are God for all eternity.

Tehillim 136

Give thanks to Hashem, for He is good,
for His kindness is forever.
Give thanks to the God of gods,
for His kindness is forever;
Give thanks to the Lord of lords,
for His kindness is forever;
To the One Who alone does great wonders,
for His kindness is forever;
To the One Who made the heavens with understanding,
for His kindness is forever;
To the One Who stretched out the earth over the waters,
for His kindness is forever;
To the One Who made the great lights,
for His kindness is forever —

אֶת הַשֶּׁמֶשׁ לְמֶמְשֶׁלֶת בַּיּוֹם, כִּי לְעוֹלָם חַסְדּוֹ:

אֶת הַיָּרֵחַ וְכוֹכָבִים לְמֶמְשְׁלוֹת בַּלָּיְלָה, כִּי לְעוֹלָם חַסְדּוֹ:

לְמַכֵּה מִצְרַיִם בִּבְכוֹרֵיהֶם, כִּי לְעוֹלָם חַסְדּוֹ:

וַיּוֹצֵא יִשְׂרָאֵל מִתּוֹכָם, כִּי לְעוֹלָם חַסְדּוֹ:

בְּיָד חֲזָקָה וּבִזְרוֹעַ נְטוּיָה, כִּי לְעוֹלָם חַסְדּוֹ:

לְגֹזֵר יַם סוּף לִגְזָרִים, כִּי לְעוֹלָם חַסְדּוֹ:

וְהֶעֱבִיר יִשְׂרָאֵל בְּתוֹכוֹ, כִּי לְעוֹלָם חַסְדּוֹ:

וְנִעֵר פַּרְעֹה וְחֵילוֹ בְיַם סוּף, כִּי לְעוֹלָם חַסְדּוֹ:

לְמוֹלִיךְ עַמּוֹ בַּמִּדְבָּר, כִּי לְעוֹלָם חַסְדּוֹ:

לְמַכֵּה מְלָכִים גְּדֹלִים, כִּי לְעוֹלָם חַסְדּוֹ:

וַיַּהֲרֹג מְלָכִים אַדִּירִים, כִּי לְעוֹלָם חַסְדּוֹ:

The Manner in which Pharaoh and His Army Perished Was Also Part of the Miracle

ונער פרעה וחילו בים סוף During the splitting of the Red Sea, the Jewish people and their Egyptian persecutors witnessed several additional miracles. Among these was the way in which Pharaoh and his army were overthrown. Normally when a horse enters deep water it rears resiliently forwards and upwards attempting to fight its way with its rider towards dry land. However, when harnessed to a chariot, the horse cannot succeed in pulling such a weight, and inevitably the horse, the chariot and the rider will sink. Yet Miriam and the

The sun to rule by day,
for His kindness is forever,
The moon and stars to rule by night,
for His kindness is forever —
To the One Who struck Egypt in their firstborn,
for His kindness is forever,
And took Israel out of their midst,
for His kindness is forever,
With a strong hand and with an outstretched arm,
for His kindness is forever;
To the One Who carved the Red Sea into sections,
for His kindness is forever,
And had Israel pass through it,
for His kindness is forever,
And stirred up Pharaoh and his army in the Red Sea,
for His kindness is forever;
To the One Who led His people through the desert,
for His kindness is forever;
To the One Who struck great kings,
for His kindness is forever,
And killed mighty kings, *for His kindness is forever —*

Jewish people sung a song after the splitting of the Red Sea describing the opposite miraculous phenomenon: "Pharaoh's chariots and army, He cast into the sea; and the pick of his officers were drowned in the Red Sea."[185] Explains Rav Yehonatan, although Pharaoh and

לְסִיחוֹן מֶלֶךְ הָאֱמֹרִי, כִּי לְעוֹלָם חַסְדּוֹ:

וּלְעוֹג מֶלֶךְ הַבָּשָׁן, כִּי לְעוֹלָם חַסְדּוֹ:

וְנָתַן אַרְצָם לְנַחֲלָה, כִּי לְעוֹלָם חַסְדּוֹ:

נַחֲלָה לְיִשְׂרָאֵל עַבְדּוֹ, כִּי לְעוֹלָם חַסְדּוֹ:

שֶׁבְּשִׁפְלֵנוּ זָכַר לָנוּ, כִּי לְעוֹלָם חַסְדּוֹ:

וַיִּפְרְקֵנוּ מִצָּרֵינוּ, כִּי לְעוֹלָם חַסְדּוֹ:

נֹתֵן לֶחֶם לְכָל בָּשָׂר, כִּי לְעוֹלָם חַסְדּוֹ:

הוֹדוּ לְאֵל הַשָּׁמָיִם, כִּי לְעוֹלָם חַסְדּוֹ:

his heavy chariots were cast into the sea they did not sink; however, the officers were drowned in the depths of the sea.[186]

Another reading of this verse, offered by Rav Yehonatan, suggests that those Egyptians who merely "drowned in the Red Sea" were those who began to question Pharaoh's actions and believe in Hashem. Notwithstanding their good intentions, these officers feared for their lives and did not dare to openly challenge Pharaoh's actions. Hashem recognized their good intentions, to some degree, by merely drowning them in the sea. In contrast, Pharaoh and his faithful servants who vociferously challenged Hashem to the very end were thrown "into" the heart of the sea. Their deaths were exceedingly painful as the horses dragged them to the depths of the sea.[187]

Miraculous Confirmation of the Egyptians' Demise

ונער פרעה וחילו בים סוף Hashem mercifully covered the Egyptian corpses with deep waters – "deep waters covered them"[188] – so that the large fish would not

Sichon, king of the Amorites, *for His kindness is forever,*

And Og, king of Bashan, *for His kindness is forever —*

And gave their land as a possession,
for His kindness is forever,

A possession to His servant Israel,
for His kindness is forever;

[To the One] Who remembered us when we were lowly, *for His kindness is forever,*

And delivered us from our enemies,
for His kindness is forever.

He gives food to all flesh, *for His kindness is forever.*

Give thanks to the God of heaven,
for His kindness is forever.

consume their bodies. Yet He knew that if the Jews did not see the Egyptian corpses they would always be afraid that the Egyptians had survived the sea and were waiting to attack. So Hashem had the bodies wash ashore near the Jews' encampment. However, He recognized that this too would not allay the Jews' fears because a drowning victim's face is often unrecognizable. Even if the Egyptians' bodies washed ashore, the Jews would continue to worry. Hashem performed a final miracle for the Jews: the Egyptians "descended in the depths like stone."[189] Just as a stone never changes its appearance no matter how deep it sinks, the Egyptians' appearances also remained the same, so that when Hashem caused their bodies to wash ashore, miraculously, the Jewish people could identify them and verify that they had perished.

נִשְׁמַת כָּל חַי תְּבָרֵךְ אֶת שִׁמְךָ יְיָ אֱלֹהֵינוּ, וְרוּחַ כָּל בָּשָׂר תְּפָאֵר וּתְרוֹמֵם זִכְרְךָ מַלְכֵּנוּ תָּמִיד, מִן הָעוֹלָם וְעַד הָעוֹלָם אַתָּה אֵל. וּמִבַּלְעָדֶיךָ אֵין לָנוּ מֶלֶךְ גּוֹאֵל וּמוֹשִׁיעַ, פּוֹדֶה וּמַצִּיל, וּמְפַרְנֵס, וּמְרַחֵם בְּכָל עֵת צָרָה וְצוּקָה. אֵין לָנוּ מֶלֶךְ אֶלָּא אָתָּה. אֱלֹהֵי הָרִאשׁוֹנִים וְהָאַחֲרוֹנִים, אֱלוֹהַּ כָּל בְּרִיּוֹת, אֲדוֹן כָּל תּוֹלָדוֹת, הַמְהֻלָּל בְּרֹב הַתִּשְׁבָּחוֹת, הַמְנַהֵג עוֹלָמוֹ בְּחֶסֶד, וּבְרִיּוֹתָיו בְּרַחֲמִים. וַייָ לֹא יָנוּם וְלֹא יִישָׁן, הַמְעוֹרֵר יְשֵׁנִים, וְהַמֵּקִיץ נִרְדָּמִים, וְהַמֵּשִׂיחַ אִלְּמִים, וְהַמַּתִּיר אֲסוּרִים, וְהַסּוֹמֵךְ נוֹפְלִים, וְהַזּוֹקֵף כְּפוּפִים. לְךָ לְבַדְּךָ אֲנַחְנוּ מוֹדִים:

אִלּוּ פִינוּ מָלֵא שִׁירָה כַּיָּם, וּלְשׁוֹנֵנוּ רִנָּה כַּהֲמוֹן גַּלָּיו, וְשִׂפְתוֹתֵינוּ שֶׁבַח כְּמֶרְחֲבֵי רָקִיעַ, וְעֵינֵינוּ מְאִירוֹת כַּשֶּׁמֶשׁ וְכַיָּרֵחַ, וְיָדֵינוּ פְרוּשׂוֹת כְּנִשְׁרֵי שָׁמָיִם, וְרַגְלֵינוּ קַלּוֹת כָּאַיָּלוֹת, אֵין אֲנַחְנוּ מַסְפִּיקִים לְהוֹדוֹת לְךָ, יְיָ אֱלֹהֵינוּ וֵאלֹהֵי אֲבוֹתֵינוּ, וּלְבָרֵךְ אֶת שְׁמֶךָ, עַל אַחַת מֵאָלֶף, אֶלֶף אַלְפֵי אֲלָפִים, וְרִבֵּי רְבָבוֹת פְּעָמִים, הַטּוֹבוֹת שֶׁעָשִׂיתָ עִם אֲבוֹתֵינוּ וְעִמָּנוּ. מִמִּצְרַיִם גְּאַלְתָּנוּ יְיָ אֱלֹהֵינוּ, וּמִבֵּית עֲבָדִים פְּדִיתָנוּ, בְּרָעָב זַנְתָּנוּ, וּבְשָׂבָע כִּלְכַּלְתָּנוּ, מֵחֶרֶב הִצַּלְתָּנוּ

The soul of every living being shall bless Your Name, Lord, our God; and the spirit of all flesh shall always glorify and exalt Your remembrance, our King. For all eternity You are God, and other than You we have no king who redeems and saves us. You deliver, rescue, sustain, and show mercy in all times of trouble and distress; we have no king but You – the God of the first and of the last, God of all creatures, Lord of all generations, Who is lauded with a multitude of praises, Who guides His world with kindness and His creatures with compassion. Hashem neither slumbers nor sleeps; He awakens sleepers and rouses those who slumber; He makes the mute speak, releases the bound, supports those who are falling and straightens those who are bent over. To You alone do we give thanks.

Even if our mouths were as full with song as the sea, and our tongues [as full] with shouts of joy as the multitudes of its waves, and our lips [as full] with praise as the expanse of the sky, and our eyes as gleaming as the sun and the moon, and our hands as spread out as the eagles of heaven, and our feet as swift as hinds – we would still be insufficient to thank You, Lord, our God and God of our fathers, and to bless Your name for even one of the millions and billions of benevolent acts that You have done for our fathers and for us. You redeemed us from Egypt, Lord, our God, and You delivered us from the house of bondage. You have fed us during famine and nourished us in times of plenty; You have saved us from the sword and

וּמִדֶּבֶר מִלַּטְתָּנוּ, וּמֵחֳלָיִם רָעִים וְנֶאֱמָנִים דִּלִּיתָנוּ. עַד הֵנָּה עֲזָרוּנוּ רַחֲמֶיךָ, וְלֹא עֲזָבוּנוּ חֲסָדֶיךָ, וְאַל תִּטְּשֵׁנוּ יְיָ אֱלֹהֵינוּ לָנֶצַח:

עַל כֵּן אֵבָרִים שֶׁפִּלַּגְתָּ בָּנוּ, וְרוּחַ וּנְשָׁמָה שֶׁנָּפַחְתָּ בְּאַפֵּינוּ, וְלָשׁוֹן אֲשֶׁר שַׂמְתָּ בְּפִינוּ הֵן הֵם יוֹדוּ וִיבָרְכוּ, וִישַׁבְּחוּ וִיפָאֲרוּ, וִירוֹמְמוּ וְיַעֲרִיצוּ, וְיַקְדִּישׁוּ וְיַמְלִיכוּ אֶת שִׁמְךָ מַלְכֵּנוּ. כִּי כָל פֶּה לְךָ יוֹדֶה, וְכָל לָשׁוֹן לְךָ תִשָּׁבַע, וְכָל בֶּרֶךְ לְךָ תִכְרַע, וְכָל קוֹמָה לְפָנֶיךָ תִשְׁתַּחֲוֶה, וְכָל לְבָבוֹת יִירָאוּךָ, וְכָל קֶרֶב וּכְלָיוֹת יְזַמְּרוּ לִשְׁמֶךָ, כַּדָּבָר שֶׁכָּתוּב: כָּל עַצְמֹתַי תֹּאמַרְנָה: יְיָ, מִי כָמוֹךָ, מַצִּיל עָנִי מֵחָזָק מִמֶּנּוּ, וְעָנִי וְאֶבְיוֹן מִגֹּזְלוֹ. מִי יִדְמֶה לָּךְ וּמִי יִשְׁוֶה לָּךְ. וּמִי יַעֲרָךְ לָךְ. הָאֵל הַגָּדוֹל הַגִּבּוֹר וְהַנּוֹרָא, אֵל עֶלְיוֹן, קוֹנֵה שָׁמַיִם וָאָרֶץ. נְהַלֶּלְךָ, וּנְשַׁבֵּחֲךָ, וּנְפָאֶרְךָ, וּנְבָרֵךְ אֶת שֵׁם קָדְשֶׁךָ, כָּאָמוּר: לְדָוִד, בָּרְכִי נַפְשִׁי אֶת יְיָ, וְכָל קְרָבַי אֶת שֵׁם קָדְשׁוֹ:

rescued us from pestilence, and extricated us from dire and serious diseases. Up to now Your compassion has always helped us, and Your kindnesses have not left us; so too, do not abandon us, Lord our God, forever more!

Therefore, the limbs that You have supplied us with, and the spirit and soul that You have breathed into our nostrils, and the tongue that You have placed in our mouth – they shall all thank, bless, praise, glorify, exalt, acclaim, sanctify and proclaim the sovereignty of Your name, our King. For every mouth shall give thanks to You, every tongue shall swear allegiance to You, every knee shall kneel to You, every spine shall bow down before You, every heart shall fear You and every organ and mind shall sing praises to Your Name, as it is written, "All my bones say: 'Hashem, who is like You?' You save the poor man from those stronger than he, and the poor and needy man from one who tries to rob him" *(Tehillim 35:10)*. Who can be likened to You, who is equal to You, who can be compared to You, the great, mighty, awesome God, supreme God, Possessor of heaven and earth! We shall praise You, laud You and glorify You, and we will bless Your holy name, as it says: "By David. Bless the Lord, O my soul, and all that is within me [bless] His holy name" *(Tehillim 103:1)*.

הָאֵל בְּתַעֲצֻמוֹת עֻזֶּךָ, הַגָּדוֹל בִּכְבוֹד שְׁמֶךָ, הַגִּבּוֹר לָנֶצַח וְהַנּוֹרָא בְּנוֹרְאוֹתֶיךָ, הַמֶּלֶךְ הַיּוֹשֵׁב עַל כִּסֵּא רָם וְנִשָּׂא:

שׁוֹכֵן עַד מָרוֹם וְקָדוֹשׁ שְׁמוֹ, וְכָתוּב: רַנְּנוּ צַדִּיקִים בַּיְיָ, לַיְשָׁרִים נָאוָה תְהִלָּה:

בְּפִי יְשָׁרִים תִּתְהַלָּל. וּבְדִבְרֵי צַדִּיקִים תִּתְבָּרַךְ. וּבִלְשׁוֹן חֲסִידִים תִּתְרוֹמָם. וּבְקֶרֶב קְדוֹשִׁים תִּתְקַדָּשׁ.

וּבְמַקְהֲלוֹת רִבְבוֹת עַמְּךָ בֵּית יִשְׂרָאֵל, בְּרִנָּה יִתְפָּאַר שִׁמְךָ מַלְכֵּנוּ בְּכָל דּוֹר וָדוֹר, שֶׁכֵּן חוֹבַת כָּל הַיְצוּרִים לְפָנֶיךָ, יְיָ אֱלֹהֵינוּ וֵאלֹהֵי אֲבוֹתֵינוּ, לְהוֹדוֹת, לְהַלֵּל, לְשַׁבֵּחַ, לְפָאֵר, לְרוֹמֵם, לְהַדֵּר, לְבָרֵךְ, לְעַלֵּה וּלְקַלֵּס, עַל כָּל דִּבְרֵי שִׁירוֹת וְתִשְׁבְּחוֹת דָּוִד בֶּן יִשַׁי עַבְדְּךָ מְשִׁיחֶךָ:

יִשְׁתַּבַּח שִׁמְךָ לָעַד מַלְכֵּנוּ, הָאֵל הַמֶּלֶךְ הַגָּדוֹל וְהַקָּדוֹשׁ בַּשָּׁמַיִם וּבָאָרֶץ, כִּי לְךָ נָאֶה, יְיָ אֱלֹהֵינוּ וֵאלֹהֵי אֲבוֹתֵינוּ, שִׁיר וּשְׁבָחָה, הַלֵּל וְזִמְרָה, עֹז וּמֶמְשָׁלָה, נֶצַח, גְּדֻלָּה וּגְבוּרָה, תְּהִלָּה וְתִפְאֶרֶת, קְדֻשָּׁה וּמַלְכוּת, בְּרָכוֹת וְהוֹדָאוֹת מֵעַתָּה וְעַד עוֹלָם:

You are *the God* – in the might of Your strength; *great* in the glory of Your Name; *mighty* forever; and *awesome* in Your awesome deeds; the King Who sits upon an exalted and lofty throne.

He abides forever, exalted and holy is His Name. And it is written: "Shout out with joy to Hashem, you righteous ones; it is befitting for the upright to offer praise" *(Tehillim 33:1)*.

By the mouth of the upright You shall be praised; by the words of the righteous You shall be blessed; by the tongue of the pious You shall be exalted; and among the holy ones You shall be sanctified.

And in the assemblies of the myriads of Your people, the House of Israel, Your name shall be glorified with joyful shouts, our King, in every generation. For this is the duty of all creatures before You, Lord, our God and God of our fathers – to thank, to praise, to laud, to glorify, to exalt, to honor, to bless, to elevate and to extol [You], even beyond all the words of song and praise of David son of Jesse, Your anointed servant.

May Your Name be praised forever, our King, the God and King Who is great and holy in heaven and on earth. For to You, Lord, our God and God of our fathers, are befitting song and praise, laud and hymn, strength and dominion, eternity, greatness and might, glorification and splendor, holiness and sovereignty, blessings and thanksgiving – for all eternity.

Those who did not recite the following paragraph earlier should recite it here:

[יְהַלְלוּךָ יְיָ אֱלֹהֵינוּ כָּל מַעֲשֶׂיךָ וַחֲסִידֶיךָ צַדִּיקִים עוֹשֵׂי רְצוֹנֶךָ וְכָל עַמְּךָ בֵּית יִשְׂרָאֵל בְּרִנָּה יוֹדוּ וִיבָרְכוּ וִישַׁבְּחוּ וִיפָאֲרוּ וִירוֹמְמוּ וְיַעֲרִיצוּ וְיַקְדִּישׁוּ וְיַמְלִיכוּ אֶת שִׁמְךָ מַלְכֵּנוּ. כִּי לְךָ טוֹב לְהוֹדוֹת וּלְשִׁמְךָ נָאֶה לְזַמֵּר כִּי מֵעוֹלָם וְעַד עוֹלָם אַתָּה אֵל:]

There are two customs regarding the conclusion of Hallel. Those who recited יהללוך *now, should conclude with the first one. For those who recited* יהללוך *earlier, there are two possible conclusions (recite only one):*

בָּרוּךְ אַתָּה יְיָ, מֶלֶךְ מְהֻלָּל בַּתִּשְׁבָּחוֹת:

בָּרוּךְ אַתָּה יְיָ, אֵל מֶלֶךְ גָּדוֹל בַּתִּשְׁבָּחוֹת, אֵל הַהוֹדָאוֹת, אֲדוֹן הַנִּפְלָאוֹת, הַבּוֹחֵר בְּשִׁירֵי זִמְרָה, מֶלֶךְ אֵל חֵי הָעוֹלָמִים:

Raise the fourth cup, and recite the following blessing:

בָּרוּךְ אַתָּה יְיָ, אֱלֹהֵינוּ מֶלֶךְ הָעוֹלָם, בּוֹרֵא פְּרִי הַגָּפֶן:

Drink the fourth cup while reclining on your left side.

[All Your works shall praise You, Hashem, our God, along with Your pious ones, the righteous who do Your will. And all Your people, the House of Israel, with shouts of joy, will give thanks, bless, laud, glorify, exalt, acclaim, sanctify and proclaim the sovereignty of Your Name, our King. For it is good to give thanks to You, and it is befitting to sing to Your Name, for You are God for all eternity.]

Blessed are You, Lord, the King Who is lauded with praises.

Blessed are You, Lord, God, King, great in praises, God of thanksgiving, Lord of wonders, Who favors melodious songs of praise, the King, the Life of the universe.

Blessed are You, Lord, our God, King of the universe, who creates the fruit of the vine.

After drinking a revi'it of the wine recite the following blessing: (On Shabbat add the words in parentheses. When the wine is from Israel, substitute the two words in square brackets for the two preceding words.)

בָּרוּךְ אַתָּה יְיָ, אֱלֹהֵינוּ מֶלֶךְ הָעוֹלָם, עַל הַגֶּפֶן וְעַל פְּרִי הַגֶּפֶן וְעַל תְּנוּבַת הַשָּׂדֶה, וְעַל אֶרֶץ חֶמְדָּה טוֹבָה וּרְחָבָה, שֶׁרָצִיתָ וְהִנְחַלְתָּ לַאֲבוֹתֵינוּ, לֶאֱכוֹל מִפִּרְיָהּ וְלִשְׂבּוֹעַ מִטּוּבָהּ. רַחֵם נָא יְיָ אֱלֹהֵינוּ עַל יִשְׂרָאֵל עַמֶּךָ, וְעַל יְרוּשָׁלַיִם עִירֶךָ, וְעַל צִיּוֹן מִשְׁכַּן כְּבוֹדֶךָ, וְעַל מִזְבְּחֶךָ, וְעַל הֵיכָלֶךָ. וּבְנֵה יְרוּשָׁלַיִם עִיר הַקֹּדֶשׁ בִּמְהֵרָה בְיָמֵינוּ, וְהַעֲלֵנוּ לְתוֹכָהּ וְשַׂמְּחֵנוּ בְּבִנְיָנָהּ וְנֹאכַל מִפִּרְיָהּ וְנִשְׂבַּע מִטּוּבָהּ וּנְבָרֶכְךָ עָלֶיהָ בִּקְדֻשָּׁה וּבְטָהֳרָה: (בשבת: וּרְצֵה וְהַחֲלִיצֵנוּ בְּיוֹם הַשַּׁבָּת הַזֶּה) וְשַׂמְּחֵנוּ בְּיוֹם חַג הַמַּצּוֹת הַזֶּה, כִּי אַתָּה יְיָ טוֹב וּמֵטִיב לַכֹּל וְנוֹדֶה לְךָ עַל הָאָרֶץ וְעַל פְּרִי הַגֶּפֶן [פְּרִי גַפְנָהּ]. בָּרוּךְ אַתָּה יְיָ, עַל הָאָרֶץ וְעַל פְּרִי הַגֶּפֶן [פְּרִי גַפְנָהּ]:

נִרְצָה

חֲסַל סִדּוּר פֶּסַח כְּהִלְכָתוֹ, כְּכָל מִשְׁפָּטוֹ וְחֻקָּתוֹ.
כַּאֲשֶׁר זָכִינוּ לְסַדֵּר אוֹתוֹ, כֵּן נִזְכֶּה לַעֲשׂוֹתוֹ.
זָךְ שׁוֹכֵן מְעוֹנָה, קוֹמֵם קְהַל עֲדַת מִי מָנָה.
קָרֵב נַהֵל נִטְעֵי כַנָּה, פְּדוּיִם לְצִיּוֹן בְּרִנָּה:

לְשָׁנָה הַבָּאָה בִּירוּשָׁלָיִם:

Blessed are You, Lord our God, King of the universe, for the vine and the fruit of the vine, for the produce of the field, and for the precious, good and spacious land that You saw fit to grant as a possession to our fathers, to eat of its fruit and be sated by its goodness. Have mercy, Lord our God, on Israel Your people, on Jerusalem Your city, on Zion the abode of Your glory, on Your altar and on Your Temple. Rebuild Jerusalem, the holy city, speedily in our days, and bring us up into it and let us rejoice in its rebuilding, when we may partake of its fruits and be sated by its goodness and bless You in holiness and purity. *(May it please You to grant us strength on this Sabbath day,)* and remember us for good on this day of the Festival of Matzot. For You, Lord, are benevolent and bestow benevolence upon all, and we give thanks to You for the land and for the fruit of the vine. Blessed are You, Lord, for the land and for the fruit of the vine [*its vines*].

Nirtzah

This is the completion of the Pesach ceremony according to its rules, in accordance with all its laws and statutes. Just as we merited to present it, so may we merit to perform it. Pure One, Who dwells on high, raise up the congregation of whom it was said, "Who can count them?" *(Bamidbar 23:10)*! Soon lead the plants of your vineyard *(Israel)*, Redeemed, to Zion, with shouts of joy.

Next year in Jerusalem!

This poem is recited on the first night (some recite it on both nights):

וּבְכֵן וַיְהִי בַּחֲצִי הַלַּיְלָה:

אָז רֹב נִסִּים הִפְלֵאתָ בַּלַּיְלָה.
בְּרֹאשׁ אַשְׁמוּרוֹת זֶה הַלַּיְלָה.
גֵּר צֶדֶק נִצַּחְתּוֹ כְּנֶחֱלַק לוֹ לַיְלָה.

וַיְהִי בַּחֲצִי הַלַּיְלָה:

דַּנְתָּ מֶלֶךְ גְּרָר בַּחֲלוֹם הַלַּיְלָה.
הִפְחַדְתָּ אֲרַמִּי בְּאֶמֶשׁ לַיְלָה.
וַיָּשַׂר יִשְׂרָאֵל לְמַלְאָךְ וַיּוּכַל לוֹ לַיְלָה.

וַיְהִי בַּחֲצִי הַלַּיְלָה:

זֶרַע בְּכוֹרֵי פַתְרוֹס מָחַצְתָּ בַּחֲצִי הַלַּיְלָה.
חֵילָם לֹא מָצְאוּ בְּקוּמָם בַּלַּיְלָה.
טִיסַת נְגִיד חֲרֹשֶׁת סִלִּיתָ בְכוֹכְבֵי לַיְלָה.

וַיְהִי בַּחֲצִי הַלַּיְלָה:

יָעַץ מְחָרֵף לְנוֹפֵף אִוּוּי, הוֹבַשְׁתָּ פְגָרָיו בַּלַּיְלָה.
כָּרַע בֵּל וּמַצָּבוֹ בְּאִישׁוֹן לַיְלָה.
לְאִישׁ חֲמוּדוֹת נִגְלָה רָז חֲזוֹת לַיְלָה.

וַיְהִי בַּחֲצִי הַלַּיְלָה:

And so "It happened at midnight" *(Shemot 12:29)*

Always, You have performed wondrous miracles on this night.

At the beginning of the watches on this night, You granted victory to the righteous convert *(Avraham)* when the night was divided in two *(Bereishit 14:15)*.

It happened at midnight.

You judged the king of Gerar *(Avimelech)* in a dream at night *(ibid. 20:3)*. You frightened the Aramean *(Lavan)* in the dark of the night *(ibid. 31:24)*. Israel struggled with an angel and overcame him at night *(ibid. 32:25)*

It happened at midnight.

You crushed the firstborn offspring of Pathros *(Egypt)* at midnight. They did not find their vigor *(firstborn sons)* when they awoke in the middle of the night. You trampled the swift army of the Prince of Harosheth *(Sisera)* by the stars of the night *(Shoftim 5:20)*.

It happened at midnight.

The blasphemer *(Sennacherib)* planned to wave his hand against the cherished Temple; You dried out his corpses overnight *(II Melachim 19:35)*. Bel *(Babylonia)* and its watchmen collapsed in the dark of night; to the beloved man *(Daniel)* was revealed the secret of the vision at night *(Daniel 5)*.

It happened at midnight.

מִשְׁתַּכֵּר בִּכְלֵי קֹדֶשׁ נֶהֱרַג בּוֹ בַּלַּיְלָה.
נוֹשַׁע מִבּוֹר אֲרָיוֹת פּוֹתֵר בִּעֲתוּתֵי לַיְלָה.
שִׂנְאָה נָטַר אֲגָגִי וְכָתַב סְפָרִים בַּלַּיְלָה.

וַיְהִי בַּחֲצִי הַלַּיְלָה:

עוֹרַרְתָּ נִצְחֲךָ עָלָיו בְּנֶדֶד שְׁנַת לַיְלָה.
פּוּרָה תִדְרוֹךְ לְשׁוֹמֵר מַה מִּלַּיְלָה.
צָרַח כַּשּׁוֹמֵר וְשָׂח אָתָא בֹקֶר וְגַם לַיְלָה.

וַיְהִי בַּחֲצִי הַלַּיְלָה:

קָרֵב יוֹם אֲשֶׁר הוּא לֹא יוֹם וְלֹא לַיְלָה.
רָם, הוֹדַע כִּי לְךָ הַיּוֹם אַף לְךָ הַלַּיְלָה.
שׁוֹמְרִים הַפְקֵד לְעִירְךָ כָּל הַיּוֹם וְכָל הַלַּיְלָה.
תָּאִיר כְּאוֹר יוֹם חֶשְׁכַת לַיְלָה.

וַיְהִי בַּחֲצִי הַלַּיְלָה:

The one who became drunk drinking from the sacred vessels *(Belshazzar)* was killed that very night *(ibid.)*. The one saved from the lion's den *(Daniel)* interpreted the frightening sight at night *(ibid.)*. The Agagite *(Haman)* retained his hatred and wrote writs at night *(Esther 5:14-6:4)*.

It happened at midnight.

You launched Your triumph against him *(Haman)* when [Ahasuerus'] sleep was disturbed at night *(ibid.)*. You will trample the vintage of the one *(Edom)* of whom it was said, "Watchman, what of the night?" *(Yeshayahu 21:11)*. God shouted back like a watchman and said, "Morning is coming, but also night" *(ibid. 21:12)*.

It happened at midnight.

Bring near the day *(of the Messiah)* which is "neither day nor night" *(Zechariah 14:7)*. Exalted One, make it known that "Yours is the day and Yours is the night" *(Tehillim 74:16)*. Post guardians over Your city all day and all night *(Yeshayahu 61:6)*. Light up the dark of night as brightly as the light of day.

It happened at midnight.

This poem is recited on the second night (some recite it on both nights):

וּבְכֵן וַאֲמַרְתֶּם זֶבַח פֶּסַח:

אֹמֶץ גְּבוּרוֹתֶיךָ הִפְלֵאתָ בַּפֶּסַח.
בְּרֹאשׁ כָּל מוֹעֲדוֹת נִשֵּׂאתָ פֶּסַח.
גִּלִּיתָ לְאֶזְרָחִי חֲצוֹת לֵיל פֶּסַח.

וַאֲמַרְתֶּם זֶבַח פֶּסַח:

דְּלָתָיו דָּפַקְתָּ כְּחוֹם הַיּוֹם בַּפֶּסַח.
הִסְעִיד נוֹצְצִים עֻגוֹת מַצּוֹת בַּפֶּסַח.
וְאֶל הַבָּקָר רָץ זֵכֶר לְשׁוֹר עֵרֶךְ פֶּסַח.

וַאֲמַרְתֶּם זֶבַח פֶּסַח:

Hashem Teaches Us How to Visit the Sick by Visiting Avraham After His Circumcision

דלתיו דפקת כחם היום בפסח According to the text of the Haggadah, when Hashem visited Avraham after his circumcision, He knocked on Avraham's door. Why does the author emphasize this particular detail? Furthermore, the *Midrash* explains that Hashem visited Avraham on the third day following his circumcision.[190] Why did Hashem visit on this day?

In order to answer these questions, Rav Yehonatan first introduces the following halachic discussion. To discourage people from transgressing the biblical prohibition of boiling water on Shabbat, the Rabbis prohibited bathing on Shabbat. However, for health reasons,

And you shall say, "It is a sacrifice of Pesach" (*Shemot 12:27*)

You demonstrated the power of Your might on Pesach.

You elevated as the first of the holidays, Pesach (*Vayikra 23:4-5*).

You revealed to the Easterner (*Avraham*) the events of the midnight of Pesach.

And you shall say, "It is a sacrifice of Pesach."

You knocked on his (*Avraham's*) door in the heat of the day on Pesach (*Bereishit 18:1*);

He fed angels unleavened cakes on Pesach (*ibid. 18:6*)

He ran to take from the cattle (*ibid. 18:7*), symbolizing the ox brought in conjunction with the sacrifice of Pesach.

And you shall say, "It is a sacrifice of Pesach."

the Rabbis made an exception regarding bathing a baby in hot water on the day of its circumcision and on the day following. On the third day following the circumcision, bathing the baby in hot water is prohibited; however, one may sprinkle hot water upon the baby by hand (not with a utensil).[191]

The Maharsha questions this ruling for the Torah itself reports, "And it came to pass on the third day [after they had circumcised themselves, that the males of Shechem...] were in pain."[192] Seemingly, the third day after circumcision is the most painful and, perhaps, the most dangerous. This being the case, the Talmud should permit cleansing and soaking the wounded area properly on the third day after the circumcision as well. Why does the Talmud permit bathing the circumcision on the first and second days because of danger and discomfort when the same should be true regarding the third day? The Maharsha explains that the Rabbis are discussing the case of babies who are in grave danger the first two days, but are in considerably less danger on the third day. The Torah, in contrast, describes the predicament of adults having undergone circumcision who are in danger even on the third day.

For this reason the *Midrash* emphasizes that Hashem visited Avraham on the third day after his circumcision, a day that could be life threatening. According to the Talmud, however, one should not actually enter the room of someone critically ill; one should visit and inquire about the invalid's health without entering. Following Avraham's circumcision the Torah states: "Hashem appeared to him ... while he was sitting at the entrance of the tent in the heat of the day."[193] Rashi comments that Hashem visited Avraham on the third day following his circumcision. If the third day is life threatening for an adult then Hashem should not have visited Avraham on that day. Why then did He do so? Rav Yehonatan explains that this is the reason the Torah states that Hashem "appeared to" Avraham. The Torah is teaching us that Hashem merely appeared to inquire about Avraham's health, He did not enter Avraham's home. Recognizing the unusual wording of the Torah, the author of the Haggadah stresses that Hashem knocked at Avraham's door to inquire about his health, but He did not actually enter Avraham's home.

AUTHOR'S COMMENTS The Haggadah recounts the story of Hashem's visit to Avraham following his circumcision: Hashem "knocked at Avraham's door in the heat of the day" in order to visit and heal Avraham. Ostensibly, the author of the Haggadah recalls Hashem's visit because it occurred on Pesach; however, there is a more profound reason. Hashem began Avraham's healing process on Pesach because Avraham was dedicated to Hashem and His commandments. The period of enslavement in Egypt scarred the Jews both physically and spiritually, like a sickness would. Hashem began the Jews' healing process on Pesach, when he took them out of Egypt, because they too would soon commit as a nation to performing His commandments.

Why Hashem Remained at Avraham's Side After His Circumcision

דלתיו דפקת כחם היום בפסח Normally after describing an ascent, the Torah describes a descent. For example, when Moshe ascended Mount Sinai the Torah says, "Moshe arose early in the morning, and ascended to Mount Sinai." Immediately thereafter the Torah records a descent, "Hashem descended in a cloud and stood with him there."[194] The exception to this rule occurs in the case of Avraham's circumcision. After Hashem commanded Avraham to circumcise himself and the members of his household, the Torah states, "And when He finished speaking with him, Hashem ascended from upon Avraham."[195] Hashem "ascended from upon Avraham" because He had finished instructing him. When Hashem returned to speak with Avraham after the circumcision, the Torah should have written that Hashem descended to speak with Avraham, but instead the Torah writes that "Hashem appeared to him."[196] Why is this ascent not followed by a descent?

Rav Yehonatan explains that the Torah's description of Hashem ascending "from upon Avraham" is actually not to be taken literally; rather, it signifies that Hashem had finished instructing Avraham. Upon hearing the instructions, Avraham immediately performed the mandated circumcision, and the presence of Hashem remained with Avraham to heal him. The Torah does not say that Hashem descended because He never actually left Avraham's presence.

זׁוֹעֲמוּ סְדוֹמִים וְלוֹהֲטוּ בָּאֵשׁ בַּפֶּסַח.
חֻלַּץ לוֹט מֵהֶם וּמַצּוֹת אָפָה בְּקֵץ פֶּסַח.
טִאטֵאתָ אַדְמַת מוֹף וְנוֹף בְּעָבְרְךָ בַּפֶּסַח.

וַאֲמַרְתֶּם זֶבַח פֶּסַח:

יָהּ רֹאשׁ כָּל אוֹן מָחַצְתָּ בְּלֵיל שִׁמּוּר פֶּסַח.
כַּבִּיר עַל בֵּן בְּכוֹר פָּסַחְתָּ בְּדַם פֶּסַח.
לְבִלְתִּי תֵּת מַשְׁחִית לָבֹא בִּפְתָחַי בַּפֶּסַח.

וַאֲמַרְתֶּם זֶבַח פֶּסַח:

מְסֻגֶּרֶת סֻגָּרָה בְּעִתּוֹתֵי פֶּסַח.
נִשְׁמְדָה מִדְיָן בִּצְלִיל שְׂעוֹרֵי עֹמֶר פֶּסַח.
שׂוֹרְפוּ מִשְׁמַנֵּי פּוּל וְלוּד בִּיקַד יְקוֹד פֶּסַח.

וַאֲמַרְתֶּם זֶבַח פֶּסַח:

According to the Talmud, Hashem who is all-compassionate remains by the sick person's bedside to heal him, even though this kindness of His goes unrecognized. Avraham who was righteous knew that Hashem would stay by his side. Thus, when the verse says "Hashem appeared to him," this means that Avraham opened his eyes and, as he expected, saw Hashem. From Avraham we learn the importance of recognizing Hashem's omnipresence at all points in our lives.

The Sodomites were damned and burnt in fire on Pesach.

Lot was rescued from among them; he baked unleavened bread *(ibid. 19:3)* at the end of the eve of Pesach.

You wiped out the land of Moph and Noph *(Egypt)* when You passed through on Pesach.

And you shall say, "It is a sacrifice of Pesach."

God, You crushed the first one of all their child-bearing on the "night of watching" *(Shemot 12:42)* of Pesach.

Mighty One, You passed over [Your own] firstborn son because of the blood of the Pesach,

Not allowing the Destroyer to enter my doors on Pesach.

And you shall say, "It is a sacrifice of Pesach."

The sealed city *(Jericho)* was handed over during the time of Pesach.

Midian was destroyed through a loaf representing the barley of the Omer-sacrifice of Pesach *(Shoftim 7:13)*.

The burly warriors of Pul and Lud *(Assyria)* were burnt in a conflagration on Pesach *(Yeshayahu 10:16)*.

And you shall say, "It is a sacrifice of Pesach."

עוֹד הַיּוֹם בְּנֹב לַעֲמֹד עַד גָּעָה עוֹנַת פֶּסַח.
פַּס יָד כָּתְבָה לְקַעֲקֵעַ צוּל בַּפֶּסַח.
צָפֹה הַצָּפִית עָרוֹךְ הַשֻּׁלְחָן בַּפֶּסַח.

וַאֲמַרְתֶּם זֶבַח פֶּסַח:

קָהָל כִּנְּסָה הֲדַסָּה, צוֹם לְשַׁלֵּשׁ בַּפֶּסַח.
רֹאשׁ מִבֵּית רָשָׁע מָחַצְתָּ בְּעֵץ חֲמִשִּׁים בַּפֶּסַח.
שְׁתֵּי אֵלֶּה רֶגַע תָּבִיא לְעוּצִית בַּפֶּסַח.
תָּעֹז יָדְךָ וְתָרוּם יְמִינְךָ כְּלֵיל הִתְקַדֵּשׁ חַג פֶּסַח.

וַאֲמַרְתֶּם זֶבַח פֶּסַח:

He *(Sennacherib)* wanted "to reach Nob that very day" *(ibid. 10:32)* – until it became the season of Pesach.

The palm of a hand wrote an inscription about the crushing of the well-watered country *(Babylonia)* on Pesach.

"The chandelier was lit and the table was set" *(ibid. 21:5, describing the downfall of Babylonia)* on Pesach.

And you shall say, "It is a sacrifice of Pesach."

Hadassah assembled the congregation to hold a three-day fast on Pesach *(Esther 4:16)*.

You vanquished the chief *(Haman)* from the wicked family *(Amalek)* on a fifty-cubit wooden pole on Pesach.

May You bring "these two things" *(Yeshayahu 47:9)* in an instant upon the Utzites *(Babylonians)* on Pesach!

Let Your hand be strong and Your right hand raised, as on the night of the sanctification of the holiday of Pesach!

And you shall say, "It is a sacrifice of Pesach."

(This poem is based on Yirmiyahu 10:7: "Who would not fear You, O King of the nations, for it is befitting to You!")

כִּי לוֹ נָאֶה, כִּי לוֹ יָאֶה:

אַדִּיר בִּמְלוּכָה, בָּחוּר כַּהֲלָכָה, גְּדוּדָיו יֹאמְרוּ לוֹ:
לְךָ וּלְךָ, לְךָ כִּי לְךָ, לְךָ אַף לְךָ, לְךָ יְיָ הַמַּמְלָכָה:
כִּי לוֹ נָאֶה, כִּי לוֹ יָאֶה:

דָּגוּל בִּמְלוּכָה, הָדוּר כַּהֲלָכָה, וָתִיקָיו יֹאמְרוּ לוֹ:
לְךָ וּלְךָ, לְךָ כִּי לְךָ, לְךָ אַף לְךָ, לְךָ יְיָ הַמַּמְלָכָה:
כִּי לוֹ נָאֶה, כִּי לוֹ יָאֶה:

זַכַּאי בִּמְלוּכָה, חָסִין כַּהֲלָכָה, טַפְסְרָיו יֹאמְרוּ לוֹ:
לְךָ וּלְךָ, לְךָ כִּי לְךָ, לְךָ אַף לְךָ, לְךָ יְיָ הַמַּמְלָכָה:
כִּי לוֹ נָאֶה, כִּי לוֹ יָאֶה:

יָחִיד בִּמְלוּכָה, כַּבִּיר כַּהֲלָכָה, לִמּוּדָיו יֹאמְרוּ לוֹ:
לְךָ וּלְךָ, לְךָ כִּי לְךָ, לְךָ אַף לְךָ, לְךָ יְיָ הַמַּמְלָכָה:
כִּי לוֹ נָאֶה, כִּי לוֹ יָאֶה:

To Him it is befitting! To Him it is becoming!

Mighty in dominion, Superior indeed, His legions *(angels)* say to Him:

To You, to You! To You, indeed to You! To You, only to You! "To You, Lord, belongs the dominion" (I Divrei Hayamim 29:11)!

To Him it is befitting! To Him it is becoming!

Outstanding in dominion, Glorious indeed, His devoted ones *(Israel)* say to Him:

To You, to You! To You, indeed to You! To You, only to You! To You, Lord, belongs the dominion!

To Him it is befitting! To Him it is becoming!

Pure in dominion, Powerful indeed, His captains *(angels)* say to Him:

To You, to You! To You, indeed to You! To You, only to You! To You, Lord, belongs the dominion!

To Him it is befitting! To Him it is becoming!

Unique in dominion, Potent indeed, His learned ones *(Israel)* say to Him:

To You, to You! To You, indeed to You! To You, only to You! To You, Lord, belongs the dominion!

To Him it is befitting! To Him it is becoming!

מֶלֶךְ בִּמְלוּכָה, נוֹרָא כַּהֲלָכָה, סְבִיבָיו יֹאמְרוּ לוֹ:
לְךָ וּלְךָ, לְךָ כִּי לְךָ, לְךָ אַף לְךָ, לְךָ יְיָ הַמַּמְלָכָה:
כִּי לוֹ נָאֶה, כִּי לוֹ יָאֶה:

עָנָיו בִּמְלוּכָה, פּוֹדֶה כַּהֲלָכָה, צַדִּיקָיו יֹאמְרוּ לוֹ:
לְךָ וּלְךָ, לְךָ כִּי לְךָ, לְךָ אַף לְךָ, לְךָ יְיָ הַמַּמְלָכָה:
כִּי לוֹ נָאֶה, כִּי לוֹ יָאֶה:

קָדוֹשׁ בִּמְלוּכָה, רַחוּם כַּהֲלָכָה, שִׁנְאַנָּיו יֹאמְרוּ לוֹ:
לְךָ וּלְךָ, לְךָ כִּי לְךָ, לְךָ אַף לְךָ, לְךָ יְיָ הַמַּמְלָכָה:
כִּי לוֹ נָאֶה, כִּי לוֹ יָאֶה:

תַּקִּיף בִּמְלוּכָה, תּוֹמֵךְ כַּהֲלָכָה, תְּמִימָיו יֹאמְרוּ לוֹ:
לְךָ וּלְךָ, לְךָ כִּי לְךָ, לְךָ אַף לְךָ, לְךָ יְיָ הַמַּמְלָכָה:
כִּי לוֹ נָאֶה, כִּי לוֹ יָאֶה:

Exalted in dominion, Awesome indeed, Those surrounding Him *(angels)* say to Him:

To You, to You! To You, indeed to You! To You, only to You! To You, Lord, belongs the dominion!

To Him it is befitting! To Him it is becoming!

Deigning in dominion, Redeeming indeed, His righteous ones *(Israel)* say to Him:

To You, to You! To You, indeed to You! To You, only to You! To You, Lord, belongs the dominion!

To Him it is befitting! To Him it is becoming!

Holy in dominion, Compassionate indeed, His *Shinanim* *(angels)* say to Him:

To You, to You! To You, indeed to You! To You, only to You! To You, Lord, belongs the dominion!

To Him it is befitting! To Him it is becoming!

Strong in dominion, Supporter indeed, His faithful ones *(Israel)* say to Him:

To You, to You! To You, indeed to You! To You, only to You! To You, Lord, belongs the dominion!

To Him it is befitting! To Him it is becoming!

אַדִּיר הוּא יִבְנֶה בֵיתוֹ בְּקָרוֹב:
בִּמְהֵרָה, בִּמְהֵרָה, בְּיָמֵינוּ בְּקָרוֹב:
אֵל בְּנֵה, אֵל בְּנֵה, בְּנֵה בֵיתְךָ בְּקָרוֹב:

בָּחוּר הוּא, גָּדוֹל הוּא, דָּגוּל הוּא, יִבְנֶה בֵיתוֹ בְּקָרוֹב:
בִּמְהֵרָה, בִּמְהֵרָה, בְּיָמֵינוּ בְּקָרוֹב:
אֵל בְּנֵה, אֵל בְּנֵה, בְּנֵה בֵיתְךָ בְּקָרוֹב:

הָדוּר הוּא, וָתִיק הוּא, זַכַּאי הוּא, חָסִיד הוּא, יִבְנֶה בֵיתוֹ בְּקָרוֹב:
בִּמְהֵרָה, בִּמְהֵרָה, בְּיָמֵינוּ בְּקָרוֹב:
אֵל בְּנֵה, אֵל בְּנֵה, בְּנֵה בֵיתְךָ בְּקָרוֹב:

טָהוֹר הוּא, יָחִיד הוּא, כַּבִּיר הוּא, לָמוּד הוּא, מֶלֶךְ הוּא, נוֹרָא הוּא, סַגִּיב הוּא, עִזּוּז הוּא, פּוֹדֶה הוּא, צַדִּיק הוּא, יִבְנֶה בֵיתוֹ בְּקָרוֹב:
בִּמְהֵרָה, בִּמְהֵרָה, בְּיָמֵינוּ בְּקָרוֹב:
אֵל בְּנֵה, אֵל בְּנֵה, בְּנֵה בֵיתְךָ בְּקָרוֹב:

He is mighty!

May He build His Temple soon! Speedily, speedily, in our days, soon! God, build, God build, build Your Temple soon!

He is superior! He is great! He is outstanding!

May He build His Temple soon! Speedily, speedily, in our days, soon! God, build, God build, build Your Temple soon!

He is glorious! He is virtuous! He is blameless! He is kind!

May He build His Temple soon! Speedily, speedily, in our days, soon! God, build, God build, build Your Temple soon!

He is pure! He is unique! He is powerful! He is all-knowing! He is king! He is awesome! He is exalted! He is all-powerful! He is the Redeemer! He is righteous!

May He build His Temple soon! Speedily, speedily, in our days, soon! God, build, God build, build Your Temple soon!

קָדוֹשׁ הוּא, רַחוּם הוּא, שַׁדַּי הוּא, תַּקִּיף הוּא, יִבְנֶה בֵיתוֹ בְּקָרוֹב:

בִּמְהֵרָה, בִּמְהֵרָה, בְּיָמֵינוּ בְּקָרוֹב:

אֵל בְּנֵה, אֵל בְּנֵה, בְּנֵה בֵיתְךָ בְּקָרוֹב:

Some begin the Counting of the Omer at this point (on the second night of Pesach):

בָּרוּךְ אַתָּה יְיָ, אֱלֹהֵינוּ מֶלֶךְ הָעוֹלָם, אֲשֶׁר קִדְּשָׁנוּ בְּמִצְוֹתָיו, וְצִוָּנוּ עַל סְפִירַת הָעֹמֶר:

הַיּוֹם יוֹם אֶחָד לָעוֹמֶר:

הָרַחֲמָן הוּא יַחֲזִיר לָנוּ עֲבוֹדַת בֵּית הַמִּקְדָּשׁ לִמְקוֹמָהּ, בִּמְהֵרָה בְיָמֵינוּ, אָמֵן סֶלָה:

He is holy! He is compassionate! He is the Almighty! He is strong!

May He build His Temple soon! Speedily, speedily, in our days, soon! God, build, God build, build Your Temple soon!

Blessed are You, Lord, our God, King of the universe, Who has sanctified us through His commandments, and commanded us concerning the counting of the Omer.

Today marks one day to the Omer.

אֶחָד מִי יוֹדֵעַ? אֶחָד אֲנִי יוֹדֵעַ:

אֶחָד אֱלֹהֵינוּ שֶׁבַּשָּׁמַיִם וּבָאָרֶץ:

שְׁנַיִם מִי יוֹדֵעַ? שְׁנַיִם אֲנִי יוֹדֵעַ:

שְׁנֵי לֻחוֹת הַבְּרִית, אֶחָד אֱלֹהֵינוּ שֶׁבַּשָּׁמַיִם וּבָאָרֶץ:

שְׁלֹשָׁה מִי יוֹדֵעַ? שְׁלֹשָׁה אֲנִי יוֹדֵעַ:

שְׁלֹשָׁה אָבוֹת, שְׁנֵי לֻחוֹת הַבְּרִית, אֶחָד אֱלֹהֵינוּ שֶׁבַּשָּׁמַיִם וּבָאָרֶץ:

אַרְבַּע מִי יוֹדֵעַ? אַרְבַּע אֲנִי יוֹדֵעַ:

אַרְבַּע אִמָּהוֹת, שְׁלֹשָׁה אָבוֹת, שְׁנֵי לֻחוֹת הַבְּרִית, אֶחָד אֱלֹהֵינוּ שֶׁבַּשָּׁמַיִם וּבָאָרֶץ:

חֲמִשָּׁה מִי יוֹדֵעַ? חֲמִשָּׁה אֲנִי יוֹדֵעַ:

חֲמִשָּׁה חֻמְשֵׁי תוֹרָה, אַרְבַּע אִמָּהוֹת, שְׁלֹשָׁה אָבוֹת, שְׁנֵי לֻחוֹת הַבְּרִית, אֶחָד אֱלֹהֵינוּ שֶׁבַּשָּׁמַיִם וּבָאָרֶץ:

There Is Only One

אחד מי יודע? אחד אני יודע. אחד אלוהינו שבשמים ובארץ The Torah describes the first day of Creation in the following manner: "And there was evening and there was morning, one day."[197] Rashi notes that the other days of Creation are enumerated in ordinal numbers. Why then does the Torah refer to the first day of Creation using the cardinal number?

Rashi explains that by referring to the first day as "one day," the Torah empha-

Who knows what one is? I know what one is!

One is our God, in heaven and on earth.

Who knows what two is? I know what two is!

Two are the tablets of the Covenant; One is our God, in heaven and on earth.

Who knows what three is? I know what three is!

Three are the patriarchs; two are the tablets of the Covenant; One is our God, in heaven and on earth.

Who knows what four is? I know what four is!

Four are the matriarchs; three are the patriarchs; two are the tablets of the Covenant; One is our God, in heaven and on earth.

Who knows what five is? I know what five is!

Five are the books of the Torah; four are the matriarchs; three are the patriarchs; two are the tablets of the Covenant; One is our God, in heaven and on earth.

sizes Hashem's singularity, His "oneness." Hashem was the only one to exist prior to creation and He is the sole Creator. In "Who Knows One?" the author of the Haggadah also stresses Hashem's "oneness" to emphasize that Hashem alone is responsible for our Exodus from Egypt and He alone is responsible for our future redemption at the end of days.

שִׁשָּׁה מִי יוֹדֵעַ? שִׁשָּׁה אֲנִי יוֹדֵעַ:

שִׁשָּׁה סִדְרֵי מִשְׁנָה, חֲמִשָּׁה חֻמְשֵׁי תוֹרָה, אַרְבַּע אִמָּהוֹת, שְׁלֹשָׁה אָבוֹת, שְׁנֵי לֻחוֹת הַבְּרִית, אֶחָד אֱלֹהֵינוּ שֶׁבַּשָּׁמַיִם וּבָאָרֶץ:

שִׁבְעָה מִי יוֹדֵעַ? שִׁבְעָה אֲנִי יוֹדֵעַ:

שִׁבְעָה יְמֵי שַׁבְּתָא, שִׁשָּׁה סִדְרֵי מִשְׁנָה, חֲמִשָּׁה חֻמְשֵׁי תוֹרָה, אַרְבַּע אִמָּהוֹת, שְׁלֹשָׁה אָבוֹת, שְׁנֵי לֻחוֹת הַבְּרִית, אֶחָד אֱלֹהֵינוּ שֶׁבַּשָּׁמַיִם וּבָאָרֶץ:

שְׁמוֹנָה מִי יוֹדֵעַ? שְׁמוֹנָה אֲנִי יוֹדֵעַ:

שְׁמוֹנָה יְמֵי מִילָה, שִׁבְעָה יְמֵי שַׁבְּתָא, שִׁשָּׁה סִדְרֵי מִשְׁנָה, חֲמִשָּׁה חֻמְשֵׁי תוֹרָה, אַרְבַּע אִמָּהוֹת, שְׁלֹשָׁה אָבוֹת, שְׁנֵי לֻחוֹת הַבְּרִית, אֶחָד אֱלֹהֵינוּ שֶׁבַּשָּׁמַיִם וּבָאָרֶץ:

תִּשְׁעָה מִי יוֹדֵעַ? תִּשְׁעָה אֲנִי יוֹדֵעַ:

תִּשְׁעָה יַרְחֵי לֵידָה, שְׁמוֹנָה יְמֵי מִילָה, שִׁבְעָה יְמֵי שַׁבְּתָא, שִׁשָּׁה סִדְרֵי מִשְׁנָה, חֲמִשָּׁה חֻמְשֵׁי תוֹרָה, אַרְבַּע אִמָּהוֹת, שְׁלֹשָׁה אָבוֹת, שְׁנֵי לֻחוֹת הַבְּרִית, אֶחָד אֱלֹהֵינוּ שֶׁבַּשָּׁמַיִם וּבָאָרֶץ:

Who knows what six is? I know what six is!

Six are the volumes of the Mishnah; five are the books of the Torah; four are the matriarchs; three are the patriarchs; two are the tablets of the Covenant; One is our God, in heaven and on earth.

Who knows what seven is? I know what seven is!

Seven are the days of the week; six are the volumes of the Mishnah; five are the books of the Torah; four are the matriarchs; three are the patriarchs; two are the tablets of the Covenant; One is our God, in heaven and on earth.

Who knows what eight is? I know what eight is!

Eight are the days until circumcision; seven are the days of the week; six are the volumes of the Mishnah; five are the books of the Torah; four are the matriarchs; three are the patriarchs; two are the tablets of the Covenant; One is our God, in heaven and on earth.

Who knows what nine is? I know what nine is!

Nine are the months of pregnancy; eight are the days until circumcision; seven are the days of the week; six are the volumes of the Mishnah; five are the books of the Torah; four are the matriarchs; three are the patriarchs; two are the tablets of the Covenant; One is our God, in heaven and on earth.

עֲשָׂרָה מִי יוֹדֵעַ? עֲשָׂרָה אֲנִי יוֹדֵעַ:

עֲשָׂרָה דִבְּרַיָּא, תִּשְׁעָה יַרְחֵי לֵידָה, שְׁמוֹנָה יְמֵי מִילָה, שִׁבְעָה יְמֵי שַׁבְּתָא, שִׁשָּׁה סִדְרֵי מִשְׁנָה, חֲמִשָּׁה חֻמְשֵׁי תוֹרָה, אַרְבַּע אִמָּהוֹת, שְׁלשָׁה אָבוֹת, שְׁנֵי לֻחוֹת הַבְּרִית, אֶחָד אֱלֹהֵינוּ שֶׁבַּשָּׁמַיִם וּבָאָרֶץ:

אַחַד עָשָׂר מִי יוֹדֵעַ? אַחַד עָשָׂר אֲנִי יוֹדֵעַ:

אַחַד עָשָׂר כּוֹכְבַיָּא, עֲשָׂרָה דִבְּרַיָּא, תִּשְׁעָה יַרְחֵי לֵידָה, שְׁמוֹנָה יְמֵי מִילָה, שִׁבְעָה יְמֵי שַׁבְּתָא, שִׁשָּׁה סִדְרֵי מִשְׁנָה, חֲמִשָּׁה חֻמְשֵׁי תוֹרָה, אַרְבַּע אִמָּהוֹת, שְׁלשָׁה אָבוֹת, שְׁנֵי לֻחוֹת הַבְּרִית, אֶחָד אֱלֹהֵינוּ שֶׁבַּשָּׁמַיִם וּבָאָרֶץ:

שְׁנֵים עָשָׂר מִי יוֹדֵעַ? שְׁנֵים עָשָׂר אֲנִי יוֹדֵעַ:

שְׁנֵים עָשָׂר שִׁבְטַיָּא, אַחַד עָשָׂר כּוֹכְבַיָּא, עֲשָׂרָה דִבְּרַיָּא, תִּשְׁעָה יַרְחֵי לֵידָה, שְׁמוֹנָה יְמֵי מִילָה, שִׁבְעָה יְמֵי שַׁבְּתָא, שִׁשָּׁה סִדְרֵי מִשְׁנָה, חֲמִשָּׁה חֻמְשֵׁי תוֹרָה, אַרְבַּע אִמָּהוֹת, שְׁלשָׁה אָבוֹת, שְׁנֵי לֻחוֹת הַבְּרִית, אֶחָד אֱלֹהֵינוּ שֶׁבַּשָּׁמַיִם וּבָאָרֶץ:

Who knows what ten is? I know what ten is!

Ten are the Commandments; nine are the months of pregnancy; eight are the days until circumcision; seven are the days of the week; six are the volumes of the Mishnah; five are the books of the Torah; four are the matriarchs; three are the patriarchs; two are the tablets of the Covenant; One is our God, in heaven and on earth.

Who knows what eleven is? I know what eleven is!

Eleven are the stars *(of Yosef's dream)*; ten are the Commandments; nine are the months of pregnancy; eight are the days until circumcision; seven are the days of the week; six are the volumes of the Mishnah; five are the books of the Torah; four are the matriarchs; three are the patriarchs; two are the tablets of the Covenant; One is our God, in heaven and on earth.

Who knows what twelve is? I know what twelve is!

Twelve are the tribes of Israel; eleven are the stars *(of Yosef's dream)*; ten are the Commandments; nine are the months of pregnancy; eight are the days until circumcision; seven are the days of the week; six are the volumes of the Mishnah; five are the books of the Torah; four are the matriarchs; three are the patriarchs; two are the tablets of the Covenant; One is our God, in heaven and on earth.

שְׁלֹשָׁה עָשָׂר מִי יוֹדֵעַ? שְׁלֹשָׁה עָשָׂר אֲנִי יוֹדֵעַ: שְׁלֹשָׁה עָשָׂר מִדַּיָּא, שְׁנֵים עָשָׂר שִׁבְטַיָּא, אַחַד עָשָׂר כּוֹכְבַיָּא, עֲשָׂרָה דִבְּרַיָּא, תִּשְׁעָה יַרְחֵי לֵידָה, שְׁמוֹנָה יְמֵי מִילָה, שִׁבְעָה יְמֵי שַׁבְּתָא, שִׁשָּׁה סִדְרֵי מִשְׁנָה, חֲמִשָּׁה חֻמְשֵׁי תוֹרָה, אַרְבַּע אִמָּהוֹת, שְׁלֹשָׁה אָבוֹת, שְׁנֵי לֻחוֹת הַבְּרִית, אֶחָד אֱלֹהֵינוּ שֶׁבַּשָּׁמַיִם וּבָאָרֶץ:

חַד גַּדְיָא, חַד גַּדְיָא, דְּזַבִּין אַבָּא בִּתְרֵי זוּזֵי. חַד גַּדְיָא, חַד גַּדְיָא:

וְאָתָא שׁוּנְרָא, וְאָכְלָה לְגַדְיָא, דְּזַבִּין אַבָּא בִּתְרֵי זוּזֵי. חַד גַּדְיָא, חַד גַּדְיָא:

וְאָתָא כַלְבָּא, וְנָשַׁךְ לְשׁוּנְרָא, דְּאָכְלָה לְגַדְיָא, דְּזַבִּין אַבָּא בִּתְרֵי זוּזֵי. חַד גַּדְיָא, חַד גַּדְיָא:

Who knows what thirteen is? I know what thirteen is!

Thirteen are God's attributes of mercy; twelve are the tribes of Israel; eleven are the stars *(of Yosef's dream)*; ten are the Commandments; nine are the months of pregnancy; eight are the days until circumcision; seven are the days of the week; six are the volumes of the Mishnah; five are the books of the Torah; four are the matriarchs; three are the patriarchs; two are the tablets of the Covenant; One is our God, in heaven and on earth.

One kid, one kid – that my father bought for two zuzim.

One kid, one kid.

Along came a cat and ate the kid – that my father bought for two zuzim.

One kid, one kid.

Along came a dog and bit the cat that ate the kid – that my father bought for two zuzim.

One kid, one kid.

וְאָתָא חוּטְרָא, וְהִכָּה לְכַלְבָּא, דְּנָשַׁךְ לְשׁוּנְרָא, דְּאָכְלָה לְגַדְיָא, דְּזַבִּין אַבָּא בִּתְרֵי זוּזֵי.

חַד גַּדְיָא, חַד גַּדְיָא:

וְאָתָא נוּרָא, וְשָׂרַף לְחוּטְרָא, דְּהִכָּה לְכַלְבָּא, דְּנָשַׁךְ לְשׁוּנְרָא, דְּאָכְלָה לְגַדְיָא, דְּזַבִּין אַבָּא בִּתְרֵי זוּזֵי.

חַד גַּדְיָא, חַד גַּדְיָא:

וְאָתָא מַיָּא, וְכָבָה לְנוּרָא, דְּשָׂרַף לְחוּטְרָא, דְּהִכָּה לְכַלְבָּא, דְּנָשַׁךְ לְשׁוּנְרָא, דְּאָכְלָה לְגַדְיָא, דְּזַבִּין אַבָּא בִּתְרֵי זוּזֵי.

חַד גַּדְיָא, חַד גַּדְיָא:

וְאָתָא תוֹרָא, וְשָׁתָה לְמַיָּא, דְּכָבָה לְנוּרָא, דְּשָׂרַף לְחוּטְרָא, דְּהִכָּה לְכַלְבָּא, דְּנָשַׁךְ לְשׁוּנְרָא, דְּאָכְלָה לְגַדְיָא, דְּזַבִּין אַבָּא בִּתְרֵי זוּזֵי.

חַד גַּדְיָא, חַד גַּדְיָא:

וְאָתָא הַשּׁוֹחֵט, וְשָׁחַט לְתוֹרָא, דְּשָׁתָה לְמַיָּא, דְּכָבָה לְנוּרָא, דְּשָׂרַף לְחוּטְרָא, דְּהִכָּה לְכַלְבָּא, דְּנָשַׁךְ לְשׁוּנְרָא, דְּאָכְלָה לְגַדְיָא, דְּזַבִּין אַבָּא בִּתְרֵי זוּזֵי.

חַד גַּדְיָא, חַד גַּדְיָא:

Along came a stick and hit the dog that bit the cat that ate the kid – that my father bought for two zuzim.

One kid, one kid.

Along came a fire and burnt the stick that hit the dog that bit the cat that ate the kid – that my father bought for two zuzim.

One kid, one kid.

Along came water and extinguished the fire that burnt the stick that hit the dog that bit the cat that ate the kid – that my father bought for two zuzim.

One kid, one kid.

Along came an ox and drank the water that extinguished the fire that burnt the stick that hit the dog that bit the cat that ate the kid – that my father bought for two zuzim.

One kid, one kid.

Along came a butcher and slaughtered the ox that drank the water that extinguished the fire that burnt the stick that hit the dog that bit the cat that ate the kid – that my father bought for two zuzim.

One kid, one kid.

וְאָתָא מַלְאַךְ הַמָּוֶת, וְשָׁחַט לְשׁוֹחֵט, דְּשָׁחַט לְתוֹרָא, דְּשָׁתָה לְמַיָּא, דְּכָבָה לְנוּרָא, דְּשָׂרַף לְחוּטְרָא, דְּהִכָּה לְכַלְבָּא, דְּנָשַׁךְ לְשׁוּנְרָא, דְּאָכְלָה לְגַדְיָא, דְּזַבִּין אַבָּא בִּתְרֵי זוּזֵי.

חַד גַּדְיָא, חַד גַּדְיָא:

וְאָתָא הַקָּדוֹשׁ בָּרוּךְ הוּא, וְשָׁחַט לְמַלְאַךְ הַמָּוֶת, דְּשָׁחַט לְשׁוֹחֵט, דְּשָׁחַט לְתוֹרָא, דְּשָׁתָה לְמַיָּא, דְּכָבָה לְנוּרָא, דְּשָׂרַף לְחוּטְרָא, דְּהִכָּה לְכַלְבָּא, דְּנָשַׁךְ לְשׁוּנְרָא, דְּאָכְלָה לְגַדְיָא, דְּזַבִּין אַבָּא בִּתְרֵי זוּזֵי.

חַד גַּדְיָא, חַד גַּדְיָא:

After finishing the poems and songs, it is customary to recite Shir Hashirim.

Along came the angel of death and killed the butcher who slaughtered the ox that drank the water that extinguished the fire that burnt the stick that hit the dog that bit the cat that ate the kid – that my father bought for two zuzim.

One kid, one kid.

Then God came and killed the angel of death who killed the butcher who slaughtered the ox that drank the water that extinguished the fire that burnt the stick that hit the dog that bit the cat that ate the kid – that my father bought for two zuzim.

One kid, one kid.

ויגד יהונתן

ESSAYS

Moshe's Ascent to Leadership

THE FIRST SIGN

Pharaoh and the Egyptian people believed in Hashem's existence but they certainly did not believe in His continued influence over the world. Egypt believed that the world was at the mercy of luck and chance, certainly not in the hands of Hashem. For this reason, Pharaoh said: "Who is Hashem that I should heed His voice to send out Yisrael? I do not know Hashem, nor will I send out Yisrael!"[198] This heresy was adopted by Bnei Yisrael as the Torah reports, "but they [Bnei Yisrael] did not heed Moshe because of shortness of breath."[199] The Rabbis explain that the word "breath" in Hebrew is *ruach,* which also means spirit, and, therefore, the shortness of breath in the verse refers to a lack of spirituality. Bnei Yisrael were influenced by the Egyptians and they began to worship idols. This caused them to experience a shortness of spiritual breath, detrimental to their existence.

Moshe, realizing the state Bnei Yisrael was in, became discouraged and doubted whether the Jewish people deserved to be redeemed from Egypt. So Moshe responded to Hashem's promise of deliverance by saying, "But they will not believe me and they will not heed my voice."[200] The following discussion ensued. Hashem responded by asking Moshe, "What is that in your hand?" When Moshe answered "a staff, " Hashem told him to "Cast it on the ground." Moshe, following Hashem's instructions, cast it on the ground and it turned into a snake. Moshe fled from the snake and Hashem instructed him, saying, "Stretch out your hand and grasp its tail." Moshe stretched out his hand, grasped the snake, and it became a staff in his palm. With this sign, Moshe could prove to Bnei Yisrael "that Hashem, the God of their forefathers, appeared to you

[Moshe], the God of Avraham, the God of Yitzchak, and the God of Yaakov."[201]

The events described in these verses raise many questions that require further clarification. Why did the staff transform into, of all things, a snake? Why did Hashem tell Moshe to grab the snake by its tail in order to transform it back into a staff? Why, after the snake turned back into a staff, did Hashem remind Moshe that He was the God of the forefathers? How is Hashem's relationship with the forefathers related to the staff and the snake?

Hashem wanted Moshe to appreciate that Bnei Yisrael had two strengths that would help them overcome their spiritual deterioration: their lineage (direct lineal descent from Avraham, Yitzchak and Yaakov), and the sign of the covenant (circumcision). Moshe need not fear, for Bnei Yisrael's lineage benefited them in several ways. Firstly, the merit of the forefathers served to protect them. Secondly, Hashem would know that they were rooted in the holiness of the forefathers, and that they would not stray too far. Therefore, it would be easier for them to repent both because they knew what true holiness is and because holiness was already an integral part of their beings. They would not have to develop into "new beings" in order to become holy because their lineage would help guarantee their allegiance to Hashem.

Hashem alludes to this message when he tells Moshe to take the staff (*mateh*) and "cast it on the ground." While the Hebrew word used in this verse to refer to staff is mateh, another word for staff, in Hebrew, is *shevet*. Shevet also means tribe in Hebrew. Thus, by referring to the staff – shevet – Hashem was alluding to *shivtei Yah* – the tribes of Hashem.[202] Originally Bnei Yisrael walked the straight and narrow path – a path as straight as a staff – believing only in Hashem. However, corrupted by the Egyptian influence, they were transformed into snakes. Moshe was afraid that no one could rectify the situation and save them. Hashem told him to grab the tail, which represented the circumcision, and the snake turned back into a staff. Hashem taught Moshe that there was hope for Bnei Yisrael to return to its original state of holiness.

THE SECOND SIGN

At the burning bush, Hashem commanded Moshe: "Go and I shall dispatch you to Pharaoh and you shall take My people, Bnei Yisrael out of Egypt."[203] Moshe responded by expressing his doubts: "But they will not believe me and they will not heed my voice."[204] To allay Moshe's fears and provide him with proof that Hashem had sent him, Moshe was commanded to bring his hand to his chest. When he did so and then subsequently withdrew it, he found that his hand was afflicted with *tzara'at*. When, at Hashem's command, he returned his hand to his chest, it was miraculously cured. This miracle proved Hashem's greatness and demonstrated that Hashem had sent Moshe. However, the Talmud contends that this sign possesses an even profounder meaning.

After Moshe claimed that Bnei Yisrael would not believe him, the Talmud reports that Hashem reprimanded Moshe telling him that the Jewish people are believers and the sons of believers. According to the Talmud, Moshe was afflicted with tzara'at for questioning Bnei Yisrael's character. The Talmud concludes that Moshe's punishment teaches us that "one who suspects someone unjustly will have his body afflicted with tzara'at."[205]

Both the Torah text and the Talmud's inferences raise questions. Why does the Torah emphasize that Moshe both brought his hand to and withdrew his hand from his chest? What does this signify? Additionally, why did Moshe doubt the Jewish people in the first place? Why didn't Moshe simply fulfill Hashem's mission?

In order to answer these questions it is important to understand the purpose of tzara'at and why the Rabbis connect it with the transgression of suspecting someone unjustly. The Rambam writes, in the "Laws of Repentance," that it is difficult to repent for suspecting someone unjustly because the sinner is unaware of having done so.[206] Afflicting an individual with tzara'at is Hashem's way of sending this person a spiritual wake-up call. Hashem punished Moshe with tzara'at because he misjudged the Jewish people, suspecting that they would not listen to him. Hashem wanted Moshe to learn from his mistake and adopt a new attitude towards Bnei Yisrael.

Yet, why did Moshe express his doubts concerning the Jewish people's character in the first place? The answer to this question stems from a Talmudic ruling regarding the law of rebuke. The Talmud says, "just as it is a mitzva to give rebuke, when rebuke will be accepted, so too is it a mitzva to refrain from giving rebuke, when rebuke will not be accepted."[207] Even omitting to inform people of their transgressions can be a mitzva because the Rabbis maintain that "it is preferable to transgress unintentionally [when unaware of the prohibition] than to transgress intentionally";[208] if the sinner would not listen, he or she is better off not knowing the nature of the sin.

However, this principle can only be applied under certain circumstances. According to Tosafot, it cannot be applied to a mitzva or concept explicitly stated in the Torah, and, therefore it only applies to rabbinically mandated laws. Moreover, if one is convinced that one's listeners will not listen when admonished, it is preferable to refrain from rebuke, allowing them to transgress in ignorance. Therefore, one who reprimands the Jewish community must consider carefully what should and should not be said, depending upon the nature of the mitzva itself and upon the nature of one's listeners.

The Talmud brings proof for this principle from the following rabbinic exchange. A group of rabbis exclaimed, "We wonder if there is anyone in this generation who knows how to give reprimand." Rabbi Tarfon responded, "You wonder if anyone knows how to offer reprimand! I wonder if there is anyone in this generation who will accept reprimand."[209] Rabbi Tarfon's response is surprising, for what does offering reprimand have to do with accepting reprimand? One can offer reprimand even though no one is prepared to accept it! Rabbi Tarfon, in answering the Rabbis' question, wanted to emphasize the true challenge inherent in reprimanding; persuading your listeners to accept your words. Particularly in a generation unlikely to accept rebuke, the speaker must first consider whether he has a realistic chance of being heard. If not, his words should remain unspoken, for it is better if the people transgress unwittingly.

Curiously enough, sometimes, rather than bettering the listeners' situation reprimand worsens it, for now they transgress knowingly and are fully responsible for their actions. However, in general, receiving a reprimand should be a positive experience, for it encourages self-improvement. Therefore, if you have an opportunity to successfully reprimand another, and do not, an opportunity has been lost. However, for this very reason, you should only reprimand out of love and concern, so that your reprimand can be accepted in the spirit that it was given.

This interpretation of the law of rebuke explains Moshe's hesitation and doubts regarding approaching Bnei Yisrael. Moshe feared that if he approached Bnei Yisrael they would not believe him and might even reject the words of Hashem. Moshe concluded that given such a likelihood it was preferable to leave Bnei Yisrael uninformed because "it is preferable to transgress unintentionally [unaware of a prohibition] than to transgress intentionally.

Hashem decided to teach Moshe an invaluable lesson. He punished Moshe with tzara'at for doubting the Jewish people, but at the same time He taught Moshe how to successfully approach the Jews: he told Moshe to draw his hand to his chest both to receive and to become cured of the tzara'at. The Abravanel explains that symbolically Hashem taught Moshe to draw Bnei Yisrael close to his heart, offering them advice and guidance, again and again. Moshe would be able to successfully convince the Jews to accept Hashem's message if he offered it with patience and compassion. Hashem taught Moshe that the concept, "it is preferable to transgress unintentionally [unaware of a prohibition] than to transgress intentionally," only applies to offering rebuke when one is absolutely certain no one will listen. In Moshe's case, although he would often be discouraged, persistence would pay off; Bnei Yisrael would finally listen. This truth is explicitly pointed out by the wording of the verse commanding rebuke, "You shall rebuke and rebuke your fellow."[210] The Torah repeats the instruction to rebuke twice because an effective reprimand must be given more than once.

Miriam the Prophetess and Her Mission

The Torah recounts after the splitting of the Red Sea, "Miriam, the prophetess, the sister of Aharon, took her drum in her hand and all the women went forth after her with drums and with dances."[211] Miriam led the women in song and dance after Bnei Yisrael was miraculously saved at the sea. Why didn't the men join the women in expressing their jubilation and gratitude for the miracle? Furthermore, why is Miriam referred to as "the sister of Aharon" when she was also Moshe's sister?

The Talmud states that "Hashem's Divine presence does not rest upon those who are in a state of sadness, but, rather, upon those who are in a state of happiness."[212] Miriam and the women had an ulterior motive for expressing their jubilation. Having witnessed the deliverance of Hashem, they wanted to take advantage of this opportunity to benefit from and partake of the *Ruach Hakodesh*. To do this, they realized that they needed to create the proper atmosphere; therefore, they went out to sing and dance. The men who were already on such a level did not need to take artificial steps to create this atmosphere; therefore, they did not sing and dance.

This insight explains why the women needed to sing and dance, while the men did not; however, it raises another question: why did Miriam, who was a prophetess, need to resort to "drums and dances" to experience the flow of the Divine Spirit? The Talmud – responding indirectly to this question – teaches us that after Moshe was born, Miriam lost her ability to prophesy:

Miriam was a prophetess, as it is written, "And Miriam, the prophetess, the sister of Aharon, took"; was she not the sister of Moshe as well? [That is to say, why does the Torah refer to her exclusively as "the sister of Aharon"?] Rav Nachman said in the name of Rav: 'Because she prophesied when she was a sister of Aharon saying, "In the future my mother will bear a son who will save the people of Yisrael." When Moshe was born the entire house filled with light. Her father rose and kissed her on the head and said to her, "My daughter, your prophecy has been fulfilled." When they cast [Moshe] into the river, her father rose and struck her on her head and said to her, "My daughter where is your prophecy?" Therefore it is written, "And his sister placed herself at a distance to know," to know what would become of her prophecy.'[213]

When Moshe, the savior of the Jewish people, was born, Miriam's prophecy seemed to have been fulfilled. However, when his mother, Yocheved, was forced to place him in a basket upon the water, the success of Miriam's prophecy was in doubt. Therefore, Miriam placed herself at a distance from the basket and waited to see not only whether baby Moshe would survive but also whether her prophecy would come to fruition. Once Miriam's prophecy reached fruition and Moshe became the savior of Bnei Yisrael, she lost the ability to prophesy. At the splitting of the Red Sea, the Torah intimates that Miriam saw an opportunity to regain the prophetic spirit she had when she was only "Aharon's sister," so she began to sing and dance hoping to arouse the necessary state of happiness for receiving Ruach Hakodesh. The Torah refers to Miriam as the sister of Aharon because before Moshe's birth – when she had only been Aharon's sister – she had the gift of prophecy. Following the splitting of the Red Sea, Miriam once again benefited from Ruach Hakodesh and hoped to prophesy once again.

The Three Festivals

The Talmud relates that Hashem gave Bnei Yisrael three gifts: the Torah, Eretz Yisrael and the World to Come.[214] Each gift is represented by one of the three Festivals. Pesach represents the gift of Eretz Yisrael because the main reason for Bnei Yisrael's redemption from Egypt was to facilitate their inheritance of Eretz Yisrael, a connection emphasized by Bnei Yisrael's celebration of Pesach immediately upon their entering the Land.[215] Shavuot represents Torah because on that day Bnei Yisrael accepted Torah and mitzvot at Mount Sinai. Sukkot commemorates the clouds of glory that represent the World to Come because being in the sukkah is like basking in the Divine presence in the World to Come. The sukkah attains this status both because it symbolizes the clouds of glory that protected the Jewish people during their sojourn in the desert and because when entering the sukkah, one is supposed to envision oneself entering the presence of Hashem. Thus, the Jews repent during the High Holidays of Rosh Hashana and Yom Kippur in preparation for Sukkot, much like a person is meant to repent in preparation for the World to Come.

Tragically, we no longer have the opportunity to celebrate the three Festivals by offering sacrifices and reciting prayers in the Temple. However, by understanding and appreciating these holidays' significance, we demonstrate how eager and ready we are for the rebuilding of the Temple. Let us hope and pray that as a result of our commemorating the Jewish festivals properly and understanding their deeper meaning we will be privileged to celebrate them in the rebuilt Temple in Jerusalem.

The Intrinsic Connection Between Shabbat, Torah and Eretz Yisrael

By observing the Shabbat as a day of rest, the Jew testifies to Hashem's creation of the world. The world did not come into existence by itself; Hashem created it over a period of six days and then on the seventh He rested. The Talmud promises that "Anyone who delights in the Shabbat is given a portion with no boundaries ... Anyone who observes Shabbat in accordance with its laws will be forgiven for his sins even if he worshipped idols like the generation of Enosh."[216] This *Gemara* raises several serious questions: Why does the Talmud specifically mention the generation of Enosh? Why is delighting in the Shabbat so important? Why was the reward of a "portion with no boundaries" promised for observing the Shabbat?

The people of Enosh's generation worshipped idols because they believed that Hashem had created the world and then left it in the keeping of other heavenly gods and supernatural forces. They kept Shabbat to commemorate Hashem's creation of the world in six days and His resting on the seventh. According to the *Zohar*, the mistake Enosh and his followers made was believing that one of the angels responsible for overseeing the world was called Shabbtai.[217] The name Shabbtai is closely linked to the word Shabbat. However, if one breaks the Hebrew name Shabbtai into two, it becomes either *Ei Shabbat* or *Oiy Shabbat*, indicating that Shabbat is a time to suffer. The generation of Enosh believed that Shabbtai had been granted dominion over the world and he had established Shabbat as a day of pain and sorrow. The Rabbis instructed Bnei Yisrael to observe Shabbat "in accordance with its laws." Although this would seem rather obvious, the Rabbis wanted Bnei Yisrael to delight in the Shabbat, showing its joy and happiness at observing this holy day. By doing so, it would show its appreciation for Hashem who created the world and continues to govern it, and thwart the beliefs of those who maintain that Shabbtai rules the world. Thus, the Talmud affirmed that even if you worshipped idols like the generation of Enosh, by keeping the Shabbat "in accordance with its laws" – that is, by rejoicing on Shabbat – you can demonstrate your rejection of that doctrine and be forgiven.

Why is Bnei Yisrael awarded "a portion with no boundaries" for Shabbat observance? By observing Shabbat, the Jew testifies that Hashem created the world. The promise of "a portion with no boundaries," on the one hand, indicates a great reward, appropriate for such vital testimony; however, on the other hand, it leaves the actual amount unspecified. Rav Yehonatan explains that had Hashem revealed the specific reward for Shabbat observance, the nations might have suspected Bnei Yisrael of accepting a bribe and observing the Shabbat in order to gain the reward. For this reason, the Talmud declares that the Torah did not reveal the exact reward for Shabbat observance to the foreign nations.[218]

What is the relationship between Shabbat, the Torah, and Eretz Yisrael? The Ramban explains that most of the mitzvot in the Torah can only be performed in Eretz Yisrael. To embrace the whole Torah, one must embrace Eretz Yisrael. Recognizing this truth, the nations of the world saw no advantage to accepting the yoke of the Torah, in order to receive such a geographically small country.

Hashem only told Bnei Yisrael that "Anyone who keeps the Shabbat receives a portion without boundaries," that is to say, Eretz Yisrael. That Eretz Yisrael is "the portion with no boundaries" may be proven from its other name: "the land of the deer."[219] Eretz Yisrael received this title because even though the Land appears small in size, miraculously it expands like deerskin (which is very elastic) and holds as many people as it must. (This miraculous trait is also why Eretz Yisrael is referred to as "the portion of Yaakov," for Rashi tells us that when Yaakov left his father's home, fleeing from Esav, Hashem folded-up all of Eretz Yisrael and placed it under his head to sleep on.[220]) The Torah was given to Bnei Yisrael at Mount Sinai on Shabbat, and after they accepted the Torah and agreed to observe Shabbat, they were privileged to receive Eretz Yisrael as well.

Observing Shabbat provides us with an opportunity to rest both mentally and physically. Shabbat observance provides us with the opportunity both to revitalize ourselves to face the challenges of this world and to earn our places in the World to Come. The unique relationship between Shabbat, the Torah and Eretz Yisrael reminds us that by observing the Shabbat we testify that Hashem created the world and that He continues to be active in it.

The Special Characteristics of Teshuva

The Talmud reports that:

> Bnei Yisrael made an improper request yet Hashem responded to them properly, as it says, 'Let us know; let us pursue the knowledge of Hashem. His going forth is sure as the morning, and He shall come to us like the rain that satiates the earth.' Hashem responded to Yisrael: 'My daughter, you request something which at times is desirable and at other times is not desirable, but I will be for you something which is desirable at all times, as it says, "I will be like the dew to Bnei Yisrael." '[221]

The verses quoted by the Talmud are cited from the prophet Hoshea and deal with the concept of repentance. The Jews request that Hashem fall amongst them like the rain, and Hashem replies that His presence will be amongst them like the dew. Hashem gives Bnei Yisrael, who only asked for Him to come occasionally, more than they requested, a commitment to consistently dwell amongst them so as to ensure their spiritual progress. While this interpretation of the midrash is profound, Rav Yehonatan explains that this dialogue contains an even deeper and more profound meaning, connected to the difference between rain and dew.

Rav Yehonatan, based upon the scientific understanding of his day, explains that rain falls as a result of water on the ground evaporating, accumulating in the form of clouds in the sky, and falling back to the ground, when the clouds can no longer hold it. Therefore if the ground is too dry, there will be no rain. Dew, in contrast, does not come from the ground. Since it derives from the dampness in the air, it can always be depended upon.

Rav Yehonatan explains that the precipitation cycle of the rain and the dew is analogous to the two forms of the teshuva process. Hashem wants His people to repent and He is even willing to assist them in returning to Him; however, ordinarily the sinner must take the first step, initiating the process by showing remorse and demonstrating a desire to change. After an individual makes the first move, Hashem responds by offering His assistance, as the *Midrash* declares, "One who comes to purify one's self, will receive assistance."[222] Similarly, another *Midrash* teaches, "Hashem says, 'If you open [yourself] to the size of the eye of a needle, I will broaden the hole to the size of a hallway.' "[223] The latter midrash teaches that if man opens himself up to atonement, even slightly, Hashem will enable his further spiritual progress. However, Rav Yehonatan notes, this rule only applies under ordinary historical circumstances. There will come a time in the future when Hashem no longer waits for man to make the first move. He will purify the hearts of Bnei Yisrael and spur the Jews on to repentance, as the time of national redemption arrives.

The dialogue between Hashem and Bnei Yisrael in the midrash now becomes clear. Bnei Yisrael asked Hashem to relate to them like rain. Rain stems from the earth and only falls intermittently. Likewise, teshuva is a process that begins on earth, initiated by man's actions and rises to the heavens. Bnei Yisrael were afraid of the daunting task of initiating teshuva constantly, so they asked Hashem to at least come to them periodically like rain to give them a break from that awesome responsibility. Hashem responded by establishing an even stronger relationship with Bnei Yisrael than they had asked for. Like dew, which begins in the heavens above and is constant, He promised to initiate the repentance process from above. This allayed Bnei Yisrael's fears as Hashem assured them that He would maintain a continuous connection with them, even when they were unable to initiate their own repentance.

AUTHOR'S COMMENTS Chazal teach that "One must look upon oneself as if he had personally left Egypt."[224] On Pesach, especially during Seder night, we fulfill this obligation. The Talmud declares: "During the month of Nissan, the Jewish people were redeemed, and during the month of Nissan, they will be redeemed again in the future."[225] We need to experience our past redemption and look forward expectantly to our future one. Therefore, we recite the prayer for dew on Pesach to remind ourselves that Hashem feels close to us and embraces us as His people. On Pesach we celebrate our Exodus from Egypt, and we renew our fervent belief in a future exodus.

Eretz Yisrael's Special Characteristics

When King David heard of Shaul and Yehonatan's deaths, he wrote a lament describing Shaul as a deer: "O precious deer of Yisrael, upon your heights lie the slain! How have the mighty fallen!"[226] Why did David compare Shaul to a deer? By resolving the apparent contradiction between two verses in *Tehillim*, Rav Yehonatan explains why David compared Shaul to a deer. In one verse David writes, "The eyes of Hashem are toward the righteous, and His ears to [hearing] their cry,"[227] while in another one he declares, "Behold, the eye of Hashem is upon those who fear Him, upon those who await His kindness."[228]

Why does the first verse refer to the "eyes of Hashem," in the plural, and the second verse refer to the singular "eye of Hashem"? The *Midrash* explains that one verse refers to Bnei Yisrael, when they follow the laws of the Torah, and the other verse refers to Bnei Yisrael, when they do not.[229] The *Midrash* does not specify which verse refers to which occasion. However, Rav Yehonatan does. Each of Hashem's eyes represents one of the two antithetical attributes: judgment and mercy. When Bnei Yisrael behave righteously, Hashem can look at them with both eyes, a statement of confidence that they are prepared for judgment. However, when Bnei Yisrael behave poorly, Hashem looks at them with only one eye – the eye of mercy – aware that they are unprepared for judgment.

Curiously, the deer sleeps with one eye open.[230] This eye represents mercy. Thus, we can explain the verse in *Shir Hashirim*, "Flee, my Beloved, from our common exile and be like a deer or a young hart in Your swiftness."[231] We ask Hashem to flee like a deer, with one eye of mercy directed towards His people, so that He will withhold judgment.

This interpretation provides us with additional insight regarding the verse in *Shir Hashirim*, "Your eyes are beautiful doves."[232] The *Midrash* explains that the "doves" in this verse symbolize the judges of the *Sanhedrin*, a body of outstanding Torah scholars.[233] Firstly, the Torah scholars are compared to doves because, as Rav Yehonatan explains, all birds, except for the dove, drink water and then spit it out. Torah is often compared to water, and the dove retaining its water parallels the Torah scholar who retains his Torah, as the *Mishna* states, "Eliezer the son of Horkenos is a plastered cistern, which loses not a drop of water."[234] Secondly, like the dove, a bird symbolizing peace and tranquility, the Torah also promotes peace and tranquility, as it is written, "Its ways [the ways of Torah] are ways of pleasantness and all its pathways are peace."[235] The judges of the high court can certainly be compared to doves. This is why the eyes of Hashem - His king, King Shaul, and His Torah scholars - are compared to those of the merciful deer and the pleasant dove, animals that embody traits characteristic of Hashem.

The Jewish leader is expected to emulate Hashem. He must control his anger and show compassion. The Rambam criticizes Moshe for losing his temper and lashing out angrily, when he hit the rock instead of speaking to it. The average person loses his patience and sometimes gets angry, but for a Jewish leader to do so is a capital offence. David praised Shaul for leading Bnei Yisrael with compassion and mercy; therefore, he compared him to the deer, a merciful animal.

Anger is a sign of foolishness. Rav Yehonatan eulogized a certain rabbi and leader of the Jewish community in Prague as a man who never showed any anger. He was tolerant of others and demonstrated tremendous patience, even though he was burdened with the concerns of the many. He greeted everyone with a gentle kindness and never expected anything in return. Rav Yehonatan writes that he experienced a renewed sense of personal loss eulogizing the rabbi for he had instilled honesty and implanted sincerity in Rav Yehonatan, himself, and for this Rav Yehonatan bore him special respect.

Why Bnei Yisrael Were Redeemed from Egypt

The *Midrash* says, "There were four reasons why Bnei Yisrael merited redemption from servitude in Egypt. They did not change their [Hebrew] names; they continued to speak the Hebrew language; they did not mingle with Egyptian women, and they were not sycophants."[236] Another midrash relates that Yosef reported to his father that his brothers were eyeing the Canaanite women; taunting their half-brothers, the sons of the handmaidens [Bilha and Zilpa], and eating the flesh from live animals. While at first glance these two midrashim seem unrelated there is a profound connection between them.

Yosef found fault with his brothers for committing three grave sins. The brothers may very well have eyed the Canaanite women, for some of them seem to have married Canaanites, as the Torah records, "Shimon's sons: Yemuel, Yamin, Ohad, Yachin, Zohar and Shaul son of the Canaanite woman."[237] Some of the brothers may also have teased their siblings, calling them "sons of the handmaidens." However it is difficult to imagine that the brothers would actually eat flesh taken from a live animal! Particularly since this act had been prohibited since Noach's time and was a capital offence. How could the *Midrash* suggest that the brothers would commit such a serious transgression? This claim requires further investigation.

Rav Yehonatan explains that the brothers really did not eat flesh taken from a live animal. They only talked as if they had done so in order to test whether Yosef would report this wrongdoing to their father. Actually they consumed flesh from an animal that had been ritually slaughtered. Yosef failed the test as he reported all their supposed wrongdoings to their father, as they had suspected he would. Yosef erred in believing his brothers capable of such sin and he erred in reporting them to his father, as the Torah says, "Yosef would bring evil reports about them to their father."[238] The brothers also erred in misrepresenting their actions, even if they only meant to test Yosef. Both the brothers and Yosef misused the power of speech.

Yosef also abused his power of speech in another venue, Potiphar's house. The *Midrash* ties the two venues together by recording Hashem's reaction to Yosef's actions: "You [Yosef] bring evil reports regarding your brothers [eyeing the Canaanite women]; I [Hashem] will unleash the bear, the wife of Potiphar, upon you."[239] Potiphar's wife attempted to seduce Yosef many times. Each time, he avoided her embrace by telling her that it was too risky, the house was too full of people. Yosef attempted to avoid confrontation by telling Potiphar's wife that he would sleep with her when the house was empty. Although Yosef's intentions were pure, he was wrong to lie and, in so doing, abused his power of speech again. Hashem punished him for again abusing his power of speech by fulfilling the condition Yosef had proposed. One day he found himself alone in the house with Potiphar's wife. She tried to seduce him, and he nearly gave in as the Torah relates:

"Then there was an opportune day when he entered the house to do his work, no man of the household staff being there in the house, that she caught hold of him by his garment, saying, "Lie with me!" But he left his garment in her hand, and he fled, and went outside!"[240]

Potiphar's wife claimed, "The Hebrew slave whom you brought to us came to me to sport with me ... Your slave did things like these to me."[241] Potiphar's wife made these false claims because she was angry at Yosef for lying to her. Hashem punished Yosef for lying, by having the Egyptians believe the lies told by Potiphar's wife.

Ultimately, as a consequence of the strife between Yosef and his brothers and Yosef's entanglement with Potiphar's wife, Bnei Yisrael was exiled in Egypt. Bnei Yisrael was redeemed from Egypt because its actions demonstrated that the sins of Yosef and his brothers had been rectified. The brothers' eyeing Canaanite women and Yosef's seduction by Potiphar's wife were rectified by Bnei Yisrael's refusal to mingle with Egyptian women. The insensitivity of those brothers, who teased their half-brothers, calling them "children of the handmaidens," was rectified by Bnei Yisrael preserving their names, as the *Midrash* relates: "Reuven went down [to Egypt] and Reuven ascended [from Egypt], Shimon went down [to Egypt] and Shimon ascended [from Egypt]."[242] Yosef's and his brothers' misuse of their powers of speech was rectified by Bnei Yisrael's decision to continue speaking the holy tongue. The Jews distancing themselves from sycophancy in Egypt rectified Yosef's evil reports to Yaakov regarding his brothers' behavior.

These *midrashim* demonstrate how much damage one can inflict with one's mouth, and how careful one must be in using the power of speech. Our Rabbis understood that the only way to avoid speaking evil is by engaging one's mouth in productive and positive activities such as studying Torah and praying to Hashem, as the Talmud says, "The only way to save oneself from speaking slander is by studying Torah and frequenting the synagogues and study houses."[243]

AUTHOR'S COMMENTS On Seder night we are commanded to speak, as the Torah declares, "And you shall tell your son on that day saying: 'It is because of this that Hashem acted on my behalf when I left Egypt.'"[244] We engage in positive dialogue with our family and friends concerning the profound depths of our history and our unique relationship with Hashem. On Seder night, we take concrete steps to rectify the sins that led to our exile in Egypt, as we sit with our children in a setting that facilitates their deeper understanding of the Torah.

Endnotes

1 *Bereishit 2:1*
2 *Bereishit 2:2*
3 Rav Yehonatan is expanding upon an idea already introduced by Rashi, *Bereishit 1:31*
4 *Shir Hashirim Rabba 8:15*
5 *Yirmiyahu 33:25*
6 *Bereishit 2:3*
7 In the previous paragraph Rav Yehonatan explained that Hashem perfected the world and here he says otherwise. It is not uncharacteristic for Rav Yehonatan to adopt diametrically opposed perspectives, for the sake of offering an additional *drash*.
8 *Pesachim 99b*
9 *Rosh Hashana 30a*
10 *Shemot 12:46*
11 For example, we wash our hands before eating the green vegetable, known as *karpas*. In the Temple period, this ritual was routinely performed to ensure that ones hands were pure before touching foods that had come into contact with water.
12 *Shemot 15:31*
13 *Devarim 6:23*
14 *Bava Metzia 114a*
15 *Yalkut Shimoni, Korach 752*
16 *Berachot 34b*
17 *Bereishit 15:3*
18 *Rashi, Bereishit 42:2*
19 *Devarim 6:20*
20 *Shemot 13:14-16*
21 *Tal Chermon, p.403*
22 *Eicha 1:7*
23 *Bamidbar 22:5*
24 *Bamidbar 22:11*
25 *Darash Moshe, p.129*
26 *Sifra, Kedoshim 10:11*
27 Rav Yehonatan's source is unclear.
28 *Bereishit 21:3*
29 *Bereishit 21:2*
30 *Shemot 15:15*
31 Rav Yehonatan's source is unclear.
32 *Shemot 1:22*
33 *Shemot 1:7*
34 *Shemot 9:29*
35 *Shemot 13:17*
36 *Tanchuma, Beshalach 10*
37 *Eicha 2:17*
38 *Bereishit 45:7*
39 *Vayikra 22:32*
40 *Sifra, Vayikra 3:3*
41 *Bamidbar 15:11*
42 *Shemot 11:2*
43 *Shir Hashirim Rabba, Parsha 4*
44 *Yoma 87a*
45 *Bamidbar 5:14*
46 *Shemot 14:15*
47 *Shemot 1:8*
48 *Shemot 32:11*
49 *Birkot Keriyat Shema* in the Morning Prayers
50 *Shemot Rabba, Parsha 6*
51 *Shemot 32:11*
52 *Shemot 32:12*
53 *Sanhedrin 94a*
54 *I Melachim 18:25*
55 *Shemot 7:5*
56 *Rashi, Bereishit 26:2*
57 *Yehoshua 5:13-15*
58 *Shemot 12:12*
59 *Shemot 23:20*
60 *Shemot 2:11*
61 *Rashi, Shemot 2:11*
62 *Shemot 3:3*
63 *Shemot 3:4*
64 *Shemot 3:8*
65 *Shemot 23:23*
66 *Berachot 33b*
67 *Shemot 7:5*
68 *Sanhedrin 97b*
69 *Shemot 4:1-4*
70 *Shemot 6:9*
71 *Midrash Aggada, Shemot 6*
72 *Bava Batra 16b*
73 *Sanhedrin 97b*
74 *Shemot 2:23*
75 *Shemot 8:17*
76 *II Melachim 2:24*
77 *Sotah 47a*
78 *Yeshayahu 6:3*
79 *Shemot 10:15*

80 *Shemot 10:2*
81 *Shemot 11:8*
82 *Shemot 10:22*
83 *Shemot Rabba 14*
84 *Bereishit 1:2-5*
85 *Bereishit Rabba 14*
86 *Shemot 10:23*
87 *Shemot 10:23*
88 *Shemot 13:17*
89 *Shemot 10:1*
90 *Shemot 23:12*
91 *Darash Moshe, p.70*
92 *Vayikra 25:3-4*
93 *Shemot 15:18-19*
94 *Mishlei 29:4*
95 *Shemot 15:1*
96 *Shemot 1:22*
97 *Yalkut Shimoni, Tehillim 247*
98 *Devarim 8:4*
99 *Mechilta deRabbi Yishmael, Yitro 8*
100 *Shabbat 118b*
101 *Sanhedrin 58b*
102 *Tehillim 19:8*
103 *Bava Batra 158b*
104 *Megilla 6b*
105 *Kohelet Rabba 1:1*
106 *Eim Habanim Semeichah, p.272*
107 *Ketubot 112a*
108 *Shabbat 118b*
109 *Shabbat 118a*
110 *Sukkah 52b*
111 *Shabbat 88a*
112 *Shulchan Arukh, Choshen Mishpat, Siman 175*
113 *Shabbat 86b*
114 *Devarim 39:12*
115 *Mechilta deRabbi Yishmael, Beshalach 12*
116 *Devarim 30:11*
117 *Bereishit 18:6-7*
118 *Bereishit Rabba 48*
119 *Bereishit 18:6*
120 *Bereishit 18:8*
121 *Sechel Tov, Bereishit 21*
122 Rav Yehonatan's source is unclear.
123 *Pesachim 36b*
124 *Bamidbar 9:11*
125 *Bamidbar 20:16*
126 *Tehillim 86:36*
127 *Devarim 16:3*
128 *Pesachim 34a*
129 *II Melachim 23:3*
130 *Shemot 12:43*
131 *Devarim 6:20*
132 *Yirmiyahu 2:2*
133 Rav Yehonatan's source is unclear.
134 *Bereishit 1:2*
135 *Berachot 34b*
136 *Sichot Mussar, p.138*
137 Rav Yehonatan's source is unclear.
138 *Mishlei 10:7*
139 *Yoma 38a*
140 Rav Yehonatan's source is unclear.
141 *Shemot 17:6*
142 *Bamidbar 20:11*
143 *Shemot 13:6*
144 *Bamidbar 9:11*
145 *Eicha 3:15*
146 *Eicha Rabba 18*
147 *Shemot 12:6*
148 The Halacha defines *bein ha'arbayim* (between the evenings) as from midday – the sixth hour of the day – until it gets dark. See Rashi, *Shemot 12:6*. However, in the context of this *derasha*, Rav Yehonatan interprets *bein haarbayim* as twilight.
149 *Tehillim 149:1*
150 *Pesachim 109a*
151 *Yerushalmi, Peah 7:5*
152 *Rosh Hashana 32b*
153 *Rambam, Mishneh Torah, Hilchot Yom Tov 1:1*
154 *Rambam, Mishneh Torah, Hilchot Megilla and Hannuka 3:6*
155 *Chagiga 5b*
156 *Shabbat 30b*
157 *Rambam, Mishneh Torah, Hilchot Klei Hamikdash 5:7*
158 *Tehillim 144:15*
159 *I Melachim 8:23*
160 *Yeshayahu 12:6*
161 *Tehillim 2:1-2*
162 *Tehillim 2:3*
163 *Tehillim 2:7-8*
164 *Meila 14a*
165 *Shemot 25:8*
166 *Tal Chermon, p.411*
167 *Bamidbar Rabba 12:8*
168 In citing the existence of four elements, Rav Yehonatan is relying upon the classical Greek conception

that the world is composed of four fundamental elements: earth, air, fire and water.

169 *Daniel 7:10*
170 *Bereishit 1:7*
171 *Tehillim 8:2*
172 *Pesikta Rabbati 25*
173 *Sanhedrin 102a*
174 *Bereishit 17:1*
175 *Zohar 3:166a*
176 *Tehillim 116:9*
177 *Berachot 54a*
178 *Bereishit 12:2*
179 *Bamidbar Rabba 11*
180 *Pesachim 119b*
181 *Eicha 2:9*
182 *Megilla 15a*
183 *Megilla 15a*
184 *Berachot 34b*
185 *Shemot 15:4*
186 This interpretation adopts the midrashic statement that Pharaoh survived.
187 This interpretation suggesting that Pharoh died at the Red Sea differs from that of the *Midrash*.
188 *Shemot 15:5*
189 *Shemot 15:5*
190 *Yalkut Shimoni, Bereishit 247*
191 *Shabbat 134b*. This ruling is in accord with the *tanna kamma*'s opinion (the first opinion recorded in the Talmud).
192 *Bereishit 34:25*
193 *Bereishit 18:1*
194 *Shemot 34:5*
195 *Bereishit 17:22*
196 *Bereishit 18:1*
197 *Bereishit 1:5*
198 *Shemot 5:2*
199 *Shemot 6:9*
200 *Shemot 4:1*
201 *Shemot 4:2-5*
202 *Tehillim 122:4*
203 *Shemot 3:10*
204 *Shemot 4:1*
205 *Shabbat 97a*
206 *Rambam, Mishneh Torah, Hilchot Teshuva 4:4*
207 *Yevamot 65b*
208 *Beitza 30a*
209 *Beitza 30a*
210 *Vayikra 19:17*
211 *Shemot 15:20*
212 *Shabbat 30b*
213 *Megilla 14a*
214 *Berachot 5a*
215 *Yehoshua 5:10*
216 *Shabbat 118a-118b*
217 *Zohar, Tikkun 21*
218 *Beitza 16a*
219 *Ketuvot 112a*
220 *Rashi, Bereishit 28:13*
221 *Ta'anit 4a*
222 *Bereishit Rabbati 49:25*
223 *Shir Hashirim Rabba 5*
224 *Pesachim 116b*
225 *Rosh HaShana 11a*
226 *II Shmuel 1:19*
227 *Tehillim 34:16*
228 *Tehillim 33:18*
229 *Shir Hashirim Rabba 8*
230 Rav Yehonatan's source for this statement about the natural world is unclear.
231 *Shir Hashirim 8:14*
232 *Shir Hashirim 1:15*
233 *Midrash Tanchuma, Parshat Tetzave 1*
234 *Mishna Avot 2:8*
235 *Mishlei 3:17*
236 *Shemot Rabba 1*
237 *Shemot 46:10*
238 *Bereishit 37:2*
239 *Bereishit Rabba 84*
240 *Bereishit 39:11-13*
241 *Bereishit 39:14*
242 *Mechilta deRabbi Yishmael, Bo 5*
243 *Arachin 15b*
244 *Bereishit 13:8*

Glossary of Names and Terms in the Haggadah and in the Commentary

Abravanel: Rabbi Isaac of the Abravanel family lived during the fifteenth century and is famous for his Bible commentary.

***Afikoman*:** Greek word meaning dessert; refers to the last piece of matza eaten (for dessert) at the **Pesach Seder**. We refrain from eating after the afikoman has been consumed.

***Akeida*:** Hashem's test of Avraham's dedication to Him wherein he was instructed to sacrifice his son Yitzchak on Mount Moria.

Amalek: The first nation to attack **Bnei Yisrael** after they left Egypt. An eternal enemy of the Jewish people.

***Amida*:** Also referred to as the *Shemoneh Esreh*. Recited three times daily as the focal point of the three prayer services.

***Am Yisrael*:** The nation of Israel (Jewish nation).

***Av*:** Eleventh month of the year according to the Jewish calendar.

Avimelech: King of the Pelishtim. Reigned during the time of our forefathers Avraham and Yitzchak.

***ba'al teshuva*:** An individual who is engaged in or has engaged in the process of repentance. See also **teshuva.**

Babylonian Talmud: A collection of discussions and interpretations of the *Mishna* compiled by Ravina and Rav Ashi around 500CE.

***Barech*:** The twelfth part of the **Seder** which includes the **Birkat Hamazon.**

***Bar Mitzra*:** A Talmudic law formulated to enable individuals to conveniently expand their own holdings by having the right of first refusal on buying fields adjoining their own.

***bechor*:** Firstborn son.

***beit din*:** A court of Jewish law.

***Beit Hamikdash*:** The Temple in Jerusalem. See also **Mikdash**.

***Berit ben Habetarim*:** Covenant Between the Pieces which was made by Hashem with Avraham (*Bereishit* 15).

***bikkurim*:** The mitzva obligating us to redeem the first fruits annually by taking them up to the **Beit Hamikdash**.

***Birkat Hamazon*:** Grace After Meals.

***Bnei Yisrael*:** Children of Israel. Refers to the Jewish nation.

***chavura*:** Group of individuals or families who choose to eat the **Pesach** sacrifice together.

***chametz*:** Leavened bread.

charoset: A lumpy paste usually made of chopped nuts, apples, cinnamon and sweet red wine possessing a thick consistency reminiscent of the mortar used by the Jewish people to build the cities in Egypt.

***Chazal*:** Acronym for *Chachameinu Zichronam Levracha* (Our Sages, of blessed memory).

***chukot*:** Decrees.

***devar Hashem*:** The word of God.

***edot*:** Testimonies.

Edom: The Edomite nation, sometimes referred to as Edom, was descended from Yaakov's brother, **Esav**.

***egla arufa*:** A calf with a broken neck. Refers to the ritual to be performed by the city elders upon the discovery of a murder victim's body near their city.

***Eicha*:** The book of Lamentations written by the prophet **Yirmiyahu**.

***Ei Shabbat*:** There is no Shabbat.

Enosh: Adam's grandson.

***Eretz Yisrael*:** The Land of Israel.

Esav: Our forefather Yaakov's brother.

etzba Elohim: The (mighty) finger of God.

Gemara: Learning. Common way of referring to the **Babylonian Talmud**.

Gilgal: The first place where Bnei Yisrael encamped after having crossed the Jordan River with Yehoshua.

Halacha: Jewish Law.

Hallel: The thirteenth part of the Seder containing a selection of psalms taken from *Tehillim*. This selection is also recited on Jewish holidays and Festivals.

halutzim: Early Zionist pioneers who built up what later became the State of Israel.

Hashem: The Name. Referring to the Lord, our God.

hekdesh: Items designated specifically to serve Hashem in the **Mishkan** or the Temple.

Hevel: Adam's second son who was slain by his jealous brother **Kayin**.

Hillel: Great Jewish leader and scholar who lived shortly before the Destruction of the Second Temple during the time of Herod and Augustus Caesar.

Jerusalem Talmud: A collection of discussions and interpretations of the **Mishna** completed in **Eretz Yisrael** at the end of the fourth century of the Common Era. Often compared and contrasted with the **Babylonian Talmud**.

Kadesh: The first part of the **Seder** containing **kiddush**.

kapandriya: shortcut

Karpas: The third part of the **Seder** in which a green vegetable is dipped in salt water.

Kayin: Adam's eldest son, who slew his brother, Hevel.

Kelal Yisrael: The nation of Israel (the Jewish people).

kezayit: A (olives bulk) measurement of solids used by Jewish law.

***kiddush*:** Sanctification of the day usually recited over a cup of wine.

***kilai hakerem*:** The produce of mixed seeds in the vineyard.

***kohen*:** One of priestly descent.

***Korech*:** The ninth part of the **Seder** in which a sandwich made of **maror** and **matza** is eaten.

***lifnei Hashem*:** Before **Hashem.** Connotes basking in Hashem's presence in the **Beit Hamikdash**.

Levi(tes): Levi was one of Yaakov**'s twelve sons. The tribe of Levi served Hashem in the Temple.**

***Maggid*:** The fifth and central part of the **Seder** wherein the story of the Exodus from Egypt is recounted.

Maharsha: Rabbi Shmuel Edels (1555-1632), Talmudic commentator.

***mamzer(im)*:** Illegitimate offspring.

***manna*:** Bread-like portions of food that miraculously fell from the sky as a gift from Hashem to provide for Bnei Yisrael during their travels in the desert.

***Maror*:** "Bitter herbs." Refers to the seventh part of the **Seder** in which the bitter herbs are eaten.

***mateh*:** Staff.

matza (pl. *matzot*): Unleavened bread eaten by Bnei Yisrael when they left Egypt.

***me'ila*:** Any use of **hekdesh** for a purpose unrelated to Temple service violates the biblical prohibition of me'ila.

***mekadesh Shem Shamayim*:** To Sanctify God's Heavenly name.

***Mikdash*:** See **Beit Hamikdash**.

mincha (*gedola, ketana*)**:** When the afternoon prayer is recited in the early part of the afternoon, it is referred to as mincha gedola. When it is recited in the latter part of the afternoon, it is referred to as mincha ketana.

***Mishkan*:** The Tabernacle.

Mishlei: The book of Proverbs written by King Solomon.

Mishna: Redacted by Rabbi Yehuda Ha-Nasi around 200 CE. The first written recording of the Oral Torah of the Jewish people.

***Mishneh Torah*:** A code of Jewish law written by the *Rambam*.

***mishpat*:** Judgment.

mitzva (pl. *mitzvot*)**:** Commandment; usually refers to one of the six hundred and thirteen commandments Hashem gave to Bnei Yisrael.

Moav: A nation hostile to the Jewish people and descended from Lot, Avraham's nephew.

Moshe Rabbeinu: Moshe our (the Jewish people's) Rabbi.

***Moshiach*:** The Messiah.

Motzi and *Matza*: The seventh part of the **Seder** in which the **matza** is eaten for the first time. Two blessings are recited: hamotzi and matza.

***nachal eitan*:** The barren area in which the **egla arufa** was offered.

***Navi*:** Prophet.

Nirtza: The concluding part of the **Seder**.

***Nissan*:** Seventh month of the year according to the Jewish calendar. The Jewish people was redeemed from Egypt in Nissan.

***Oiy Shabbat*:** Woe is Shabbat.

***Orla*:** The fruit of a tree during its first three years.

Pesach: The Festival of Passover.

***pidyon haben*:** The biblical commandment to redeem one's firstborn son.

Rabbeinu Asher: Also know as the Rosh, he was a thirteenth century Talmudist and Halachist.

***Rachtza*:** The sixth part of the **Seder** in which we wash our hands before eating the **matza**.

Rambam: Rabbi Moshe ben Maimon, also known as Maimonides. Twelfth century author of the halachic code, the *Mishneh Torah,* and of the *Commentary on the Mishna.*

rebbe: Term of endearment used to refer to one's own personal rabbi.

***revi'it*:** A quarter. A halachic measurement of liquid volume.

Rosh Hashana: The first day of the Jewish new year.

***ruach*:** Breath or spirit.

***Ruach Hakodesh*:** Divine Spirit.

Sanhedrin: Jewish High Court of Justice.

Seder: Order. Refers to the ceremony the Jewish people perform on **Pesach** night.

Sefer Tehillim: The book of Psalms.

Sennacherib: Ruler of the Assyrian Empire from 720 BCE to 683 BCE. Attempted to conquer Jerusalem during the reign of King Chizkiyahu.

Shaul: (King) Saul. The first king of Israel.

***Shabbat*:** The Sabbath.

Shavuot: The Festival of Pentecost.

Shehecheyanu: Blessing recited upon fulfilling a seasonal **mitzva**, thanking Hashem for having enabled us to reach this moment.

***Shechina*:** Divine Presence.

shekel (pl. *shekalim*)**:** Coin used in biblical times.

***Shemitta*:** The Sabbatical year. Every seven years Jews are forbidden to work the land in **Eretz Yisrael** for an entire year, thus demonstrating their faith that the produce of the Land is dependent exclusively upon Hashem.

shevet: Staff or tribe.

shiur: Amount or class.

***Shir Hashirim*:** The Song of Songs written by King Solomon.

***shivtei Yah*:** The tribes of Hashem.

Shmuel: The prophet Samuel who anointed both **Shaul** and David kings of *Yisrael.*

***Shulchan Orech*:** Set table. The tenth part of the **Seder**; the Festive Meal.

***simcha*:** Joyousness or happiness.

Sisera: General in the Cannanite army; a sworn enemy of the Jewish people.

***Sivan*:** The ninth month of the year according to the Jewish calendar.

Sukkot: The Festival of Tabernacles.

***Talmud Yerushalmi*:** See **Jerusalem Talmud.**

***Targum Onkelos*:** A translation of the Torah into Aramaic written by Onkelos, the convert.

***Tehillim*:** The book of Psalms. See also *Sefer Tehillim.*

***teshuva*:** Repentance. See also **ba'al teshuva**.

Tosafot: Commentary on the Talmud compiled by a group of western-European Torah scholars during the twelfth and thirteenth centuries; these scholars were known as the Ba'alei Tosafot, and their commentaries were referred to as "tosafot," literally meaning additions (to the Talmud).

***tzaddik*:** A wholly righteous individual.

***Tzafun*:** Hidden. The eleventh part of the Seder in which the **afikoman** is eaten.

***tzara'at*:** A skin affliction. Often mistranslated as leprosy.

***Urechatz*:** The second part of the **Seder** wherein we wash our hands before we perform the **Karpas** ceremony.

Yaakov: Jacob, our forefather.

***Yachatz*:** The third part of the **Seder** in which the middle matza is broken in two.

yad hagedola: (His) great hand.

Yechezkel: Ezekiel the prophet who lived during the Babylonian Exile around 597 BCE.

Yehonatan: King Shaul's son; King David's best friend.

Yehoshua: Joshua.

Yeshayahu: The prophet Isaiah.

Yirmiyahu: The prophet Jeremiah, who foretold the Destruction of the First Temple and the exile of the Jewish people to Babylonia in the sixth century BCE.

Yishmael: Avraham's son who became the father of the Arab nations.

Yisrael: Israel. Referring to the nation of Israel, or to **Yaakov**, our forefather.

Yitzchak: Our forefather, Isaac.

Yom Tov: Jewish Festival.

***Zohar*:** The main kabbalistic work authored by Rabbi Shimon Bar Yochai (2nd century CE).

Zuz(im): A coin used in Talmudic times.